Contents

HERRING

There are patterns in the scales which tell
how many years since they were spawned;
how many seasons they have circled;
how often they have swum through storm
and calm, slipping beyond the links and coils
thrown out from a vessel's side or stern.

And each year they must count their chances
(that thought streamlining through their heads)
whether passing through tight channels
or straits where shoals are often brought or led.
Or while they race through deeper waters,
quicksilver over ocean beds,
wondering if their track is clear
or if they'll be reined by fishing nets.

'I know of a cure for everything: salt water . . . Sweat, or tears, or the salt sea.'
Isak Dinesen (Karen Blixen), *Seven Gothic Tales*

The Major Herring Ports of Northern Europe

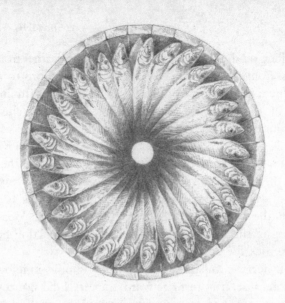

CHAPTER ONE

'Them Belly Full'

The ghost of Marley – Bob, that is, not Jacob – has done his share of haunting me during my times at sea.

On a particularly ferocious trip from south Harris to the far western isle of St Kilda, his songs spun on a continual loop, played by one of the yacht's crew. I was reassured by continual reminders not to 'worry about a thing', while the waves crashed, thunderous and white around me, lashing the back of my life jacket, rendering me wet, cold and miserable. I looked out into the blackness of the skies and heard the words of 'Exodus' echoing, the beat of the song a frenzied rhythm through the darkness. The lyrics made me long for the solidity of earth, even wilderness or desert, anything except this constant pitch and roll beneath my feet.

On this occasion, however, the waters soothed me almost as much as the music of Mr Marley. I was part of a group

travelling on the *Atloy*, an old, restored fjord steamer from the
1930s, from the western Norwegian port of Florø to a fish
restaurant located in a converted warehouse in Knutholmen –
one of those rare places where the menu matches the
magnificent setting. Accompanying the thrum of the
engines was the voice of Michael, the lead singer of a Marley
tribute band called Legend, which had come all the way
from the Caribbean via, give or take a generation or two, the
city of Birmingham, United Kingdom. With his backing
group, the aptly named Elaine Smiler and Celia Heavenly,
joining in the lilting harmonies, he kept instructing people
not to rock the boat.

The ferry companies of the world should employ this
band because, true to their word, the *Atloy* did not rock. It
barely trembled, steaming calmly around the small islets and
cliffs that are to be found on the west coast of Norway,
untroubled by any of the strong winds that so frequently
haunt us in the north. It was a glorious day, made bright and
special by the company I kept, including the extraordinary
figure of our Norwegian host, Per Vidar Ottesen, who sang
'Buffalo Soldier' while decked out in a jacket stitched
together from the bright green, yellow and red colours of
the Marley flag. Like a Cuban revolutionary, a beret marked
with a crimson star was perched upon his head.

There was, too, an Irish band who called themselves
Tupelo, after a town in far-off Mississippi and the birthplace
of that other musical giant, Elvis Presley. To add to my
musical and geographical confusion, the first song these
young Irishmen played later that evening was called 'Down
to Patagonia', the southern, snow-smothered edge of the
world. Its chorus boomed over the narrow streets of Florø
where a crowd of Filipinos, Americans, Swedes and visiting
Norwegians had gathered to celebrate the herring, the fish
that provided the most important reason for this community
ever coming into existence. As both visitor and native
stamped their feet and joined in with the singing, I could

not help but look around the small island town to see how the most important meal of my childhood had been marked within its boundaries.

Reminders of its existence were everywhere. Florø's municipal crest carried echoes of that of my hometown of Stornoway, the largest community of the Western Isles. Just like the one to be found in our town hall, Florø's crest was decorated by three herring, but there were important differences. These herring swam on a simple red background; Stornoway's biblical injunction 'God's Providence Is Our Inheritance' was not scrolled below. Nor did the fish share their space on the shield with a castle or the birlinn, the single-masted vessel associated with the Western Isles and the West Highlands of Scotland. The Florø herring swim in a trio, slimmer than their Hebridean counterparts.

On the town's edge, too, a circular steel statue stood. With tiny jagged teeth, it was meant to resemble the open mouth of a fish but could just as easily have been a visual metaphor for the opening scene of a bad horror movie or a toothy version of the Rolling Stones' logo. Atop a huddle of stone was the iron silhouette of a fisherman. One hand stretched out, the other dragged his catch by its gills as he marched onwards. A stone sculpture of a woman with a creel on her back stood not far from the town's municipal buildings. Determined to defy the wind that must so often whistle down the street, she ignored the young, bawling child who plucked at her skirt. Elsewhere, two oilskin-capped young faces grinned at people from a stone plinth. An odd-looking boy with a cap and short trousers dangled a clutch of herring in his hand, as if he were taking it home for his grandmother to fry. (She sat elsewhere, a stout, grim-faced, elderly woman occupying her own stone stool in one of the few sculptures in the town that appeared, at first glance anyway, to have little connection with fishing.) There was also a ring of herring carved from stone, circling endlessly a tiny space beside a glass-fronted office. Later that evening, as the few

short shadows of midsummer fell, electric light gleamed
from below the sculpture, its brightness catching and
illuminating the underbellies of the fish. One could imagine
how it might appear in the gloom of midwinter, as luminous
and elusive as the shoals that once circled the waters of the
North Atlantic and beyond, well outside the nets of men
fishing at sea.

And then there were the tables that lay stretched out on
the Strandgata, the town's main street. Bare throughout
much of the morning, they were then draped with blue
plastic sheets resplendent with the words 'Norway Pelagic'.
On the benches alongside, people crammed and squeezed,
their places at the table watched jealously by those who had
come late to the party, arriving, perhaps, by the National
Road 5* that linked the town to the rest of the country or,
like me, the fast passenger ferry from Bergen. (There were
even a few Fjordtaxis tied up at the harbour, bearing those
from other, smaller islands nearby to the town's biggest night
of the year.) Some people clearly planned to be ensconced
there for hours – to listen to Tupelo with its singer from
Dublin, its fiddler from Ballina in County Mayo; to watch
the local Herring Prince having a gold medal pinned on his
chest for all he had achieved for the community; to receive
the free cans of (weak) beer and lemonade their hosts were
handing out; to eat the huge variety of herring the people
had prepared for this special day, the third Friday in June,
coinciding with the closing day of the island's schools.
Together with paper plates and plastic forks, young people,
perhaps pupils kitted out in fisherman's jumpers, brought to
our table plastic pails with lids that had to be squeezed and
prised open. Inside them was the herring that was to be our

---

*Much of this was built by the Germans during the Second World
War, one of the few good outcomes of their occupation of
Norway.

feast and fare on the *sildebordet*: what the organisers told us was the Longest Herring Table in the World.*

There was certainly enough herring available to grant both spice and substance to that boast. It arrived in many forms and flavours, far more than the narrow choice of varieties I had witnessed in my youth. It was dipped in mustard; mingled with nuts; given added zest and flavour by tomato; mixed with red and white onion, carrots and herbs; sprinkled with spice; served both sour and sweet (with sherry); cooked in curry. (I missed out on the last.) For an hour or two, until people had scraped their platters clean, it seemed as if the whole town had been restored to its glory days in the middle of the nineteenth century, when both ports and harbours were awash with what men in Scotland termed 'the silver darlings', or what those in Norway called 'the silver of the sea'. This was riches indeed, both a transformation and a celebration of Florø's history as a place where the herring was brought ashore, albeit without the screech of gulls as used to be the case, and with condiments and seasoning not employed by the townsfolk when the industry was at its height.

In a small marquee tent off the town's main street, one could, however, gain a real sense of the older traditions that lie behind the celebration. Around the tables there, a large number of locals gather, paying a few kroner for – what they believe to be – the highpoint of the night's celebrations. Washing down their meal with another mouthful of beer, a small glass of honey-flavoured aquavit, they eat a banquet of potato and (the inevitable) herring. Yet this one is very different from the super-spiced, super-scented models that were served outside. It has been dried in the original,

---

*This honour used to be claimed by the more southerly town of Haugesund. Now it boasts of its Sildajazz, or Herring Jazz, festival, the scales played by the disciples of Louis Armstrong and Benny Goodman replacing those that used to be found on fish.

authentic manner probably employed since the likes of Egil Skallagrimsson, the outlaw, poet and central character of *Egil's Saga*, fished in these waters in the tenth century. Together with such everyday practices as setting a horse's head on a nithing pole and cursing Norway's king and queen, he probably sat in a small building where both fish and seabirds hung from the rafters, lifting to the wind whistling through gaps between the stone. Along with salt, created from seawater, drying was the means by which food was often preserved back then. The coastline of Norway with its dry, windy winters and temperatures that rarely go below zero was ideal for this purpose. This only began to change in the early seventeenth century, when inexpensive, purer Spanish salt started to be introduced throughout Europe; this was a better preserver than the poorer quality version they possessed before.

Like several others I lifted this gastronomic delight gingerly with my fingers, making sure first of all that the last layer of skin had been removed. (I failed to do this the first time.) And then came the treat, that moment of magical indulgence when I chewed and nibbled my way through the meal that had been prepared for me. Requiring the full force of my molars and incisors to make any real impression on its flesh, I finally bit my way through it, aware it was like a mixture of kipper and beef jerky, a dry piece of salt leather difficult to chop or swallow. One could imagine that, far from it being eaten, the fish might have been used in the past as a restraint for a Norwegian fjord horse, a halter to hold and control the dun-shaded breed that was used for centuries to carry loads and men, and plough barren acres in this far, north-western edge of Europe. Or perhaps, too, a string of dried herring might have harnessed a boat to harbour, rendering it impervious to the threat of any storm.

Yet eat it they did, and the others at this feast – largely men, it has to said – all provided testimony to this. We all gnawed through it as if it was the best gourmet meal or a la carte dinner that had been ever served up to us, relishing each bite. And it was as if, by its taste, something of the Norwegian's ancestry and identity had been restored to them. They were once again kindred of Eric Bloodaxe, the tenth-century Norse king who even had my native Hebrides under his control; this method of preserving fish was mentioned as far back as 875 when, in *Egil's Saga,* the Viking businessman Torolf Kveldulvsson is referred to as sending dried cod all the way to England. Judging by the reaction to the meal, for all that the historical connection had clearly frayed a little in my case, it still remained strong within these men, their appetite apparent in every bite, their hunger for this food reinforced by the town's location, the most westerly town in Norway, peeping out over that country's edge.

In some ways this was strange, for far from being an old settlement, the city of Florø was, in fact, a relatively new one, some distance from Norway's ancient capital of Bergen. It was true that people had always fished nearby, particularly from the early years of the nineteenth century when the country was still under the jurisdiction of Sweden. By the time the mid-point of that century had passed, there was a growing awareness of the need for a commercial centre somewhere in the county of what was then known as Northern Bergenhus, one which would enable the people of that area to develop the fishing industry more. It was this that led in 1858 to the creation of a commission which chose the place then called Florøven, one that was 'located near the inner shipping lines', beside the sea with its crowded depths. Slowly but surely, Florø took shape, its existence depending on the rich harvest of herring shoaling in nearby waters. There was even some settlement, which the military officer who had first sketched out the beginnings of the town might not have envisaged. Sometimes this added to the town's appeal; the old wooden houses still at its centre are largely built in a Swiss style first developed in Berlin by the architect Karl Friedrich Schinkel, among others, and adapted to the salt and stormy conditions prevalent on the Norwegian coast. Others are based on the style found in Bergen in the nineteenth century. And then there is the wonderfully distinctive Stabben lighthouse built in 1867 not far from the town's harbour. Built to ensure the safety of boats fishing in these waters, its strong, high walls, too, are shaped like the bows of a boat, one that could meet the challenge of the mountainous seas and storms that frequently whirl in its direction.

Yet for all its charm and beauty, the astonishing vigour of Florø's setting among fjords and high cliffs, and the high slopes of Rognaldsvåg nearby, there was squalor also to be found within the town during these years, a quality some might associate with America's western frontier rather than the Norwegian version. There were those who drew their open boats upon the town's shoreline, turning them over and sleeping beneath their upturned bows. Others slept standing all night, crammed into tiny rooms. For instance, there is a case recorded of 150 people squeezed into a room of 88 metres square (950 square feet). There is little record, however, of these grim realities in the plaques that decorate the houses in Strandgata, which display rather bland information like: 'Strandgata 29 is a special storehouse adapted in a narrow site towards the harbour . . .'

There is also little about how Florø's time as a major herring port was relatively short. The herring did as they have often been known to do, leaving the area for waters new in 1872. It was a shift of direction that had an enormous impact on the human population that had either settled or come to that area each spring. Writing of them, a local doctor wrote: 'The plight of these people over the last autumn and winter has been lamentable. What they have suffered through hunger, thirst and general deprivation is almost beyond belief.'

While this may not have been as bad as the mass starvation that affected Norway's population in 1812, it, too, had its legacy. Like this community's counterparts in places as close as Unst in Shetland or as far away as the west coast of Ireland, it could – and in some places continues to – be seen in the ruins of curing houses, fishermen's huts and boarding houses found in various locations not far from Florø, the wind and weather curling around their crumbling walls until they toppled and fell, leaving nothing but the building's foundations behind them. The people, like the herring, moved elsewhere, perhaps in the direction of Ålesund, now the country's most important fishing harbour, or Haugesund, miles further south in that long western coast of Norway, near bays and inlets where the fish still thronged and swam. The latter community had, for years, a herring barrel on its crest, accompanied by an anchor and three seagulls. This was in tribute to the thousands of barrels that were stacked upon that town's quaysides, ready to be sent to places like Russia or even the Caribbean, where the British fed much of the people there with what the slave-owners termed 'slave herring', a rich source of minerals and vitamin D for a population on the edge of hunger. The herring was stockpiled and distributed when a hurricane or other storm had destroyed their usual food of maize and plantains. It was not, however, doled out in vast quantities. In 1737, for instance, John Woolman writes how 'in Barbadoes and some of the other islands, six pints of Indian corn and three herrings, are reckoned a full week's allowance for a working slave'.

A taste for herring remains a small part of the Jamaican menu even today. It comes in the form of a fish paste based on smoked red herring they call Solomon Gundy. Minced and spiced with chilli pepper – including the Scotch Bonnet, so called because of its resemblance to the Tam O'Shanter hat – and various seasonings, and served with crackers or bread, its strange name may have come from the word 'salmagundi' used by the British to describe a salad. There is also a suggestion that the dish's title may have been derived from a nursery rhyme of similar name: 'Solomon Grundy'. An equivalent fare from Nova Scotia, which, unlike the

Jamaican variety, only involved herring, pickle and onion, is said to be linked, too:

> On Monday the Herring was caught, gutted and salted.
> On Tuesday the Herring rested in salt.
> On Wednesday the Herring was stripped and put in vinegar brine.
> On Thursday onions and spices were added to the Herring in brine.
> On Saturday the Herring, onion, spices and brine were packed in bottles.
> On Sunday the Herring was eaten and given away as gifts.
> And that was the end of one tasty batch of Solomon Gundy.[*]

No doubt Bob Marley and his contemporaries would have looked wryly at both this verse and the form of sustenance. Reflecting on it, he might have been inspired to write some of the lyrics of 'Them Belly Full', part of the repertoire of Legend, the reggae group that would stand on the open stage in Florø during the second night of the Herring Festival. Pointing at stouter, rounder men, they might have noted that the salt herring served on the street tables earlier was part of the diet of the hungry throughout the world. It united many who came to Florø that particular evening, linking the ancestors of those whose people came from the Caribbean with the ones who came from Scotland, the Irish musicians with the Swedes and Danes among their audience. There was a good reason for this, though one now misted over and forgotten within our collective remembrance.

[*]www.merseypointfish.ca/index.php/about/a_bit_of_history/nova_scotian_solomon_gundy/

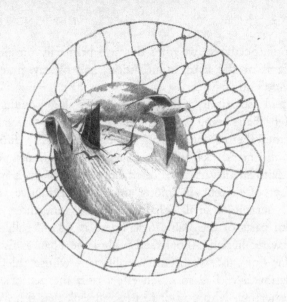

CHAPTER TWO

'When the Seagulls Follow the Trawlers'

At one time shoals of herring used to stipple the oceans around much of the world's coastline; in the years before the First World War, an average of between two and three million barrels a year stood on the harbours of Scotland alone. Like a host of blades and bayonets, flashes of silver, the fish cut through dark waves as if they were a military force that might sometimes be counted in the millions. The territory in which they operated was huge. They thronged the North Atlantic. Found off the shores of places as far apart as Iceland, the Netherlands, Ireland, the United States and Southern Greenland, they stitched together a patchwork of places that seemed – at first sight – quite different and distinct, giving these localities similarities in their ways of life no matter what kind of landscapes their ports and harbours occupied, whether this was primarily prosperous farmland or the bare, mountainous soil of, say, much of Scotland's north-west.

These variations applied to the fish they sought too. Rather than being utterly identical, as my forefathers presumed them to be, herring can be divided into different types and races, each with its localities to swim and patrol, each with small variations of shade or size, or even in the number of vertebrae. Among the most distinctive is the Baltic herring, a small fish living in the innermost, most hidden parts of the Baltic Sea. There is a kind called the Blackwater herring, too, found within the Thames Estuary, not far from the Westminster politicians whose rules and legislation have had so much effect over the centuries on the fishermen who go out to net and seek that fish. Pearly and iridescent, it is smaller and paler than most fish that bear the name. It still remains the centre of its own distinctive industry, with a small fleet of some half-dozen boats setting out to catch it with their nets – a small, faint glimmer of what was found on the edges of this country for much of the previous century. There are also the Down herring and Bank herring, based in the North Sea, Icelandic herring, White Sea and Norwegian spring-spawning herring. Each kind is both different from other types of herring and the same. Like the ethnic differences that are found within humanity, there are variations within them for all they share the same biology.

And then there are the relatives. The family Clupeidae to which the herring belongs has many cousins throughout the world. They include some freshwater fish, such as the skipjack shad, which apparently leaps out of the water while feeding in places like the upper Mississippi river near the mouth of the Ohio river. There is the alewife or gaspereau, found again in fresh water in North America, where its slightly rounder shape is said to resemble a stout tavern-keeper. Between Japan and Australia, there can be found the wolf herring. As ravenous as its name suggests, it is not really part of the Clupeidae family. One difference is its ability to bite morsels out of fish swimming nearby.

There are also other kinds of freshwater herring swimming around the lakes and rivers of Australia, South America and Africa. The African continent boasts a pygmy herring among its family. Another tiny member of the clan is the pilchard or sardine, crammed normally in the British Isles within a can that can only be broken into with its own key. Much of the variety caught off the south-west of England was sent to the Catholic areas of Europe for eating on Fridays and during the period of Lent, which inspired Cornishmen to compose this mock toast, an attempt to persuade those of that faith to eat even more of the fish at great profit to themselves:

Here's health to the Pope, may he live to repent
And add just six months to the term of his Lent,
And tell all his vassals from Rome to the Poles
There's nothing like pilchards for saving their souls.

Another of the herring's cousins to be found in these waters is the sprat. It is fished throughout European waters, in areas like the Minch and elsewhere by men from ports such as Mallaig in the north-west of Scotland. Sitting at his front window on the warm day in June I visited him in his home, Michael Currie, a former fisherman and coxswain of Mallaig lifeboat, and I looked out at the various strata of red light as the sun set, framing the outline of the Cuillins and Isle of Skye we could see across the Sound of Sleat from his home. While he did this, he described a fish that was easily confused with others.

'Sometimes sprats end up in a sardine can along with pilchards. At other times, people mix them up with young herring. But if you rub their stomachs with your fingers' – he imitated the motion with a broad, expansive hand – 'it's easy to tell the difference. A herring's belly is smooth. There's a roughness to the sprat's scales.'

Yet it is the larger, free-range and free-swimming battalions that were once the focus of a huge fishing industry in the North Atlantic that one thinks of normally when we refer to the fish of that name. Though we now associate the herring with the names we heard on the Shipping Forecast on either the Home Service or BBC Radio 4 in our youth, the Malin, Hebrides, Fair Isle, Forties, Dogger and Lundy that surround our coast, there was a time when this was not the case. Until about 1425, the bulk of the herring swam not towards Cromarty, Forth and Tyne but thronged the Baltic Sea, adding to the riches of such Hanseatic towns as Bremen, Lübeck and Riga, and much of the coastal settlements of the Baltic States, as well as north Germany and parts of Scandinavia. Suddenly, showing a reputation for fickleness that still follows the fish today, they largely deserted these areas, never to return in such vast numbers again.

These shifts have occurred through the history of the herring. The small rocky island of Klädesholmen, which lies in the Skagerrak Strait, between south-east Norway, south-west Sweden and Denmark's Jutland peninsula, has seen six vast shoals of the fish in its history. One was in the sixteenth century. Another was between 1780 and 1808. The people there fished and boiled the herring in two large plants, owned by merchants from Gothenburg and Stockholm, sending the oil that rose to the surface in their vats to light up the streets of London and Paris. When the fish disappeared, there were a number of people who thought that the herring plants dumping their waste into the ocean nearby were responsible for the aversion of the fish to these waters. The stink and, perhaps, the punishment being meted out to some of their number resulted in them veering away. They only returned afterwards between 1880 and 1900, giving the community that worked there forgiveness and a second chance. This did not last long. They did not return in the twentieth century.

There have been other suggestions made as to the reasons why these sudden changes in direction have been made by the fish; why, for instance, they deserted Florø in 1872 and darted southwards, arriving, perhaps, in Klädesholmen a few years later. A slight alteration in the level of light or the strength of the prevailing winds might have sent them elsewhere. Perhaps, too, a shift in the ocean's temperature or even in the Earth's geomagnetic fields influenced them to move somewhere else, leaving men and women in some ports and harbours without work, seas where they once thronged now empty. However, nobody is certain why the shoals concluded it was best to wander to other parts – one of the major reasons why fishermen switched to the more dependable and far-flung cod in the fifteenth century.* It was, to parody Denis Norden and Frank Muir's own parody of the Shipping Forecast, as if the herring had come together and suddenly decided:

in Ross and Finistere,
The outlook was not too sinisterre.

This is not to say there were not herring already present in areas like the south-east of England before. The records of various monasteries show that their monks enjoyed a taste for the fish, those at Evesham savouring the salt variety brought to them on the backs of packhorses. A rental of 30,000 herring was also paid to the Abbey of St Edmund in Beccles in Suffolk, giving an additional smack and fervour to their prayers. Consumed especially on fast days – including Fridays and throughout Lent – they were an essential part of both the churchman and church-goer's diet, less expensive than meat. As a result, their presence in the ocean brought some measure of prosperity to a number of ports.

*Another reason is that herring tends to spoil more quickly than cod, largely as a result of its high oil content. In a dry, cool environment, cod can also be air-dried without salt, a huge benefit in northern latitudes with high winds and with salt relatively scarce.

The town of Great Yarmouth illustrates this long historical pattern perfectly. In 1067, the town already had a herring fair, the local baron having appointed bailiffs to govern the celebrations. Later, some time between the eleventh and thirteenth centuries, it became the task of the Cinque Ports – Hastings, New Romney, Hythe, Dover and Sandwich – to regulate the industry. In addition, the port is noted as having '24 fishermen' and '3 salthouses' in the Domesday Book of 1086, the small beginnings of an industry that lasted at least 900 years.

In the far north of Scotland, the populations of Orkney and Shetland are also recorded as having traded in salt fish from early times, while the records in Iceland provide us with evidence that far-travelled men were not always well behaved when following the herring and far away from home. In 1415, the King of Denmark had cause to complain when some visited that far-flung part of his domain, acting riotously after they landed there. There was even the 'Battle of the Herrings'. This took place when in February 1429, Sir John Fastolfe, the prototype for Shakespeare's character of a similar name, was taking barrels of salt herring to France to feed the English troops fighting both the Scots and French at the siege of Orleans. En route he encountered a French force determined to prevent these supplies being delivered in time for the meat-free days of Lent.

All this is evidence of how the herring journeys huge distances in its lifetime, a 30cm-long fish travelling at about 6km an hour through the sea. (This is relatively slow compared to certain other species. A 50cm cod swims at 8km during the same period, a mackerel manages 10km, while the sea trout, clearly the Michael Schumacher of the fish world, succeeds in reaching the heady speed of 12km an hour.) The herring can be seen at their giddiest in the Sea Life Centre in Oban, travelling around the doughnut-shaped glass circuit that has been designed specifically for their use. And on their real life Grand Prix, they speed much vaster distances. Some herring spawn off the Scottish or English coast before whizzing east towards the west coast of Jutland in Denmark and swimming – as mature fish – back towards the waters around Unst or Yell in Shetland. Another kind, the Norwegian herring, might – in one season – head north to the Barents Sea, near such exotically named islands as Svalbard and Novaya Zemlya to the north of Norway and Russia, before zooming off in the direction of the slightly cooler waters near Iceland. That they can do this without sinking is largely a result of the swim-bladder which the herring, like the cod, sardine and other pelagic fish that – by definition – live near the surface, possess. Heavier than water, they would not remain afloat without an air-filled sac of connective tissue. This lies above the digestive tract and allows the herring to regulate its own density. A gland in the bladder's wall enables it to do this, the air coming from its blood, ensuring that it retains the hold of gravity and keeping it buoyant. This changes as the fish rises or falls, surging or ebbing as its need and direction requires.

And as they swim, herring feed on plankton sieved from water with the assistance of gill-rakers, small structures that resemble fine mesh connected to their gills. It is these that help provide the rations they depend on for their lives. They filter the tiny crustaceans and planktonic organisms that sustain them as the ocean's flood surges through their mouths and flows out over their gills, winnowing out all they require for their survival. It is a source of food that is there in abundance. Within the North Sea, it has been estimated that there are about 10 million tons of animal plankton, which the herring, among other fish, can plunder and swallow. Over six million tons of this is a tiny crustacean, the copepod. Like other planktonic animals, copepods endlessly shift, up and down, seeking plant plankton as if they were miniature puppets tugged by darkness. In daylight, they retreat to deeper water. By night, they shift to the surface, grazing on the plant plankton to be found there in the long daylight hours of summer. There is less available in winter, unlike in warmer seas where these microscopic plants are available all year round, allowing for a longer spawning season for the fish that cluster there.

At the same time, the herring imitate their prey, taking part in a huge and continual vertical movement, higher and lower, up and down, through the Minch and North Sea, the Irish Sea or Pentland Firth. For some, this movement may be as much as 300 metres every day. Aware that, like every army, the herring swims or 'marches' on its stomach, fishermen in trawlers haul nets over the bottom during the hours of day to catch them. At night, they used to suspend drift nets from floats, hoping to catch herring that veered close to the surface. For the keen-eyed fisherman, there are signs that the fish are rising. Millions of gas bubbles come to the surface if the sea is still and the shoal large when the herring rises, bubbles that spurt from a special duct in their swim-bladders, enabling them to adjust to the difference in depths. It is as if the sea is bubbling, the ranks breaking strict commands to be silent as they rise. There are even reports that the herring made peculiar noises when they came to the surface, sounds made by the gas being expelled from their swim bladders. Sometimes it was a 'plout' in still water. Francis Day in his book *The Fishes of Great Britain and Ireland* goes further. In that late nineteenth-century work, he noted that:

> the noise made by herrings when captured is peculiar, and has been likened to various things . . . to the cry of a mouse, to the word 'cheese', a sneeze or a squeak.

The Scottish artist Will Maclean told me of one of his relatives, Donald Reid from Kyleakin in the Isle of Skye, who had the skill of listening for herring in abundance. A remarkable individual who had gained the Croix de Guerre from the French in the Second World War, rowing small boats with muffled oars to take members of the Resistance to shore, Donald was skilled at listening for herring – a talent he said he had learned from the men from Avoch on the opposite, east coast of Scotland.

'He could hear their plop even in winter time,' Will said. 'And he'd sometimes bang the anchor chain at night, watching out for their movement when the fish were frightened. If it was a star shape in the water, he'd know they were mackerel. If there was a flash, he could tell it was herring. "I can see them in the fire," he used to say.'

The tall, lean figure of Donald has inspired some of Will's art. In one sculpture, for instance, he portrays the fisherman in the form of a sculpture with a glass eye observing all that is going on, a herring in his head portraying the single-minded focus that a man or hunter-gatherer of his kind must possess. It is a skill that was sometimes valued by those on land. On the west coast of Norway, for instance, this idea of the lookout was taken seriously to such a degree that men were sometimes positioned in 'herring temples' along the coastline, concealing themselves behind a shelter of stone to see if they could see the flash and fire of the fish burning on the surface of the water. They had to take care, however, that they were not seen by the herring. According to legend, should this happen, the fish might veer in another direction and race off elsewhere, never to swim that way again.

In the days before echo-sounders and sonar, it was techniques like these that sometimes allowed men to look below the thick grey camouflage of the sea, to pinpoint where a trap might be sprung and a good catch obtained. Alternately, a whale, porpoise, shark or seal could splash or squadrons of seabirds touch down on waters to try and pluck some fresh food for their own empty beaks and those of their chicks, easy signs for fishermen to note and spot. A Gaelic proverb says this succinctly: *Far am bi an t-iasg, 's ann a bhios na h-eòin* (Where the fish are, there will be birds), a neat inversion of Eric Cantona's famous phrase, 'When the seagulls follow the trawler, it is because they think sardines will be thrown into the sea.' One has to admire, too, the exactness of that French footballer's knowledge. It was indeed the gull that fishermen relied upon, more even than the gannet, say, or guillemot – known as *eun dubh an sgadain* (the black bird of the herring) in Gaelic. A flock of seagulls resting noisily on the water, swirling their heads around, then taking off, flying away before settling down again, was a certain sign that a shoal of herring was in the vicinity. Sometimes fishermen would take notes of any evidence of that kind of behaviour, building up a pattern of where birds or fish had been. It was for this reason that, for instance, there was, under Manx law, a £5 penalty for every gull killed when the herring was in season.

In the Isle of Man, even insects played their role in predicting whether herring would appear or not. Eyes would look out for signs of a daddy-long-legs early in the year. If one appeared, it was evidence that there would be fresh herring around. Another portent was a moth that Manxmen and women sometimes saw dancing around their home. They called this *lhemeen y skeddan* (the herring moth). If it appeared in the evening, it meant there was herring to be caught.

Yet the most reliable evidence was always on the sea itself – a multitude of scales glimmering like a trail of flame on the water's surface would carry greater conviction than the presence of seagulls or insects. It would be as if there had been a sudden shower of snowflakes when twilight fell, a shimmer of silver, say, at other times of day, drawing the attention of others to the presence of a shoal within the water, the prospect of a harvest to bring home. To those who possessed my native Gaelic, this resembled the blaze of phosphorescence known as *a' losgadh* (the burning). In Shetland, this was given the infinitely more poetic name of 'mareel', which, to my ears at least, suggests a dance, the continual switching and circling of partners going on below. Peculiarly, this is not the only shade that revealed the presence of a shoal of herring. Sometimes, a deep green might show that a large number of that particular fish were 'grazing' there.*

And when this occurred, it was a sign that herring were present in numbers like the vast 'army' from which their name is sometimes said to derive: the word *heer*, a Teutonic word all too appropriate to the huge, serried ranks of fish that once encircled islands or swam into deep water. They would invade inlets and bays for a short time before hastening onwards, swirling north or south as the season or the compulsions of nature urged and willed them to do, returning to the same spawning grounds year upon year, occasionally twisting and turning in another direction. Unlike in most other species, the eggs of the herring are not free-floating, shifting back and forth in open water. Instead, they sink to the bottom, adhering to rocks or fronds of seaweed until their larvae hatch out, generally from places where the seabed is full of gravel or 'maerl', a pink, coral-like substance sometimes found close to the shoreline. And with that, thousands of new recruits are added to the ranks, each female laying between 50,000 and 100,000 eggs, an astonishing rate of production for any part of the natural world that surrounds us. To begin with, the larvae into which these eggs are transformed do not look like herring. Growing slowly into their adult shape, they move towards coasts and estuaries nearby when they are about an inch and

---

*There were other methods employed to locate herring. Fish were sometimes found through underwater binoculars or a lead-line drawn through water which vibrated in the presence of fish. In the 1930s, the Finns used small aeroplanes to try and determine where shoals swam – a technique that was also employed by those from other nations. This was also the beginning of Icelandair, a far cry from its current role taking passengers from the capitals of Europe to Keflavík.

a half long. It is only then they begin to obtain the silver shimmer we associate with the fish, its first scales appearing. When they are around three years old, they desert the areas where they have spent the early stages of life. Having developed a roe, they are then ready to spawn – and also, most likely, to negotiate the dangers of a fisherman's net for the first occasion in their existence.

Throughout the ten or eleven years of life they can then be granted, constant travel sums up the herrings' existence. It is a pattern of migration that begins in their first three to four years of maturing, a manner of behaving in which these silver troops start to move and manoeuvre, appearing in the early part of the year in places like Ireland, the west coast of Scotland and the Western Isles, and later on elsewhere. It is a mystery what dictates these movements; some prompting in their blood, perhaps, a set of mystical coordinates that are charted for them somewhere in the stars, their silver reflecting the silver of the fish. It is this far-fetched comparison that even sprinkles its enchantment into a nursery rhyme, the marvellous 'Wynken, Blynken, and Nod' by the American poet Eugene Field, a work that includes the verse:

'Where are you going, and what do you wish?'
The old moon asked the three.
'We have come to fish for the herring fish
That live in this beautiful sea;
Nets of silver and gold have we!'
Said Wynken, Blynken, and Nod.

Later it goes on to note how similar the stars were to the herring fish 'that lived in that beautiful sea', following ley-lines or invisible charts that lay just before the surface. Whatever the reason, fanciful or otherwise, for their movements, the results are beyond doubt. Ports like Ardglass and Dunmore East in Ireland, Aberporth in Wales, and Oban, Mallaig, Ullapool and Stornoway in Scotland used to throng with men and women who came there to net their share of that bright and shining prey, battling the sometimes stormy seas often found at that time of year in order to harvest the *Clupea harengus,* the scientific name for the fish men had caught there perhaps even before the Pict or Gael, Jute or Saxon had ever dipped lines into these waters.

And between May and August, what appeared to be the relentless advance continued. During these months, the fishing would commence in the Orkney or Shetland Isles, before moving south to the Moray Firth and beyond. Much of the fishing occurred in ports like Lerwick, Baltasound, Scalloway, Kirkwall, Scrabster and Wick one week; the next it might be Nairn, Burghead and Lossiemouth. Yet still the progress of boats continued south. From September to November, the vessels had journeyed to the east coast of England, the flotilla of drifters, trawlers and other fishing boats sailing to places like Hull, Scarborough, Grimsby and the far southern ports of Yarmouth and Lowestoft. The fish were in season there from May to February, and at their finest during July and August. This is in contrast to the cod, which is in season from September to March and at its best from November to January, the colder, more dangerous parts of the year. Yet contrary to popular belief, as noted previously these herring congregating around East Anglia do not mirror exactly those which men might have hunted before in the north of Scotland. There are small, subtle differences between the herring caught outside Wick and those found off Lowestoft, spawned in different locations by the fish who had visited these coastlines, for all that they appear the same as one another in the gaze of most humans, who see them as members of an identical brigade. This confusion is not assisted in the way they cluster together – members of the north-west of Scotland regiment swimming alongside, their companions from Tyne and Wear without any clear distinction between them.

Like an army, however, each fish had its rank – or at least one awarded to it by the herring girls who, along with the fishermen, coopers and curers, followed the herring around the coast. They grasped the fish with their fingers from farlans, the large wooden troughs filled with fish lined up for them on shore. They were sprinkled with salt to prevent them from slithering from fingers, falling from grip. At the same time, too, they would have to make sure that both the herring's pancreas and part of the digestive tract, little pouches in their stomachs called pyloric caecae, were still intact. (If either the pancreas or the part of the stomach that contained this pouch was cut, allowing the enzymes to escape, the fish would not keep for long in the brine in which it was packed, a fact that many believed for years was discovered – probably by accident – by the Dutch at the beginning of the fifteenth century. These fishermen from the ports of, what is now called, the Netherlands also reputedly found out that the complete removal of these parts of the fish diminished their flavour.)

Together with doing all this, the more experienced of the women would judge the size and condition of the fish almost without thinking, those like Rita MacNab, originally from the Hamilton area in Scotland's Central Belt but now living in Shetland. Now in her eighties, she first worked as a herring gutter in Peel in the Isle of Man, a location she was sent to by her local Labour Exchange, presumably on the basis that part of her working life when she was in school involved dipping fish in batter in a local fish and chip shop. The only person from a relatively urban, inland area among the crew, she soon learned to join in with the other women who all came from coastal areas of these islands, placing the right fish in an instant in the basket that had been put out for that particular size and scale.

'That one's a *matje*,' one might say, using a term for a mature herring that came from the Dutch, a corruption of their term for 'maiden' or, more specifically, 'Virgin Mary'.

'A mattie . . .' A woman lifts a young maturing fish not much more than 20cm in length.

'That's a spent,' another might proclaim, picking up a less valuable fish that had spawned but was not smaller than 28.5cm in length.

And so it went on, an endless grading that would not shame the ranks of the British Army to which many relatives of these girls belonged. Seven grades in total including the following:

Large full – a large fish not less than 11 1/4 inches (285mm) in length and full of milt (male semen) and roe.

Full – an inch smaller than the large full at 10 1/4 (260 mm) and also full of milt and roe.

Filling – a maturing fish not smaller than the above.

Medium – a maturing fish not smaller than 9 inches (230mm) long.

Matfull – a fish not smaller than 9 1/4 inches (235mm) in length but full of milt and roe.*

Difficult though the size and scale might have been to differentiate and divine, it would have been harder still sometimes to describe the appearance of an individual herring. There are aspects of how the fish looks that are beyond dispute – its strong tail fin, the continually changing fins on its back like the hairstyle of one of either the last of the Mohicans or their punk-rock successors, three smaller versions of the same below, its slightly prominent lower jaw, weak teeth, even the way the dark pupil appears to swim at the centre of a white iris. The position of that eye underlines how it is a forager fish, feeding largely on the ocean's surface. Bottom feeders need to have eyes near the top of the head, looking out continually for predators from above. And that gaze is set within a narrow skull, designed, like its fins, to cut quickly through water.

*There is also in some of the literature a reference to another, self-explanatory category: 'tornbelly'.

However, the herring's colour seems to be altered continually by the eye of its beholder. Its back is a greeny-blue shade, designed to mislead a seabird which, looking from above, might think it is only sea underneath its wings. From below, it appears grey, allowing it to deceive predators that stare at it from below, the shade blending with the steel-grey sky most commonly seen by those who live close to the waters of the North Atlantic. Taken in its entirety, too, the fish might seem to possess a silver shade, but one by one its individual scales shimmer, sparkling orange, red, blue, sometimes even a rich dark green or purple when it is lifted in a human hand, its skin linked together in some neatly patterned chain at its top that might appear fit to decorate a woman's neck with a diamond or pearl at the end of one of its loops. It is the microscopic rings, however, forming upon the fish's scales which – like those found within the trunk of a tree – determine the herring's age, accruing over years like wrinkles, one for every year the fish are in season. As the Basque writer Kirmen Uribe points out in his work *Bilbao–New York–Bilbao*, it is winter that creates these rings. 'It's the time when fish eat least, and that time of hunger draws a dark trace in the fish scales', as if the ring were 'a wound'. Unlike humans, though, these fish do not stop growing but continue to do so until they die, never shrinking or stooping with age. They only grow more slowly as they stretch into the fish equivalent of middle or old age.

It is not the only alteration that takes place within the fish. Some changes even occur after it dies. It seems to change its shade the longer it is left lying dead, losing the scales that cluster on it, becoming brighter for a day or two, dulling later as blood or life stops surging through its flesh. It is not for nothing that its sparkle is found within the nail varnish and lip gel that glitters on young girls' mouths and fingers, allowing them to cast their gleam on the gaze of the young men whom they attempt to catch. Or that, too, the herring features in the German writer W. G. Sebald's dreamlike and hypnotic prose. In *The Rings of Saturn,* while wandering around the Lowestoft area, he writes of how:

> *Around 1870, when projects for the total illumination of our cities were everywhere afoot, two English scientists with the names of Herrington and Lightbown investigated the unusual phenomenon [of the herring glowing] in the hope that the luminous substance exuded by dead herring would lead to a formula for an organic source of light that had the capacity to generate itself.*

This is a notion that goes back a considerable time. In *A Description of the Northern Peoples,* written in 1555, the Swedish writer and ecclesiastic Olaus Magnus picks up on this phenomenon, noting: 'In the sea at night its eyes shine like lamps, and what is more, when these fish are swimming rapidly, and the huge shoal turns back on itself, they resemble flashes of light in the churning sea.'

And, of course, boiling herring to extract the oil and create this illuminating way of lighting up the streets of Paris and London was part of the work going on at Klädesholmen, that small island lying just off the Swedish coast in the Skagerrak, bringing ecological disaster in its wake and perhaps deterring shoals of swerving, dipping herring from nearing the shoreline. Yet before we run away with the notion that Manhattan might have sparkled with herring light or the outline of the Arc de Triomphe could ever have glimmered and shimmered with fish scales, perhaps we should hesitate for a moment. There is no evidence that this was a great success. The House of Commons is unlikely to have ever been lit up with fish gills (the shade of kippers, perhaps, to cover up the murky deals within), or the streets of the nation's cities flashed with the lustre of fish tail-fins. The failure of the 'eccentric undertaking' described by Sebald was so great that it left little of lasting legacy. It is tempting to conclude that the author's odd choice of names for his scientists – Herrington and Lightbown – is a quirky invention, one of his own 'red herrings', sending the reader off on every bit as much a wrong scent as the fox in that ancient practice, when that strong-smelling fish was employed to trick the hounds from following in their quarry's tracks. For all that the practice of generating light from herring occurred in the late nineteenth century, there does not appear to be a record of the existence of any two English scientists with their names.[*]

There was little sense, however, of the herring's artistic or aesthetic qualities when the men and women involved in the herring trade handled and divided the fish. Written in the early twentieth century, the novel *Gillespie* by the minister and Scottish writer J. MacDougall Hay provides a wonderfully evocative description of the fishermen, the fishermen arriving in 'Brieston', the fictional name he gives to his home port of Tarbert, Loch Fyne.

> *Standing on the Quay and looking down upon these fishermen in their loaded boats, one caught a look of pathos upon their rugged faces, tawny with sweat threshed out of them in a fifteen-mile pull in the teeth of the tide. Their tired eyes were grey like the sea, their blue shirts with short oilskin sleeves were laced with herring scales; and herring scales smeared the big fishing boots which come up over the knee; their hands were slippery with herring spawn; even their beards and pipes were whitened.*

Similar descriptions were written of the young women involved in this work, how these same fish scales gleamed and sparkled on the clothing of the groups of three – two gutters and a packer – who worked together, tangled too in any lock of hair that might have worked loose from the headscarves fastened tight, and how 'the tang of fish and savour of brine' pervaded their clothing and skin. One observer,

[*] It should be noted that whale oil and peat oil, as well as herring oil, were also used for this purpose.

James Wilson in his work *A Voyage Round the Coasts of Scotland and the Isles in 1841*, noting the sheer quantities of blood and fish slime upon the women, declared: 'From what we witnessed of their process, we doubt not if they were arranged in battle array they would have gained the day at Waterloo.'

And there were other problems, ones that did not afflict Wellington's troops, such as the clouds of gulls that hung over the quays of these small fishing ports, squawking at them, battling over each scrap of fish. Sometimes the birds would spurt in their direction, staining the clothes of those who had the audacity to stand below. The women would ignore these small showers of shit, aware that they had little time to wash their clothing. None of the various Factory Acts that were passed throughout the nineteenth century and early twentieth century appeared to apply to them, the nature of their work allowing their employers to avoid limiting the time these women could be employed. Instead, they started early in the morning when the fish were landed from the boats, bending over barrels till the job was done, be it early afternoon or late evening, or occasionally even midnight and beyond. It is also the case that in the huts provided by the curers where most of the women stayed, there was little opportunity of getting clean. These buildings often had no lighting, heating or water; candles and paraffin lamps providing the only glow of comfort. Generally, these buildings had two bunk beds inside. Sometimes three women were squeezed together within a single bed, wrapped in a blanket to keep out the cold.*

Even those few who were lucky enough to stay in guesthouses had their own indignities to bear. Like their counterparts in the huts, they would have to share beds and possessed little opportunity to wash their working clothes,

---

*The working conditions of the herring girls and the government's response to them is discussed in greater depth later.

with many landladies forcing them to remove these at the front door. Such was their obsession with the taint of fish these girls carried around with them that several landladies were known to cover the rugs in the house with dustsheets or to pin sheets of newspaper over the walls. On a Saturday night the women would bathe, washing their hair sometimes as much as six times to remove the last tang of herring. Cleanliness was required for Godliness, the aroma of Lux or Sunlight soap accompanying them as they walked to church the following day. On Monday they might have the opportunity to wash their oilskins, splashing paraffin and scrubbing to rid them of fish grease, making sure that not one glimmering fish scale clung to their Baltic boots.

Yet far more than being spotless, one of the most important tasks in their daily routine was to avoid cuts on their own fingers, wounds upon their flesh. Every morning their hours awake would start with a reminder of this, the day beginning with the cry of 'Get up and tie your fingers' echoing around their lodgings. This would be done, their fingers fastened with the strips of coarse flour sacking or sometimes yellow calico known as 'cloots' or 'clooting', used to protect their hands from being cut with sharp gutting knives.

And there were reasons for this. Those who were 'gutting quines' worked at great speed, fish passing through their fingers at the rate of around sixty a minute, one a second. During this time they would lift up each herring, and in a swift, sudden movement, split it open from head to tail, removing the guts deftly at the same time – a monotonous, repetitive tempo which Shetland poet Laureen Johnson catches well in her poem 'Rhythms':

> Knife point in
> twist and rive
> gills and gut
> wan move.

Left hand
fish tae basket.
Nixt een.

The 'long gut' which they removed with this move was also useful. It dropped into a 'gut cog' or 'gut tub', which was emptied into a large 'gut barrel'. This was used later by one of the local farmers for fertilising the soil, or brought, in some places, to the local 'gut factory' or fishmeal plant, where it was made into fishmeal and fish oil. There it too might be processed into fertiliser or chicken feed – an early example of local recycling. The guts could also be delivered to the many fishmeal plants found around the country.

For the more experienced women at the farlans, this was a simple, undemanding task, though occasionally their concentration might lapse and they could end up cutting themselves. It was less so for the younger women, working, perhaps, in their first season. They would often cause injury to themselves. The 'howkett' fingers where their flesh had been cut would sometimes be contaminated by the very substance of their work, the entrails of fish perhaps, or the burn of salt. As a result, many of the fishing girls often had cracks, abscesses, wounds and even infections on their hands. Their fingers were often sore, raw and bleeding, rarely having the opportunity to heal. One major problem was the way that a fish scale sometimes became caught in an eye, affecting the girls' sight. For this difficulty, rather grotesquely, there was one woman in the party whose task it was to 'lick' the eye clean. Or else the tail fin of a herring might be used, shifting the impediment.

This was probably the least of the fishing girls' difficulties. Even travelling between ports was often arduous and problematic, with some of the fishing girls from Orkney, Shetland and the Western Isles voyaging across the Pentland Firth or the Minch to go to mainland herring ports; others made that same voyage in reverse. The late Joan Afrin recalled her own first voyage from her home in Stornoway, Lewis to Lerwick in the Shetland Isles:

> *There were about three hundred of us on board, and we left Storno-way at ten o'clock at night and didn't arrive till ten the following night – but we were so thankful we made it at all. It was a terrible night, and about halfway we were thrown with the cargo to one side, then to the other. We were sure we were all going to be lost. Eventually, the boat listed and limped into Lerwick harbour with its gunwales under water. We still expected it to sink but it didn't.*

This standard of seaborne transport brought its share of casualties. The *Scotsman* of 11 July 1893 tells the sad story of one.

> *A very unusual and affecting scene was witnessed in Peterhead yesterday afternoon at the funeral of a Highland girl named Jessie Campbell, seventeen years of age from Tolsta, Back, Stornoway. The girl caught cold on the voyage from Stornoway, and inflammation threatening into fever, was removed to the hospital, where she died on Saturday. The Rev Walter Ross, the Free Church delegate at Peterhead during the season, conducted Gaelic services on the green in front of the hospital yesterday, surrounded by those who were to attend the funeral – about fifty Highland fisher girls. Owing to the hysterical clinging of two sisters of the deceased to the closed coffin, it was with difficulty that the undertaker could get it removed. The hearse containing the coffin was followed by all the girls and two brothers of the deceased who were fishing at Peterhead, these latter being the only males present. At the graveside, where another Gaelic service was conducted, the girls so clung to the coffin that interment was impossible. Mr Ross advised them to withdraw outside the gate which they ultimately did, on his undertaking, to see the lass laid reverently on the grave.*

Another account tells of a crew of three young girls from Cromore in the Isle of Lewis who were at the summer fishing season at Wick, when they contracted measles. All of them died and were buried at Wick. Two were sisters, Mary and Peggy, born in 1867 and 1869. The third was Mary Macleod, born 1870, daughter of 'Murchadh Aoghnas Ruadh'. They were buried at Wick because it was not possible to bring the remains home, as that town was considered to be too far away in the context of the transport available at that time. While we cannot say for definite, they may have been *cuibhlearan* or 'coilers' – the first-year girls who were paid less than older ones due to their slowness and lack of experience. They also suffered more in other ways – the legacy of an industry which was hard enough when you were healthy, but brought illness and death to those who were sometimes already not that strong before their journey to and from Shetland, due to the harshness of their voyage across the Minch.

Even when they arrived on shore, there were problems. The existence of rheumatism and tuberculosis is, for instance, recorded in the Factory and Workshops Annual report for 1905, where it is noted that: 'Strong and vigorous as these women are, they are by no means proof against rheumatism from which many suffer greatly.'

The inspectors, Mairi Paterson and Emily Slocock, who composed that report, also wrote that in Lewis and Shetland, two areas where a large number of the women were engaged in herring gutting, 'the phthisis [tuberculosis] death-rate is a high one'.

In his book *Portrona*, the late Lewis writer Norman Malcolm Macdonald introduces his book with what is possibly an apocryphal story about the death of a young woman he names as Catherine MacKenzie. In an act rare in the mid-nineteenth century, her body was brought home to be buried. Published posthumously in 2000, the work tells of how: 'A Lewis Herring girl died in Fraserburgh 150 years ago. Consumption, hurried along by pitiless night-and-day working on gluts of herring, gutting and packing barrels and ships to feed the hungry of eastern Europe.'

'The fit girls,' Norman writes on, 'could take it for a time, a hard but well-paid season.'

There were others, however, who could not; their bodies now lie in unmarked graves throughout northern and central Europe, in countries such as Poland, the Baltic States, the Netherlands, Germany and Norway, or below lichen-cloaked stones in the cemeteries of Shetland, Orkney, the north of Ireland and my own native Lewis. Yet it is doubtful whether even they suffered as much as those employed in places like North Carolina on the other side of the Atlantic, in the USA, where the trade also existed. In these areas it was often slaves who 'worked' the herring, the women gutting and beheading them, the men hauling in nets on the foreshore at night. In this area salt herring was often called 'corned herring' – a reminder that 'corned beef' was created in a similar way, dipped in a salt cure. Even until recent times, blacks played a major part in that industry, unloading the fish from small boats on the Chowan river, gutting freshly caught river herring with their hair tightly wrapped under scarves not unlike those my aunts wore during the heyday of the industry here. One can imagine the rhythm of their fingers, the sharpness of their knives as they worked over containers that looked like old-time bathtubs, filling them up inch by inch.

Their story is probably even more wordless and forgotten than those of their counterparts in Europe, unrecorded in any inspector's report, remembered mainly in a few etchings that appeared in an issue of *Harper's New Monthly Magazine*. In them, the women gut the fish and mend the nets in much the same way as their counterparts on the opposite side of the Atlantic.

Yet, the terrible evils of slavery aside, there were gains from this travelling too, the endless migration of female labour across the world where the herring swam. The improvement in the architecture of, say, my native Hebrides dates from this time. The women would look at the houses of, perhaps, Great Yarmouth or Lowestoft and note the improvements that could be made to their own homes, making them more 'modern' and convenient for both themselves and others who lived in their households. It altered the attitudes of the herring girls, too. No longer were they content to accept the traditional, male-dominated world in which they were raised. Instead, they were more inclined to question long-established practices, often urging their menfolk to examine the ways in which, particularly in terms of the construction of their houses, things had always been done.

It liberated women in other ways, too, affecting even those who were not in themselves 'herring girls'. Born in 1879, Margaret Murray from the small township of Bettyhill in Sutherland began work for the Post Office in 1914. Her occupation was a highly specialised one. Being bilingual, she followed the girls around on their journey. Her task was to transcribe the girls' messages – in both Gaelic and English – for the telegrams that were the main means of communication at that time, tapping their short notes in Morse Code from offices in places like Wick, South Shields and Great Yarmouth. Later, she extended even these horizons by moving to New York, no longer accepting the limits by which the lives of the women of Bettyhill had traditionally been constrained and curtailed.

And in doing this, she was probably a model for many other women who watched her at her work and thought that this was an existence they might recommend for their own sons and daughters, a glimpse of another way of seeing the world.

CHAPTER THREE

'Return to Sender'

Kenny Maciver is a difficult man to topple. A former university boxing champion, he still has the bulk and frame of that particular breed, for all that the breadth of his arms and shoulders is now hidden beneath the restraint of the Harris tweed jacket that serves almost as his uniform while working as an early-morning presenter on BBC Radio nan Gàidheal, the Gaelic-language radio service. His hands are broad, too, though one of them is more likely to clutch a microphone these days than to be concealed within a boxing glove. His gentleness is such that the only knockout he might conceivably throw would be in the form of a question directed at a local councillor – and even that would be a rare event. His trademark is an inquisitive and impish humour, rather than a body-blow or jab to the ribs.

On a quiet Monday afternoon, I head in the direction of his Stornoway studio, clutching – as my ancestors sometimes did – an offering of fish. However, these are not strung together on a piece of string like the ones the narrator of George Mackay Brown's fine short story 'Silver' took with him when he set off to try and woo a young lady in the community – a traditional romantic technique throughout the north of Scotland, and a pleasant and reliable substitute for a bouquet of roses. Neither are they contained within an enamel bucket, as I recall my fellow villagers doing when they had obtained a rare catch and wanted to keep in with their neighbours. They are stored within a plastic bag scrolled with the name of a Norwegian supermarket. Instead of writhing free, they are also contained within a collection of jars, a sealed silver packet, a bulging tin and a plastic bucket – the last of these circled and surrounded by parcel tape, just in case there might be a volcanic explosion while it is being shoogled about in the cargo of a plane.

I am bringing this gift not just to Kenny but also to other people I know: my contemporary, the manager of the Gaelic publishing firm Acair, Agnes Rennie, and local councillor and bon vivant Alasdair Macleod. The latter has something of a reputation as a food buff. Not only has he swallowed our local delicacy, the guga or gannet, despite hailing from another district of the island, but he has also eaten puffin while visiting the Faroe Islands, as well as preparing other food far removed from the salt herring he was undoubtedly fed on during his youth. In short, this was a man who enjoyed more than a little dash of paprika to spice up the food of life.

And so now to the herring laid out before us within the studio. Alasdair opens jars of pickled herring, some soused in tomato, others in mustard or a sweet and sour sauce. In some ways the fare is similar to the food served to me and thousands of others in the picturesque town of Florø, in Norway. The guests pick at this with their forks, making judicious remarks about both the flavour and the sheer quantity of onions contained in the mix. They speak, too, about the herring they ate in their childhoods.

'The most exotic thing we ever added to it was oatmeal,' Agnes says, recalling the manner in which it was fried in our kitchens.

They also test buckling, a form of smoked herring which, wrapped tightly within a bag, I took back for them from the fish market in Bergen. Unlike what happens with that other hot-smoked fish, the kipper, the roe or milt remain in the body of the fish, which has been beheaded and gutted. It can also be eaten hot or cold. Again, they peck at this, slicing small segments from its flesh.

'I was looking forward to this, but I'm a wee bit disappointed. It's kippery but not kippery enough,' Alasdair declared.

It is at this point that I remove from the plastic bag my *pièce de résistance* – a tin of fermented herring called *surströmming* I obtained from a friend in Sweden. It sits bulging on the table, looming like a thundercloud in our midst, ready to burst, boil and bubble in all directions, spitting a poisonous potion from the tiny cauldron in which – from all appearances – it might have been brewed. I tell them tales of the dish's origins – how just enough salt was added to prevent the fish becoming rotten; how it had been a feature of northern Swedish cuisine since the sixteenth century; how a pensioner from Norway had called in his country's bomb squad to open a 25-year-old can that had been discovered in the loft of his cabin. (Apparently it had raised the roof a perilous inch or two.) I talk, too, of the German landlord who was given legal backing after expelling one of his tenants for spilling some of this liquid on the outside landing. 'He had just cause,' they decided after a quick sniff of the tin.

'We'll have to open it outside,' I tell them.

Kenny raises a sceptical eyebrow.

'Well, if you ever want to use the premises again …'

Finally, he accedes to this request, leading the four of us outside the studio. The microphone bobs above Alasdair as he crouches on the pavement to open the can, tugging at the ring-pull with all the intensity and deliberation a soldier might display while withdrawing the pin of a grenade. A few seconds later and there is a small, muted explosion, the kind of bubbling that might accompany the opening of a bottle of champagne.

And then there is the smell ...

Agnes is the first to notice it, her face grimacing in disgust. Alasdair recoils. Perched on his haunches, his knees knock and tremble. Finally, there is Kenny. His microphone moves away as if he is trying to open up greater distance between himself and a particularly aggressive opponent. His legs – in tribute, perhaps, to the fish he had eaten earlier – start buckling. After a short time, he can stand it no longer. In response to a stink that seems to mingle rotting seaweed, cat urine and vinegar, he does what he never did during his years in the boxing ring.

He runs away.[*]

★ ★ ★

As members of a generation that grew up alongside the ghosts of herring girls and fishermen, one would have thought that we were immune to all the smells of the sea. They loomed everywhere in our childhoods, even the air itself reeking of fish.

A walk around Stornoway harbour, for instance, and all its heady scents haunted nostrils, filled lungs. There was the tang of mackerel, a fish as clean as the blue steel of a bullet if you weighed it in your hand. There was the salt, slightly curdled aroma of prawns, bright and orange as they lay curled in their fish boxes, topped and tailed, ready for the UK scampi market. There might be, too, a brown crab lurking, its pincers sharp and deadly, waiting, it seemed, to grasp an outstretched finger or toe. It might be on its way to Billingsgate, packed in straw in tea chests. (Those who sent them south once or twice obtained in return a note back marked 'Dead on arrival' and a

---

[*]The author is guilty of a little dramatic exaggeration here.

bill for their carriage.) Around the town, there was often, too, the all-pervading stink of *Taigh nan Guts*, the fishmeal factory in Newton on the edge of Stornoway. It was powerful enough to mask even the strong aroma of tobacco that clung to my clothes as a teenager. We walked through a fog of rancid fish smells and cigarette smoke, somehow possessing the confidence to believe that despite the smell, our long, greasy hair, platform soles and flared checked trousers, we were still among the most attractive creatures that had ever stalked the planet, or at least the small part of it that had the good fortune to name us as among its younger citizens. Both the volume of our voices and our youthful arrogance used to compete with the raucous chorus of seagulls, drawn by the fishmeal perfume with which Stornoway seemed sometimes to have been sprayed for weeks on end.

The smell of fish even accompanied you into certain houses in my home village, lingering within whitewash or brightly coloured wallpaper. In these cases it might be a legacy left behind by some bachelor fisherman, exiled to the rocks by his good and holy spinster sisters. He would invariably stand there with the bamboo pole – *slat-creagaich* – that served as his fishing rod, lashing the waves with a furious cast of his line. His penance for his sins – stemming from a night out on the town, perhaps – would only be complete when he returned to his home with ling or some pollock, a bucket or two of *cudaigean* (coalfish, or 'cuddies'), from which good, strong souse could be made.

There were other ways in which fish could be brought to the village. Our house, for instance, had 'shares' in a small, eight-man rowing boat which ventured out from the village of Skigersta or Port of Ness. For all that its catch would be doled out among our friends and neighbours when it sailed out, there were too often times when it seemed to net more quarrels than fish. One household might complain that the bulk of repairs to the boat was falling too heavily on its shoulders, or that it was the only household that ever lifted a paintbrush in its direction, ensuring that the wood was dry and watertight. Soon the vessel would be in dry dock, lashed and harnessed beside one of the co-owners' peat stacks, waiting, perhaps, until the next generation found both nerve and forgiveness enough to suggest it might sail out from these waters again. Yet on the occasions when it did go out, it was a boon for all our fellow villagers. A trailer would be hitched on to one of the local tractors and putter down the village doors. All the households in the village would have that day's catch bubbling away on the stove for the following few evenings; that shared harvest of fish a source of sustenance for them.

And this tradition had long historical roots. In the course of writing this book, I received a phone call from my son, Angus, who, working in the Museum Service of the Western Isles Council, had obtained an enquiry from that area's archaeological service. Apparently, the foot of the family croft had been washed away, revealing a strange stone structure with a neat cobblestone floor which they thought was pre-nineteenth century. Did I know what it was? Another quick call to Donald Macleod – or Dòmhnall Aost – in the village and I obtained an answer. At one time an old salthouse had stood there, before grass and soil had concealed it from view. A short distance away, on a neighbouring croft, there had been a wood store for boats. In short, on what would seem at first glance an unpromising stretch of shoreline, where hull and keel might be broken and dunted by rock, there was at one time an industry, one that traded with ling (mainly), coalfish, mackerel and an occasional herring or two.

There were times when both the young and those from elsewhere would grow sick of this salt food. This was especially because of the lack of variety involved in its preparation. For people who had emerged from generations of their kin existing on a near-starvation diet, there was little sign of seasoning or spice in the preparation of food, or even storing some away and allowing it to ferment in a tin as was done by the citizens of northern Sweden. There is a story, for instance, of a family of people from Glasgow who came up to spend time with their Hebridean grandmother one summer. Each day boiled fish – perhaps ling, haddock or herring – appeared on the plate before them. Each day they grew more and more nauseous at the sight. Finally, they took the opportunity to go into Stornoway and buy a few pounds of sausages from one of the local butchers. They presented this to their grandmother, who thanked them profusely for their gift and assured them that the sausages would be prepared for the next meal.

Shortly afterwards, the long-awaited dinner arrived. They trekked into the kitchen to find the potatoes and a few miserable skins lying ready for them on the table. They turned to question the grandmother to find out what had happened to their anticipated feast.

'By the time I gutted them and took off their heads and tails, that's all there was left,' she explained.

Yet all this is understandable. When hunger haunts, the most important aspect of any food is to wolf it down quickly, satisfying the immediacy and urgency of the human appetite. The culinary arts are the preserve of the prosperous and content, not for those who exist on the edge of starvation, as the people in Norway and the Scottish islands often did. Their chance of experimenting in the kitchen was also affected by the lack of reliable ovens in many homes, providing them – sausages aside – with little option but to boil their food. As a result of this, the worst prediction of armchair politicians in the Western Isles – and professional ones in the Isle of Man – is the threat of a 'return to a spuds and herring economy', a life of poorly paid drudgery and toil, something that is bound to happen if their electorate or colleagues reject the unquestionable wisdom of their vision and advice.

Another method some used to catch fish involved the *taigh-thàbhaidh*, a large, spoon-shaped object that appeared to have been designed for a race of giants, allowing them to scoop their meals from some gargantuan dish. One end was a long bamboo pole, the other a circle of pliable wood to which a net had been attached. Bait was used, designed to catch as many cuddies or tiny coalfish as possible from the edge of a crag where a man stood. Two of my uncles possessed this item, one even having his photograph taken for a history book of the island of Lewis with it in his possession. It was a picture his wife, my aunt, thoroughly detested, not because of the ancient fishing implement her husband clutched within his fingers, but because he was wearing an old pair of dungarees at the time. She would shake her head at the shame she felt at her man's five minutes of fame, complaining that he had never changed his clothes to allow a decent photograph to be taken.

Yet, above all fish, it was the existence of herring that dominated my home in Ness in Lewis. While it may have lacked the potency of a tin of *surströmming*, its power was evident throughout many of the conversations that took place around our household fires. Some of my aunties had been herring girls in the 1920s and '30s. One had stopped off in Wick in mainland Scotland's top right-hand corner, meeting and marrying a Caithness man there. Another had taken welcome respite from both salt and barrel in Inverness, finding a husband and setting up her family home in that urban hubbub. 'I was never very good at it,' she used to confess. 'Cut my fingers with the blade too many times.' Despite her avowed clumsiness, she had been an attractive young woman. It was her face they used to decorate some of the promotional material for a Gaelic language book, *Clann-nighean an Sgadain*, written by my friend Norman Malcolm Macdonald nearly thirty years ago. Again, like my other aunt, she was not altogether comfortable with the notoriety of this, shivering with embarrassment each time her scarf-covered head was pointed out.

It was my favourite aunt, Bella, who had remained in the village, who had the greatest experience of 'following the fishing'. She had even ventured as far south as Lowestoft in pursuit of the herring and the exchange of silver that accompanied it. She rarely spoke about the trade, yet she was the one among all the sisters who had inherited the greatest, most terrible legacy from the work. Her fingers were twisted and crippled with the arthritis and rheumatism that plagued her entire body in later life. Devoid of self-pity as she was, I cannot recall her ever blaming her physical conditions on the ardours of the life she experienced at a young age, going from port to port in the company of other Gaelic-speaking girls, slashing the belly of each fish from gills to tail, tossing away the guts that would later fertilise the soil nearby. Suffering was a fact of life for her. There was neither point nor pleasure in complaining about her lot.

In fact, these herring girls did the opposite. In a number of Gaelic songs, their hard way of life is both celebrated and eulogised, remembered for its joys and sorrows. As my friend Margaret Stewart has informed me, the journey from one port to another is mentioned in the hundreds of Gaelic verses about the trade. Place names pepper the lines as the experiences of young men and women recall what it was like to follow the herring, such as in the two verses of the Gaelic song below:

Ma thèid mise tuilleadh a Leòdhas nan cruinneag,
Ma thèid mise tuilleadh a dh'innis nan laoch,
Ma thèid mi rim bheò dh'Eilean Leòdhais nam mòr-bheann,
Cha till mi rim bheò às gun òrdugh an Rìgh.

Mu dheireadh an t-samhraidh, 's ann thàinig mi nall às –
Bha 'n teas orm trom, anns an àm bhithinn sgìth,
Ag iasgach an sgadain a shamhradh 's a dh'earrach
Sa Bhruaich 's ann an Sealtainn 's an Arcaibh nan caol.

If I go again to Lewis of the maidens,
If I go again to that heroic land,

If I go again to the high hills of Lewis,
I will not leave its shores without the King's command.

I left towards the end of summer,
The heat so exhausting and I was so tired
Fishing the herring throughout spring and summer
In Fraserburgh and Shetland, Orkney with its kyles.

Sometimes these songs read like letters home, providing 'all-the-news-that's-fit-to-sing'. Not only place names and communities are mentioned, but even sometimes the names of the curers and employers who are mistreating them. The revenge of the herring girls is sometimes to immortalise those who oppress them, echoing their names through the reciting and repeating of their music.

There is a similar link between herring and song to be found in the Isle of Man. Sitting in a hotel bar in the south end of that island, I was entertained by the voices of Ruth Keggin and others who sang the words of '*Arrane y Skeddan*' (Song of the Herring). A gentle, soothing piece of music, it told of what happened one year when the fishing and sea brought them 'heaps of money to get food and meat'. The words reverberated, too, with the religious faith of that island: its harmonies recalling a Welsh or Methodist hymn, its words asking for the blessings of the Creator on all that they had done.

Both herring and fishing found its way, too, into much of the Presbyterian faith followed in my home district, its language and imagery understandable to both men and women in a fond and fitting manner for a religion in which four of Christ's apostles, Peter, James, John and Andrew, were reputedly fishermen. I recall sitting once in the front pews of the tiny Church of Scotland in South Dell, uncomfortable both in my new suit and in being within range of my neighbours' eyes. In front of me was the Reverend MacSween, short and broad in his minister's black clothes, impressive, too, in his thick grey hair and the strength of the hands that clutched the edge of the pulpit. It was there that my gaze kept returning again and again, noting how these were not the fingers of a scholar but possessed might and force, the lines and bruises of one who had known harsh, physical work. He had been, so I was told later, a Scalpay fisherman, used to the haul and heave of herring-filled nets.

Yet even before I had been given this explanation, I knew that this had been his trade. These fists were not those that grasped a teacup easily, raising it to his lips to sip. His words and language were not, like those of so many of his counterparts, found within the world of books. Instead they came, rich and gleaming, from another source, a life in which wages were hard earned, from the depths of the Atlantic or the Minch. His experiences and fingers gave weight and ballast to the words he chose, those like the following from Matthew's gospel:

> *Again, the kingdom of heaven is like unto a net, that was cast into the sea, and gathered of every kind: which, when it was full, they drew to shore, and sat down, and gathered the good into vessels, but cast the bad away. So shall it be at the end of the world: the angels shall come forth, and sever the wicked from among the just, and shall cast them into the furnace of fire.*

After this, he told a story I can still recall to the present day. It was of a cloudy night when the Scalpay fishing boats were returning home empty, following in each other's wake across the narrowness of the Minch. One of the older men on board a particular vessel was praying to himself, uttering the words below his breath as he often did. Suddenly he stopped and turned to the others:

'Let's put the nets down here.'

After a moment or two in which minds were clouded, too, with doubt, they did as he suggested, casting their nets overboard. The men on the other boats followed suit, letting slip their scepticism as they allowed their coils and loops down into the darkness of the water, its surface seeming as thick and viscous as blood. Yet below, the bright gleam of herring massed and accumulated, filling the tangle of the nets. When the men lifted them once more, the clouds shifted, and the skies turned bright with the shimmer of the moon. They sang to celebrate their catch, voices mingling together in a psalm that, because someone had left on the radio in the boat, reverberated around the Minch and the waters of the Atlantic. Others in different boats joined in, taking up the words and music, a performance that only came to an end when the coastguard's voice crackled on the air, asking them, respectfully, to at least switch off their radio when they sang, because their praise was putting the lives and vessels in danger if anything happened on that night.

Give praise and thanks unto the Lord,
for bountiful is he;
His tender mercy doth endure
unto eternity . . .

And then there are stories of another kind of faith, those that may well precede belief in Christ upon the Cross on these shores. Some of these note the fickle, unpredictable nature of the herring, the manner in which they might shoal around a particular shoreline and then, suddenly one year, disappear from the vicinity, turning ports and harbours that had been created almost as 'reception areas' for the fish into empty, isolated places, bereft of the silver darlings they had relied upon for some time before. They would try and provide explanations for their absence. In some areas adultery among the fisher folk was responsible for herring diving, ducking and dodging a particular stretch of coast. Sometimes, as in Martin Martin's account in his *Descriptions of the Western Isles of Scotland* (1703), it was claimed that it was human quarrels and bloodshed that had compelled herring to swim away from a particular stretch of land: 'It is a General Observation all Scotland over, that if a Quarrel happen on the Coast where Herring is caught, and that Blood be drawn violently, then the Herring go away from the Coast without returning, during that season.'

While one might be tempted to dismiss the entire notion of the prophetic skills of herring, it should be noted that one year they swerved and avoided the British coastline was 1939. Perhaps they had an inkling of the bloodshed to come, the fishing industry giving way to warships and submarines following in the wake of where fish had often swum.

Other legends exist. In one of the many tales of its kind that flood and ripple around the Western Isles, the old storyteller Angus MacLellan gives an account of a boat from South Uist on which the crew manages to net a huge harvest of herring. The vessel wobbles and trembles below the weight of its catch, the huge bulk of the ocean thunking and thudding beneath its bow. Calum Ruadh, a young man who is on board, sees a mermaid in the distance. He points her out to the others, wondering for a moment if she has emerged from the depths of his imagination. But he is wrong. The others see her too.

'Each of us throw a fish towards her,' the skipper says.

'All of us?'

'Aye . . .'

One crew member after another tosses a herring in the mermaid's direction, the bright gleam of silver whirling above the watery darkness. The mermaid continues to swim after the vessel, moving relentlessly through the waves.

'Now you.' The skipper nods in the young man's direction.

He grasps hold of fin and tail, hurling the fish towards the mermaid. No sooner is it out of his hand than she dips back below the water, breaking through its surface. The skipper turns to him, saying nothing, but his face pales, a hand touching the young man's shoulder for an instant.

'I don't want you to go to sea again,' he says when the boat touches land, and the young man promises to do so.

It is a year before he breaks that promise. Calum approaches him to go on a voyage from Lochboisdale to Loch Skipport. At first he shakes his head, remembering how that mermaid shimmered in the water, following in the boat's wake. The memory has begun to seem insubstantial to him, a trick, perhaps, of the light.

'Oh, go on!' Calum laughs.

It is the last people see of them, the moment they step into the vessel heading north. Someone observed that it shook and trembled as it set off from the shore . . .

It is perhaps tales like these, stories of both everyday and transcendent miracles, that have made my fellow islesmen on occasion value the herring highly, even causing them to view the fish with something that approaches both wonder and sentimentality. Michael Iain Currie in Mallaig – the brother of the other Michael Currie in Mallaig – reminded me of a story I recall my uncle telling me when I was young. He lifted up a herring head in his fingers and showed it to me, shifting it back and forth in his hands.

'The five predators of the herring can be found within its head,' he declared in Gaelic. 'If you open up its mouth, you can find a small mark like a candle, representing the light that draws it to the surface to be killed. Look down its throat and you can see the shape of a whale. Examine the gills from the inside and you can glimpse the shapes of oars. Push them forwards, see them from the outside, and they look like the wings of a gannet. And, of course, the fine mesh of the skin that covers its head looks like a herring net, stretched out and ready to capture a shoal.'

The herring is a dish that represents the simplicity of an old way of life, particularly potent and rich with flavour for those who turned their back on it, for all that they were much more dismissive of it if it lay before them day after day. When they gathered together in exile in the city, it was its flesh and bones, scales and gills which, together with the *buntàta* (potato), lay at the centre of their plates. (Very like the Lowlander who, when gathering away from home, invariably stood with knife gleaming above a stuffed and steaming sheep's stomach, addressing this strange object with a few pious words.) The exiles would forsake their customary cutlery as they plunged their fingers deep into the flesh of the fish, carefully removing the bones that clustered there, quaffing down any flesh that remained with a quick dip and swallow of milk or even something stronger. Sometimes, too, their thirst was made all the more powerful by the fact that the herring was sprinkled with salt, a justification for another pint or two of pale ale or lager. Then, when the meal was over, there would be more Gaelic songs, with words, perhaps, that might have been echoed by one of the fishermen who had sailed out to catch the very fish that had arrived on the table before.

> 'S truagh nach do dh'fhuirich mi tioram air tìr:
> 'N fhìrinn a th' agam nach maraiche mi . . .

> It's a shame I didn't stay dry on the land.
> It's the truth I am telling. Have pity on me . . .

Yet this sentimentality wasn't present without good reason. The herring in all its various forms had been omnipresent in their childhood homes. It had a number of shades and flavours. Not only was it boiled and salted, but it could also be dipped in oatmeal and fried. (In later, more refined times, the frying pan was put aside and the grill put in its place, a dash of mustard splashed over the catch's ribs, spare or otherwise. On these occasions we would pick vigorously at its bones, complaining, as young children, that there were too many 'hairs' in it.) It also arrived looking like a bronzed and exotic intruder into our pallid lives in the form of the kipper, with a smell so indelible when it landed on a plate that it even compelled that famous Englishman in New York, Quentin Crisp, to break his own hygiene rule and wash his dish when he consumed it for his breakfast. There is little doubt that it came, too, to an Englishman's tongue in other ways. As well as a 'red herring', he might have spoken of 'to throw a sprat to catch a herring', which involves baiting your hook with a tiny piece of fish in order to catch a larger one or, in other words, foregoing the chance of a small advantage to ensure you later have a greater one. Who knows? If he had East Anglian connections, he might even have described someone as 'herring-gutted' if he was a tall, thin streak of a man. And then there is the occasional expression in Shakespeare's plays. When Toby Belch complains of 'a plague o' these pickled herring' in *Twelfth Night*, he is talking of a persistent habit summed up by his own surname.

Yet all in all, the fish only features in an English expression or two. Its Gaelic equivalents shoal and sparkle throughout the language. It even had the honour of being one of the few words of Gaelic that the English-speaking housewives of suburban Stornoway deigned to recognise, casting away all their pretensions and social snobbery when a cry of *sgadan ùr* (new herring) was heard in the street. They would put on their twinsets and pearls, slip a headscarf around their heads to protect their new perms and go out to buy a fresh catch of fish from the young women or, later, mobile shops who were selling these goods. And then the herring would be cooked. There was even a mock grace said before these meals in which Gaelic and English jostled together.

> Old man,
> say the grace.
> *Buntàta 's sgadan,*
> *sìos leis . . .*

> Old man,
> say the grace.
> Potato and herring.
> Stuff your face.

Someone from Barra has told me that when they were young and mischievous, they used to parody the 'Hail Mary' in their night-time prayers. Referring to their evening meal, most often herring, they would mutter: '*Fàilte dhut, a Mhoire, tha thu làn dhan bhuntàta, tha an t-iasg math dhut.*' (Hail, Mary, you are full of potatoes and fish is good for you.)

If a child gulped or gorged down that food, however, they might be chided with the words: '*Beagan is beagan, mar a dh'ith an cat an sgadan.*' (Little by little, as the cat eats the herring.)

If two individuals acted or looked like one another, they would be said not to be 'like two pins' but '*cho coltach ri dà sgadan*', as alike as two herring. Even doorknobs and dodos weren't said to be dead in Gaelic. That rather dubious honour went instead to the herring; the expression '*cho marbh ri sgadan*' related to the way the herring did not survive for very long when taken from salt water, gulping when other fish writhed and wriggled on the deck. This expression was developed further in the assertion '*Thèid an sgadan marbh leis an t-sruth*' (the dead herring will go along with the flood), an insult directed at an individual who floated along with the crowd and had no mind of their own.

Another well-known phrase related to herring's place in the pecking order in the dietary requirement of the Gaelic speaker is '*Seachd sgadain sàth bradain, seachd bradain sàth ròin*'. (It would take seven herring to be the equal of one salmon and seven salmon to be the equivalent of one seal when it arrives in your kitchen cauldron.) Clearly this was back in the days before the ubiquitous farmed salmon. Both its taste and flavour were very different from what we experience while shopping at the local supermarket.[*]

And then there was the way some of the old men from the district employed the herring as some kind of IQ test, particularly for young boys. On your way home from school, they would look at you with a Grand Inquisitorial eye, asking a question which they felt was bound to undermine all the confidence you had in the worth and value of your primary education.

'Tell me – just to find out how much they're teaching you in that school of yours – how many herring is there in a cran?'

It was a query that would leave you stumped for a short time, until you remembered that a few days before, the same old man had requested you to ask your father for a loan of, perhaps, a sky hook, a tin of tartan paint or a left-handed screwdriver. It didn't take too high a percentage of your IQ to work out that this was a question which belonged to that same category. If you had come out with the correct response, of around a thousand, they would have gaped at you in disbelief.

---

[*] A German book, *Philologische Studien* (1896) by the scholar O. Schrader, made a very interesting claim that the word 'Scandinavia' is derived from the Irish form 'scatan' or Gaelic 'sgadan'. For all that this seems extremely unlikely, it does have real imaginative possibilities. Did the Celtic residents of Iona, Skye, Muck and Barra all point to the horizon when Viking raiders came, and yell: 'Here comes the Sgadan-navy-ians'?

Comparisons with herring were not always, however, complimentary. Occasionally, and with utter exasperation, some would cry: '*Tha mi seachd searbh dha sgadan*', a statement in which the speaker declared simultaneously how he or she was fed up with both herring and the everyday routine of life. If someone was said to be '*cho sùmhail ri sgadan*', it was as if they possessed unctuous, Uriah Heep qualities, being slippery and greasy in their mock humility. (Anyone who has to scrape out the bottom of a large catch of herring, as I did on a few occasions one summer, will know exactly what is meant by that expression. Their wet, moist touch does tend to stick to the palms.) These insults even extend to its by-product, the kipper.

One former colleague of mine was described to me in the following way: 'He's like a Stornoway kipper . . . two-faced and no backbone.'

The entire way of life embodied by the herring did not simply, however, add decorative qualities to the language spoken by people. Instead, on these bare headlands and places on the edge of the moorland, it provided its own splash of colour. As flowers are notoriously difficult to grow in the north of Scotland, and considerably less important than grazing for sheep, they were replaced in many gardens by the glass bowls once used as floats for fishing nets, which sparkled green, yellow and dark brown in the grass. These were also placed on tops of pillars that marked out household gates, making them look like tiny lighthouses each time they reflected the rare summer sunlight. Fishing nets played a role too. They were stretched across croft gates and fences, preventing sheep from wandering back and forth. They held down haystacks, hitching them down upon a stubbled field or behind one of the barns and outhouses. Old and useless when cast upon the waves, they could still play an important role on land.

A fishing net was also an important feature in one of the most shameful trials ever held in my native isles. This occurred when the first Catholic priest for decades arrived in Stornoway to minister to the small, largely Italian Catholic population there. In 1961 when a photograph appeared in the *Stornoway Gazette* of the youth club the newly arrived Father Ryland Whittaker had set up beside the crumbling building that served as the town's Catholic church, some keen-eyed Presbyterian spotted that there was a fishing net draped along one wall. Opportunity beckoned; the danger of the Pope reaping the souls of the town's youth could be averted. A day or so later and the police arrived at the priest's door, accusing him of receiving stolen goods. It was a case that fell apart shortly afterwards in the courtroom, where the fisherman who had accused Father Whittaker of this heinous crime watched while the defence lawyer, Laurence Dowdall, tore apart the evidence – and net – with his fingers, revealing what a flawed and flimsy piece of equipment this 'new' net was. It was clearly one that had lain rotting in the harbour for quite some time before.

However, it was the fish boxes that were the most prevalent feature of the fishing trade found within a crofter's life. Once upon a time, the fish box was the one item lying around the barn of almost every croft in the islands that was guaranteed not to have been honestly obtained. The instruction on its side asking people to return it to, say, Lochinver, Mallaig or even Stornoway was ignored as a matter of course. Instead, it would be kept by the crofter who had – somehow! – managed to obtain and use it in a thousand different ways. These ranged from being the basis of a makeshift stage – where Elvis impersonators could sing 'Return To Sender' while mocking the instructions on the side of the box – to acting as a receptacle for sprouting seed potatoes. They were a trough for sheep in midwinter, a table on which their slaughter might take place at another time of the year, a container to store nets, nuts and bolts, fishing lines. Some young lads from my district even used a number of the boxes to help shore up the walls of a *bothag* (turf-hut) built on the edge of the moor. At other times it sprouted a rope, a few pieces of wood, some nails and a set of wheels to become a go-cart, steered around the curves and slopes of our island roads. There was a house in Mallaig where I once sat and admired a wonderfully varnished coffee table, complete with a hinge for placing magazines within. A moment or two later and I noticed the words 'George Walker and Sons' printed on its side.

Yet the fish box served as more than a toy or tool for crofters and their offspring. The boxes – with their owners' names or ports of origin inscribed on their sides – acted as a reminder of both the surges and the dips in the fortunes of the fishing industry. They chronicled the titles of the boats and firms involved in that trade, providing a record of the growth and dwindling of harbours at the nation's edge. If they were dated and placed side by side, they could show the time when ports like Wick gave way to, for instance, Fraserburgh, when areas once famed far and wide for their herring – such as Tarbert, Loch Fyne – rose and ebbed in importance.

However, the fish box provides, too, a way of illustrating the changes in the technology and approach of the fishing industry over the last hundred years or so. Until the late nineteenth century, it is likely that the fish box did not exist. Its place both below deck and on the country's quaysides was occupied by its larger, tubbier 'cousin' – the fish barrel.*

---

*The fish barrel, too, had its multiplicity of uses. A friend of mine, Donald William 'Ryno' Morrison, had a grandfather nicknamed Gladstone who had seventeen children in total – and two wives called Christina (not, it should be noted, simultaneously). One day he was lifting his youngest child up and down, pretending to let him fall into the water barrel at the end of the house but catching him an instant later. A stern Free Presbyterian elder passed by. 'I see you've got so many these days that you're beginning to have to salt them,' he declared. Those in the MacNab household in Lerwick also used a half-barrel for their own variety

At this time, most fish was dried or salted, stored within these barrels and shipped to the mainland's towns and cities at a later date.

It was probably the railway that led to the invention of its replacement, the fishing box. In the beginning, its original model – the shipping box – was larger than those seen around crofthouses today. The box had rope handles and a lid. When the latter was nailed down, a card bearing the despatcher and buyer's names and the route the box had to take was tacked to its top. It was a way of delivering fish copied by a number of fishing boats, using them – and vast quantities of ice – to send their catch as quickly as possible to market.

Later, in the early years of the twentieth century, the form of wooden fishing box familiar to most of us today was introduced. These boxes were open-topped, and possessed handholds at their ends and wooden bars along the top edges of each side. Thousands were made between, say, the 1920s and '70s, each one bearing the name of its firm and fishing port.

The way these wooden boxes could be stacked gave them an important advantage over what many saw as their modern replacement – the tin box. Made – oddly enough – from aluminium, tin boxes were not quite the success their makers had clearly imagined they would be. Unable to lock together in the same way as their predecessors, they slid off one another when they were stacked upright. They were easily bashed; their sides bent and battered when they were thrown noisily

Continued from p. 65:

of childcare. Their daughter was sometimes left in one when the others in the family worked. Apparently, her first words were related to the trade. She learned to shout 'bottom' after the gutters used to announce that they had finished the bottom layer of the barrel. She also used to create confusion – and loss of earnings in the curing yard – when she would shout 'Tea's up!' at odd intervals.

on to shore. Unlike the names stencilled on to old wooden boxes, it was hard to make out the words etched into their sides. As a result, boat crews and quayside workers used paint to try and claim them and keep them for their own.

And so to plastic fishing boxes – ones that, like their predecessors, are beginning to gather in the barns and garages of island crofthouses. (Invariably they are marked with their new place of origin, 'Lochinver'.) Doubtless, both crofters and their children are discovering a thousand uses for their dubiously acquired possessions, failing to return them to their owners in much the same way that their ancestors once did. Perhaps, too, they even still use them as makeshift stages, standing on them to sing songs like Elvis Presley's 'Return To Sender', mocking the inscriptions on their sides, or others like these:

> *Fàilte gu fearann air balaich an iasgaich,*
> *'G iomradh tarraing 's a' gearradh a' bhiathaidh 's a';*
> *Coma leam leabaidh no cadal no biadh*
> *Gu 'm faigh mi mo lìon an òrdugh . . .*

> Welcome ashore to the lads who were fishing,
> Rowing and pulling and cutting the bait.
> I don't care for bed or sleeping or food
> Till I put my lines in order . . .

They were words we sang with a great deal of energy when we were young, our elbows pumping in and out as we sat in our school desks, occasionally tugging at the ponytails of the girls who sat in front of us, especially where the lyrics seemed to offer us leave to do so. Our voices boomed out the place names we would visit in our imaginary journeys, exotic locations like 'Peterhead', 'Caithness' and 'England'. We even rejected the domesticity promised to us by the young women in our midst. As opposed to the appeal of a fishing life, 'Christina' was offered little in terms of either completion or comfort. Instead, there was only 'a drab little bothy' with:

> A stable and byre and a well for my milk cow and calf,
> A little brown horse and yearling sheep . . .

For all that it was a song that was composed by a man from Lewis, the words conjured up a vision for young boys that resonated throughout the Outer Hebrides – and particularly its eastern coastline. (For many reasons, the western edge of that archipelago was never as promising for the establishment of fishing ports and harbours. Not only was it further away from both the mainland and markets of Scotland and England, it had fewer inlets and sheltered bays suitable for safe anchorage. It also bore the full fury of Atlantic waves and winds coming in, sometimes it seemed, all the way from America.) As a result, it was in places on the eastern edge, like Castlebay in Barra, Stornoway in Lewis, the tiny isle of Scalpay off the coast of Harris and Lochmaddy in North Uist, that the ghosts of the herring industry could be found.

From the window of the art gallery and museum Taigh Chearsabhagh in Lochmaddy, Norman 'Curly' Macleod brandished an arm in the direction of an empty harbour.

'There was a time when there used to be a string of fishing boats at the mouth of the harbour, from one side to the other of the bay.'

Nowadays, however, he largely stares out at a vacancy, the small port only coming to life for a short time each day when the ferry either arrives from or sails to Uig in Skye, the hotel not far from the pier welcoming new arrivals to its doors.

There was a similar stillness in Eriskay when I arrived there last spring to speak to former fisherman Michael Mackinnon on the island. It is a place that is dominated by the Catholic church one sees shortly after going across the causeway, built in 2001 to allow its inhabitants greater access to nearby South Uist and all the world beyond. Step near the causeway and you can find reminders of the ocean nearby, seen in the church bell that comes from the German battlecruiser the *SMS Derfflinger*, scuttled in Scapa Flow in June 1919. Step within the church's doors and you can see the bow of a lifeboat from the aircraft carrier, *Hermes*, washed ashore nearby, its polished wood forming the centrepiece of the altar. The same sense of the heavy toll of the sea is present if you go in the direction of Michael's house. It overlooks the graveyard with its array of crosses, many dedicated to the memory of sailors and fishermen. The pub named Am Politician is also close at hand, given that title in tribute to the celebrated vessel of that name which sank, with its cargo of whisky, in the Sound of Barra. Michael's front window gazes out at the tides and drifts of the sea, the small reminders of its fluctuations everywhere on that tiny, beautiful island.

Michael's words drift, too, back to the 1960s or so when there were fishing boats aplenty sailing out of the island. He names them, the words strange and exotic on that Hebridean landscape, all very different from the ones that were heard on the Presbyterian island of my childhood.

'There's the *Santa Maria 1* and *2*. *Ave Maria*. *Virgo*. *Our Lady of Fatima*. *San Miguel*—'

'Why *San Miguel*?'

Michael shrugs before smiling and remembering. 'I think it was after the place where there was a Catholic college in Spain. Father Allan, the man who built the church, went there. It was also there that our old parish priest, John Archie MacMillan went.'

I nod, recalling that priest, famous in his day for playing the bagpipes while waterskiing. He has since left the Church and now, among other work, presents religious programmes on Gaelic television.

'But all that was in the Sixties. When the industry was at its height . . . Nowadays it's just a few small boats that come here looking for crabs and suchlike.'

'Why do you think it died here?'

'Oh, there were loads of reasons. We didn't get a proper pier till the early Seventies. That didn't help. It meant that instead of tying their vessels up on shore, people came ashore here in small rowing boats. Sometimes you had to wait until the middle of the night till the sea was right to do that. A tricky business. It might have been different if that hadn't been the case.'

I think of the new pier, sheltering the few boats that fish from the island, and reflect on the way that the lack of both natural harbours and other facilities has often been a problem in the Hebrides, hampering the development of the industry there. This was also true of islands like Tiree in the Inner Hebrides, where I had spent a month a few summers before. For a place with no sheltered bay or inlet, its community had quite remarkably spawned a large number of sailors and sea captains. The west coast of the Outer Hebrides had similar problems. The only natural harbour there was in Carloway, one of the villages that Lord Leverhulme, the old Lancashire soap baron, had tried to develop in the 1920s when he had attempted to make the Isle of Lewis, and Stornoway, the centre of a worldwide herring industry. That madcap venture had failed for a variety of reasons. Among them were the collapse of the Russian market following the First World War and the introduction of Prohibition in the United States. There was also an old North American tradition that bars would serve little scraps of herring along with their beers, increasing the thirst of their clientele for the product. It was more difficult to do that when there were only soft drinks like sarsaparilla on sale.

Yet geography, too, had played its part in the demise of the herring industry on the islands, in the way that much of the shoreline of the islands was open to the fierceness of the wide Atlantic. Due to the manner in which it stormed and raged there was little safe anchorage for either men or boats in these parts.

That did not mean there weren't the ghosts of the old herring trade there. In the Outer Hebrides these seemed to linger everywhere.

CHAPTER FOUR

'There's a Ghost in My House'

It is not only my hometown and village that contain the spirits of the herring trade. Its apparitions are to be found everywhere throughout the north of Europe, occupying crumbling buildings beside old harbours that once serviced the industry, places where curers and coopers, herring girls and fishermen once followed and practised their trade. Their presence might even be seen in small gestures – the briskness of fingers holding a small kitchen knife at a counter, each tiny movement, perhaps, showing that there is some faint recollection of how these people's ancestors used to cut and gut; the precision of a man's grip as he undertakes some task like baiting a hook or even threading a needle, both legacies of lives that have been and gone before.

Yet there is sometimes more to it than this – a craft that is sometimes valued for its own sake and passed on to those

who come afterwards. This may be something like the skill
of knitting, which often accompanied herring fishing on
the periphery of the country. In Shetland, for instance, it
dated right back to around the ninth century when Norse
settlers arrived with their native breed of sheep, the Villsau,
one that interbred with the primitive Soay sheep that was
already found within these islands. The soft, light and warm
wool this produced was first woven, then kneaded into a
cloth called *wadmal*, a product then discovered to be ideal
for knitting. By the late sixteenth century hundreds of
Dutch fishing vessels arrived in Shetland waters, anxious to
buy stockings and mittens produced from that wool. During
the seventeenth and eighteenth centuries, both Dutch
fishermen and Hanseatic merchants from Germany and
Norway established a trade in stockings from Shetland. In
1736, over 800 pairs were exported to Oporto in Portugal.
A decade later the same merchant was sending 1,590 pairs to
Hamburg.

Knitting was a task that women throughout the north
undertook while they performed other work. There are
countless photographs taken throughout the country's edge
of women with their hands intent on the movement of
knitting needles, while their backs are bent below the weight
of a creel of peats, or even in those rare moments when their
fingers were resting from the dip and weave of gutting
knives. To paraphrase a Shetland expression, the hands of
these herring women 'dunna sit idle'; instead they 'tak dee
sock'. Sometimes they did this for their own families; just as
often it was work they undertook as a means of paying the
rent. This was a task that even preceded the coming of large
catches of herring in some parts of the country. Brian Smith
in the book *Shetland Textiles – 800 BC to the Present* notes
that one landlord in 1724 provided a merchant in Lerwick
with a thousand pairs of 'good and sufficient coarse
stockings'. He concludes this by declaring: 'This transaction
leads me to believe that he was getting the stockings from

his tenants, perhaps as part of their rent, just as Shetland landlords in the new eighteenth-century regime demanded their tenants' fish. As sure as sure can be, the landlord wasn't knitting them.'

And this practice continued till quite late on, even if the landlord – and later the merchant – now had less of a role in it. A report published by the Highlands and Islands Development Board in April 1970 on the Shetland woollen industry declared: 'Earnings from hosiery are as widespread as earnings from crofting and in many cases they are both more substantial and certain. Fishermen, crofters and housewives alike enjoy the advantages of this system, which in many cases can make a crucial difference to their standard of life.'

One could argue that, within Shetland at least, it played a greater role in the female existence than, say, the gutting of herring. On the island of Unst, for instance, Paterson and Slocock observed that there were 2,865 women employed in the curing yards of Baltasound, Uyeasound and Balta island in 1905. Only 195 of them were Shetlanders, the bulk coming from the Moray Firth and the east coast of Scotland, which made up 1,710 of that total, with 948 coming from the area defined as the west Highlands. (Only twelve came from south of the Forth.) Perhaps it is for this reason that, as Lynn Abrams notes in her book *Myth and Materiality in a Woman's World*, 'herring girls have not been appropriated as representatives of a Shetland way of life'. They are certainly not commemorated in the way they are in some locations elsewhere. No sculpture exists of a fishwife and child the way her counterparts occur in Florø and Peterhead. No granite slab and bronze plate is etched with images of women gutting in the manner of the one that also appears in that last-named community. No fishwives are sculpted – as they are by the skills of Ginny Hutchison and Charles Engebretsen – in towns like Nairn and Stornoway. It is a textile museum – and not one that commemorates the herring girls – which exists on the outskirts of Shetland's main town, Lerwick.

Yet it was still fishing and the contact between people across seas that this work often entailed which led to the intricate knitting patterns found throughout the edge of northern Europe. For instance, there is evidence of this in the pendant-shaped Fair Isle kep or cap that is the earliest surviving form of knitting from that island, the most southerly in the Shetland Isles. Described as 'variegated worsted'* by medical student Edward Charlton in 1832, this headgear is 'immediately recognisable through a colour palette' of both largely imported and domestic shades. Like the natural colours of white, moorit and Shetland Black from the backs of the local sheep, shades like red and gold came from the island, drawn from the colours of the dye plants found upon its shores. The indigo blue was imported from elsewhere, bringing together a 'Rainbow Nation' of which the late Nelson Mandela might have been proud.

This mixture of the native and the exotic was part of the inheritance of the fishing trade, found in both Fair Isle and other communities; the kind of knitting developed on that small island, as Sarah Laurenson notes in *Shetland Textiles*, being 'a form of the stranded colourwork knitting seen in coastal areas throughout Europe'. Far from being remote from other parts of the world, Shetland has patterns based on techniques found in communities that might seem at first sight scattered and distant – from Iceland to Holland, the Baltic States to the coastline of north-east England, Scotland and Sweden. Unlike inland communities in both continental Europe and mainland Britain, both tide and current linked Fair Isle with tight and intricate stitches to the other extremes of this northern world.

---

*The rest of his portrait goes on to compare the Shetlanders to 'some of the Esquimaux tribe'.

When the herring boom was at its height in the nineteenth and early twentieth centuries, this exchange between different cultures was at its richest and most fruitful. Even outside the distinctive traditions of Fair Isle, women working on the quayside would note the clothing of, say, a Norwegian or German fisherman arriving on the shore, judging with a glance the intricacies of the patterns that he wore. Some would seek later to imitate the distinctive design or decoration they had seen, mimicking the stitches that had been used in its creation, 'reading the pattern' as I heard it described in a film involving Estonian women. And then there was the talk between the women, often passing on to one another the little tricks and twists of wool that went into the creation of the images and motifs they had knitted with the click of needles, the turn of their hands. There was pride and standing in being the most creative knitter among the women, a sign that there was intelligence, imagination and insight within a particular individual.

Yet, as with most human endeavours, even though this was a wonderful and rich exchange, something was also lost. At one time the women from different districts who worked at the herring wore different-coloured plaids. This allowed onlookers to differentiate where they came from at a glance. For instance, in the villages around Fraserburgh, the women from Inverallochy were always bedecked in red and black, those in Pitullie wore grey and white, and the girls from Broadsea looked resplendent in black and white, while their counterparts in St Combs were garbed in blue and black. And so it went on throughout many of the coastal villages in that area.

There was a similar distinctive quality to the 'gansey' the fishermen wore to both work and kirk. (They often put aside a spare, best one for Sundays.) The patterns were handed down by word of mouth or old hands teaching young fingers through example. It is for this reason that families all added their own small variation to the whole, for all that it could be identified as belonging to an area. Places like Whitby, Filey, Scarborough, Mallaig, Arbroath, all the way to the Norfolk ports and across to the Dutch ports from the North Sea coast to the Zuiderzee, Friesland to North Holland: each had its own individual way of knitting a pattern. A mixture of flags, zigzags, diamonds, trees and bars adorned the men as they set off in fishing boats to follow the herring. Like the thresher in the traditional folk song 'One Misty Moisty Morning', the fisherman 'wore no shirt upon his back but wool unto his skin', with the only exception sometimes* being a pure silk scarf that was worn at the neck to stop wet wool chafing him. There was a diamond patch underneath the armpit to make the garment more durable and flexible there. The sleeves were on the short side to prevent the men's wrists from tangling with hooks and machinery. The majority of the designs tended to be on the upper part of the jersey, enabling the fishermen to keep their chests warm with the extra layer of wool that this entailed. There is little doubt, too, where the 'gansey' or 'geansaidh' originated. Its beginnings were to be found in the Channel Islands, and more specifically Guernsey, which had been exporting such clothing since the sixteenth century. Both the Dutch and English adopted and adapted it to make it their own, before it travelled elsewhere.

Few of these different patterns have survived. One that did was worn by the herring fishermen of Eriskay, the skills that went into its creation found not only on that island but also on the southern end of South Uist. Among others, it is practised there by the likes of my old friend and former colleague Marybell MacIntyre, who learned it once again at

---

*This did not occur everywhere. In the Hebrides, for instance, the fishermen tended to have a three-button stand-up collar. This allowed the gansey to be a better fit.

the classes taught by two ladies who live nearby in her community, Mayag MacInnes from Eriskay and Mary Sarah MacInnes from South Uist. Marybell spoke to me about it from her home in Bornish at the southern end of South Uist, her sitting room looking out at a loch which hen harriers and short-eared owls occasionally visit. The soft brush of their wings is like wool being drawn slowly through the twilight, the hush belying the firmness of purpose behind every move as they circle a stretch of bare ground, targeting their prey. There is something in their progress that is not unlike the art of knitting itself, the needles clicking gently as the complexity of a pattern takes shape.

'I love doing it, love the intricacies it involves,' Marybell tells me.

I do not need to be told this, for in Marybell's case, enthusiasm spills over into all that she does. It is present in her teaching of both Gaelic and English to the classes of the local secondary school where she has worked for years, the pupils sensing in her sparkle her fondness for them, her two subjects and the community in which she has lived most of her days. This is evident, too, in the way her love of tradition flows through her life. It can be seen in how she enthuses about the novels of Anthony Trollope, offering proof of his own dictum: 'that I can read and be happy while I am reading is a great blessing'. There is, too, her faith, which has strengthened her through hard and difficult times, and the Gaelic music in which she and so many of her family had been involved. (She has pointed out, for instance, that the Eriskay knitting was accompanied by prayer for the individual who was going to wear it – a practice, I think, that was common for most of the more religious communities on our coast.) And there is the agility she displays when practising Hebridean – aka 'Scotch' or 'Cape Breton' – step-dancing. This form of dancing was prevalent in the Hebrides many years ago but lost out over much of the twentieth century when the formality of Scottish country dancing held sway, surviving only in Cape Breton on the eastern seaboard of Canada. That it is back, and practised both in South Uist and Eriskay once again, owes much to the energy of Marybell and her friends at the local music festival, Ceòlas.

There is a nimbleness required in both skills – the ticking of knitting needles not unlike the rhythm of a Hebridean step-dance, the tap of shoes like percussion following the beat of the music. Unlike in its Irish equivalent, there is little movement below the ankles, no high steps à la Michael Flatley, each tap as much accompaniment as an embellishment to the tune. Her voice, too, has a similar flow, that distinctive Uist accent possessing a melody of its own. She even attempts the impossible, trying to teach me how to make an Eriskay jersey. I take down notes, for all that they are hieroglyphics to a man with the limits I have set to my life, never having picked up a set of knitting needles since the days my fingers – and those of my poor and suffering primary teacher – wrestled with them during my early years in primary school.

'They were knitted in a special way with 3.5mm steel gauge needles. Five-ply pure wool. Sometimes very oily for warmth and rain. It is all done in the round. An utterly seamless garment with no sewing involved. This made it more difficult to tear, remaining tight against the skin in all eventualities. Unlike the way the designs form vertical or circular stretches on other forms of knitwear, the Hebridean version – of which only the Eriskay one survives – was often patterned in blocks.'

And then she tells me about the designs that were knitted on the garment. They include the starfish, the anchor, the cable, the open tree, the horseshoe – called fish tails in Eriskay . . .

'Some of them were borrowed by the people down south. For some reason, Scottish knitting was always more innovative and imaginative than that found there. Possibly because they travelled more, saw more distinct and different landscapes and communities. Possibly because the more pattern that was on them, the warmer they were. It gave them extra layers to protect them from the cold.'

She goes on to describe how, in other ways, Eriskay knitting was distinct and different from other forms. Unlike Fair Isle knitting where, according to Sarah Laurenson, 'the motifs do not directly represent symbols or images of things, such as stars and flowers, but form abstract patterns', Eriskay jumpers were designed for the individuals that wore them. The St Andrew's Cross that might form the yoke of the gansey, for instance, was an indication of the Catholic faith followed by most of the inhabitants, the means to ensure that any Eriskay fishermen washed up on shore were not buried in the wrong graveyard. Yet there was more to it than that. From a glance, one could tell whether a man was single or married; the latter's jumper was 'marked' with the double zigzag of waves within a block. These men being crofters, there might be 'lazybeds' or 'ears of corn' to be found within the pattern, or the 'harbour steps' seen from a man's home. There might even be 'closed diamonds' or 'nets' flanking the design, with a double plait suggesting hoofprints in the sand if the family house overlooked, say, Prince Charlie's Beach. Sometimes there was even a deliberate flaw within the pattern, a stitch or strand of wool placed to help identify one brother from another if there was a drowning.

Much of this work was done by women waiting at home for their men in Eriskay. Or else by the women who waited for boats in other ports and places – the gutters and packers in Yarmouth or Wick as they stood anticipating the arrival of a loaded fishing boat into the harbour, or perhaps late at night in their huts. Some knitted with the customary two needles; others, too, with the additional aid of four small needles held in a special horsehair-filled pouch around the waist. At other times, with their hands once again stained and silvered, the packers would be at work taking the gutted fish from the tubs at the call of the three gutters. They would soak or dunk them in a barrel of brine, known as a 'rousing tub', designed to 'rouse' or clean off any blood or loose guts. Discarding any parts of the catch that had been damaged, the clean fish were salted and placed in the barrels, belly down with tails at the centre, heads at the outside; layer after layer of salt and fish being made until the barrel was full. (If a less than competent packer was found to be 'bulking', throwing the fish any which way for several layers before completing the task in the proper way, there would be instant dismissal.) Around ten minutes and between 900 and 1,200 herring later, and the barrel would be full, approximately twenty dizzying flights of fish. This meant that with the whirl of her fingers, a good worker could pack thirty barrels – or 30,000 herring – a day. Included among this was an extraordinary amount of salt. For the curing of every twenty crans of herring, about one ton was used, mainly in the pickle, one part to every twenty parts of the silver darlings. It was a substance that came by ship largely from Russia, the salt outcrops of Perm or Prikamye, perhaps, or Astrakhan lake salt, though sometimes it arrived from France or Spain. They used this carefully and accurately, aware exactly how much was needed for the mix.

And then, there would follow the 'pining'. This came after a period of around eight to ten days, depending on the size of the fish and quality of the pickle, when the herring were allowed to settle in their barrel. As the content shrank as a result of the interaction between the salt and the juices from the herring, the 'blood pickle' created by this process was poured away, then 'top-tiered' with about four rows of fish 'pined' from the same cure. The lid was then refitted and sealed. After that the barrel was laid on its side and the bung removed. Again this allowed it to be refilled with pickle before it was 'bung-packed' again, the wooden stopper pressed into place once more.

It was work of the most extraordinary care and precision, a wonderful exactitude which was only complete when the fisheries inspector strolled around. It was his task to check four barrels out of every hundred that were stacked upon the pier, first of all discovering if there were leaks, any cracks in the wood or lids where the pickle spilled, letting slip salt on to the ground. He would then proceed to open the lid or 'head' of the barrel, discovering if the size of the fish within was similar, if the packing had been done correctly, and if there was enough or too much salt found within. Sometimes the inspector might be exceptionally enthusiastic about this task, his hand digging deeper than normal into the barrel to find out if the girl had been 'bulking' below the top few layers. Some buyers, too, had their own procedures, independent of the inspectors; a few Russians in particular had a reputation for taking a bite out of the fish, seeking to discover if it was to their taste. If this was not the case, there would be a wave of fingers, a rejection of the goods on offer. Sometimes, too, this would have been done in great style, such as by the *Cailleach Ruiseanach*, the Russian lady buyer who was remembered by many in Stornoway. The girls would look at her enviously, conscious that this was the sole woman they saw in their proximity who possessed not only great power but also well-tailored suits and a fur coat that would protect her from the chill of winds that often blustered around the harbour.

Alternatively, if the barrel met the required standard, the fish which had been removed would be restored. A stencil would be stamped with a hot iron on the wood – 'Scotland Fisheries Crown Brand' – with a reference to the size of the fish, the curer and the year. This would signify and guarantee that the contents had been processed within twenty-four hours of being caught.

The detailed care and attention the curers gave to the herring that had been landed on their harbour were not always extended to the women who were employed by them. The report for 1905 written by Paterson and Slocock makes this clear. Writing of various locations in Shetland, they make the following observations of Baltasound: 'the wetness of the ground in the yard, right up to the huts, is made offensive by the tramping into it of herring and all sorts of refuse and is an objectionable feature, which might be remedied by some form of paving allowing for drainage, and permitting thorough swilling down with seawater.'

And of Lerwick: 'In the town of Lerwick, the conditions are worse, if there could be any comparison drawn at all, because all round is a thickly populated district, and the absence of any efficient means of scavenging causes a continual menace to health.'

They condemn, too, the living quarters in which the women are forced to stay, writing of how they live in overcrowded huts and, in one case, a section of a disused chapel which was partly in 'great despair', with 'the whole place damp and littered with refuse'. Among other aspects of this accommodation which draws their ire is 'the want of water supply or wash house'. This seems to be the case throughout Shetland, but it is particularly pronounced on Balta Island, which despite having 'five curing stations, and a population of almost 900 in the fishing season', has no water supply at all.

'The curers bring water with them from Aberdeen or some other Scotch town in barrels, bringing 200 to 400 at a time. Drinking water, when this is wanted fresh, has to be paid a shilling a barrel if brought from the Laird.'

With more than a little understatement, the report goes on to conclude: 'this, of course, makes the question of sanitary accommodation very difficult.'

The lack of this provision is illustrated time and time again in the report. It tells of how at Cullivoe, in Yell, the privies are only convenient to use at low tide, being placed on the beach instead of within the yard. It informs us of how in Smith Quay in Lerwick, where 247 women worked, there was one three-seated privy. At the time when Paterson and Slocock were on their rounds, this was occupied by a man. In Balta, the tiny structures which served as the toilets sat upon the sea edge, 'overhanging the beach', not far from where the coopers were employed and fishermen came and went; the swirl of the sea flushing all that was deposited there. As a result of these design faults, little or no use was made of this accommodation. Instead the sole alternative was to 'go over the hill', a course of action that 'in this flat country involves a long walk to reach any place, and that this necessarily leads to delay and difficulty which cannot be without serious result to health'.

One of the most remarkable aspects of Paterson and Slocock's report is that it not only provides us with insight into how women from these islands were treated while they were curing herring, but also portrays how other nations considered their welfare. They note, for instance, that the Dutch herring fleet employed different practices from those found in other nations, with gutting and packing done at sea and young boys frequently employed for some of the work. While the authors were in Lerwick, they also visited four foreign ships – the *Serla* from Gothenburg in Sweden and three ships from Norway. These were the *Thor* and *Alstein* from Bergen, and the *Nicolai Knudzen* from Haagesund. All had women on board, ranging from eight on the *Alstein* to twenty on the *Thor*. In some ways they were employed under similar conditions, the curer owning or chartering the boat and engaging the worker to be employed for – what seemed to be – 'long hours'. For this, they received a piece-work rate, lower than the Scottish equivalent,* and a fixed weekly

---

*Not that the rates were all that high even in the British Isles. Here are the Scottish rates from a 1911 wage chart:
Helmsdale: 230 women earning an average of £19/-/- in 15 weeks
Wick: 1,140 women £12/-/- in 12/13 weeks
Shetland: 1,492 women £14/-/- in 18 weeks
Orkney: 282 women £20/-/- in 15 weeks
Stornoway: 2,433 women £8/14/3 in 16 weeks
Barra: 704 women £13/12/- in 29 weeks

allowance for food. Considering Paterson and Slocock's interests in such matters, the comments about the sanitation and decency on these ships is especially damning. Even less favourable in general than those found in Shetland, they would 'tend to lower the standards for our own women'.

It is the authors' account of the *Serla* – with thirteen women on board – that underlines this. Admitting that it is 'difficult to write moderately about the living and sleeping quarters provided for these women', Paterson and Slocock compare their treatment with that of some Shetland cattle lowered into similar conditions a night or so later. They go on to note that: 'down in the hold of the ship, boards were laid on top of the herring barrels, and on these with some tarpaulin laid on them, the women slept, and not only slept but cooked their food; the hatch above the hold if open would admit the light but would also of course admit the rain'.

Barely able to control their outrage, Slocock and Paterson stack further nouns and adjectives in order to convey their disgust at the horrors their fellow women endure. 'Disorder', 'slippery', 'filth', 'unventilated', 'crowded', 'dirty', 'repellent' . . . At the same time, they praise the women who experience this, singling out only a few 'among the East coast women, chiefly from Aberdeen and Peterhead' for being 'rough undesirable women'. They – and especially the 'fine type' of the Highlanders – are praised for their 'modesty, reticence and making the best of their material'. They also note that these women 'with the resignation characteristic of them . . . accept the conditions with little complaint'.

There may be a large number of reasons for this. As can be seen from the wage chart, some of the women from the West Highlands were receiving much higher rates of pay through working in faraway places than they would be back home – indeed, if they were receiving any money at all at times. In these cases they might have seen themselves as truly having

'little complaint'. For instance, the £14 that was their *arles**
while working in Lerwick was considerably more than the
nearly £9 that would slip into their wage packet if they
were employed back home in Stornoway. It is also the case
that many of these women did not rely solely on this money
to keep themselves alive. People, particularly those from
crofting townships, are not reliant on a weekly wage in the
same way as those who live in, say, a mining community.
They have seasonal work to do, like attending to the crops,
sheep and cattle on their land. They might also gain money
from their crafts.

It may be the case that the temporary nature of the work
of those who were employed as herring girls in itself
prevented solidarity with one another, especially during the
early years of the twentieth century. There was little tradition
of political action among women, especially during the years
before they obtained the vote – for all that they were united
in their basic humanity. In the course of their work, they
probably drifted in and out of various yards and locations,
most of the time on short-term contracts, unlike their male
and largely inland counterparts who worked down mines
and lived in communities that lay below slag-heaps and
mineshafts. There was also the linguistic confusion with Gaels
and Shetland girls working together side by side, their
distinctive vowels and consonants jostling together as they
bent over barrels, those from Lewis and Buckie mutually
unintelligible. This must have affected their ability to explain
their grievances to their owners, or to work together in
presenting a common cause.

Yet there was an attraction in this, too, especially for
young women who came from isolated crofthouses and
small towns on the islands. It gave them the opportunity to
mix and mingle with those who came from outside their

---

*Also called *erles*, which is related to the Gaelic term *eàrlas*
meaning 'an approved deposit'.

immediate background. It might even have provided an opportunity for some of them to misbehave. In some, this was by being sexually adventurous. For the burghers of Great Yarmouth, this was one reason why some of the herring girls were distrusted. They feared the sexual confidence that a number possessed. In others, it was the attraction of the demon drink. The Orcadian writer George Mackay Brown gives us a portrayal of a trio of whom Paterson and Slocock would certainly have disapproved in his short story 'The Ferryman' in *A Calendar of Love*. Introducing them first at the pier in Stromness, where they stand wanting to sell a basket of herring to the islanders on Hoy, he notes them later as being on his boat where one of them, Seenie, 'took a half-bottle of rum from her skirt-pocket, and we all began to drink, the flask going from mouth to mouth'.

Later, after another girl, Margaret, becomes sick in the Sound, the ferryman of the title notes sardonically: 'I did not charge a fare. They gave me a bunch of herring for nothing.'

Even for those on whom Paterson and Slocock smiled benignly, their time away must have brought hints and whispers of romance into lives that might have seemed bleak and unforgiving. There were the church services every Sunday morning and evening, after which the young men and women would walk home together. Letters written home in Gaelic tell their readers, too, of dances in Shetland on a Saturday night. *Nach ann an siud a bha a' chlann-nighean a' faighinn nan gillean?* (Isn't it there that the women got the men?) They speak of how the Bucaich, or men from the north-east fishing port of Buckie, were in their company as often as the Gaels, entertaining them with Gaelic songs while they were there. They also recall dancing in Scalloway in Shetland with *balaich bhàna Dhonegal* (the fair-haired men of Donegal). Apparently, they had built a platform in front of their huts and they would organise dances with the little melodeon they had brought along with them on their journeys, playing songs like the Irish traditional tune

'McGinty's Goat'. No doubt it provided them with an answer when they were questioned by their own mothers back home.

> Mrs. Burke to her daughter said, 'Listen, Mary Ann,
> Who is the lad you were cuddlin' in the lane?
> He had long wiry whiskers hangin' from his chin.
> ''Twas only Pat McGinty's goat,' she answered with a grin . . .

At Shetland's book festival, Wordplay, in November 2014, my friend Lawrence Tulloch from Unst told me how they used to communicate with each other at these dances in Shetland. Instead of being confused by the babble of different tongues and accents, they used to slip conversation lozenges to one another – musk, rose and violet flavours, and supplied by the local merchants who bought several hundredweight at a time. There would be a paper bag stuffed with lozenges within a young man's pocket as he asked a young lady to partner him in a reel, all bearing legends a little less direct and more subtle than modern Love Hearts. 'You Charm Me' one might read. 'Can I See You Home?' could be inscribed upon another. Some might even bear the simple word 'Hello'. There was little of the 'Sweet Talk', 'Hugs', 'Kiss Me' or 'Let's Kiss' of their modern equivalents.[*]

Then there were the quite different attractions of the English towns where they travelled. Not only could they meet similar (or even the same!) young men to those they met up north, but they could also attend the dance halls and cinemas that existed further south. There was the attraction of places like the Regal Cinema in Great Yarmouth, and the Regent and Tower in Hull, where they might see Laurel and Hardy attempting to mend a fishing boat or Buster Keaton catching himself on a hook as he tried to land a fish. In addition, there was also the

---

[*]These sweets were also a way of teasing the older men. Many would scratch their grey heads, believing their sexual charisma had been miraculously restored after being slipped a lozenge with the words 'Walk Me Home' incsribed on its surface.

existence of many shops in locations as far apart as Hartlepool in the north of England and Douglas in the Isle of Man, South Shields and Lowestoft. The women would jostle around their aisles and counters on their days off, trying on blouses, skirts, and a good pair of shoes or two. For their little sisters and the girls back home in the village, there might be the purchase of ribbons or brooches, or a comb that might curl their hair till it looked like that of silent-movie star Mary Pickford.

Yet it went further. Lists of requirements would be sent from home to herring girls, requests from relatives, friends and neighbours for goods to be carried home with them. These could range from tea sets to rolls of wallpaper, sheets of oil-cloth to bedspreads. This arrangement gave them access to small luxuries with which they had little contact either in their huts or lodging houses, or in the crofthouses they called home. In their own way, these experiences transformed the house they had left back, say, on the islands. Their heads crammed with new ideas, both in terms of architecture and household furniture, they would return to their parents, brothers, sisters and boyfriends with suggestions for change – the possibilities of toilets, upstairs bedrooms, a separation even of kitchen and sitting room. No longer would women settle for what they had put up with for centuries. This slow process of revolution began with the gifts and goods they took home with them, the purchases that made the *kists* (chests) they carried back either by train or ship extremely heavy. Flat-topped and locked away, as well as containers for new dreams, they sometimes made seats or tables for the women in their huts.

All this made life bearable. And then there is the fact that improvements in their working conditions eventually came. Political pressure from the government assisted in this process. There was no real hiding place for the curers as they came under the onslaught of Mairi Paterson and Emily Slocock's words. Matters had to improve. As curing began to centre on particular ports, with steam-powered drifters replacing those with sails, there was more money, too, for investment in improving the huts and accommodation where the women lived. Small medical stations provided by such groups as the Red Cross, the Free Church of Scotland and the Fisherman's Mission became more and more a part of the scene. In addition to providing the girls with books, knitting materials and sometimes games, they would bandage the girls' wounds and treat them for any illnesses from which they suffered. Sometimes the nurses employed there would accompany the women throughout the season, travelling to various ports with them on the train.

For some of these workers the problem of low wages proved more intractable. This came to a head during the years of the First World War. This was a time when – due to the threat of enemy warships – the entire fishing industry shifted lock, stock and herring barrel from one edge of Scotland to the other. Together with their curers, the east-coast girls brought their relatively higher wages with them to the west. It was a situation that clearly sparked some resentment among the girls from Lewis and the West Highlands. Early in 1917, the gutters, together with the herring girls, went on strike, demanding parity with their visitors. One morning, we are told rather sniffily in the pages of the *Stornoway Gazette*, 'a number of women failed to turn out to their work and the malcontents proceeded to other places and induced – in some cases intimidated – the girls to knock off work'. Following this, the scenes in the town of Stornoway were a shade more buoyant than they were when there was a midweek church meeting as 'the more ardent spirits paraded the streets carrying flags and singing popular songs, to an accompaniment beat out of empty biscuit boxes'. For all the rat-tat-tat, the strike did not last long, the employers not giving way to their demands. After a week the girls were once again bent over their barrels, their knives once more dipping and rising like the waves that washed against the harbour, the sea that would take so many young men and women away from these shores in the years of want that followed the war.

There were a number of reasons for people leaving. Despite their absence, the work continued as it had always done, the women standing in Yarmouth and other harbours sorting out the herring as they had done for many years. Some herring might be salted. Others could become kippers, gutted, split and lightly salted before being smoked over oak chippings and sawdust for around twelve hours. Invented by John Woodger from Northumbria in 1843, this was the variety for which towns like Stornoway, the Isle of Man, Mallaig and Tarbert on Loch Fyne were famous. Then there was the red herring, popular in some Mediterranean countries because it resisted rotting into mush in the heat. This was because, unlike the kipper, it was not split into a butterfly shape before smoking. Instead, after being soaked in brine for twenty-four hours, it was speared with a 'speet' through its gills and smoked with oak chips for around forty-eight hours – and sometimes considerably longer – till it became crisp and quite hard. Former herring girl, Rita Macnab, now living in Lerwick, helped to make red herring at one time during the years she spent travelling around the ports of the British Isles. She couldn't imagine how anyone could possibly enjoy them. 'Hard as a rock,' she declared. Yarmouth also had its own speciality, about which Rita was kinder – the Yarmouth bloater invented in that port in 1835 by a curer called Bishop. In this case, the fish were not gutted but left whole and lightly or cold smoked. They also had to be eaten within a few days before their flavour was lost.

Antarctic explorers may have been keen on the bloater. The New Zealand poet Bill Manhire noted the presence of bloater paste in the shed occupied during the 1910–1912 expedition to the North Pole. Preserved in the cold, a jar sat not very far away from a tin of kippered herring, its container beginning to turn as brown as its contents with the passing decades. The poet listed what he found on the shelves in a few verses that summed up what people ate back then, so different from present decades. The only item that is left out of the poem is Carnation Herring Roe, sold in a similar rose-shaded tin to the evaporated milk that is still on supermarket shelves.

More occasionally in the days after the First World War, there might also be buckling, a gutted and beheaded herring with its roe left intact. This would be cooked and smoked within a special oven, and eaten hot or cold. Even nowadays, this is still one of the common ways of eating herring on the Continent, its golden shade lying beside dark whale meat in the open air fish market of Bergen.

Following the war, however, there was less evidence of this, and no sign of German buyers, common before the conflict, making their way through the herring barrels lined up on the quay at Lowestoft or Yarmouth. The collapse of their economy had seen to that. There was no sign either of the *Cailleach Ruiseanach*, the Russian lady buyer who had once so fascinated the young girls in Stornoway. She is portrayed in Norman Macdonald's novel *Portrona* as Madame Wolkova, a woman with 'thick eyebrows and wide mouth, boot swaggering, cigar smoking, fur-collared, great-coated', who came all the way from St Petersburg 'to buy and cure herring for the Russian hinterland'. She and her kind had been swept away by war and revolution, her cigar butt perhaps extinguished forever in the Siberian gulag.

The effects of this are seen in some of the political essays written by Neil M. Gunn, the author of what is probably the greatest book about the herring and the way of life it spawned: the novel *The Silver Darlings*. Born in 1891, he writes of the contrast between what he saw as a young boy in his childhood home in Dunbeath in the north-east of Scotland and what he witnessed in 1930. In his youth, there had been 'the boats, the East Coast skippers, the Gaelic crews, the women gutters, the curers' agents, the brown sails going out at evening – most lovely of all sights, except perhaps the sight of them coming in at morning when excitement and anticipation quicken tongue and eye at the great gamble of the sea'.

In 1930, however, he notes that: 'Now, in that particular harbour, which in its heyday fished two hundred boats, there are five small boats . . . The harbour walls, the pier-head, the breakwater are sinking and bulging and rent. The basin is silted up. The cooperages and curers' premises are roofless, their windows boarded. Even of the legion of flashing gulls, only a few are left to cry disconsolately and whiten the last remnants of scentless tar and pitch.'

Change and decay in all around he sees – and Gunn inveighs against it, taking a side-swipe and strike at the many targets that come within his range. The modern industrial system, and the Church and its values, are two that appear within his gun sights again and again. He also condemns the government for failing to establish or even police its territorial waters with due care and diligence, noting how 'Dutch trawlers can cut up and destroy our fishermen's nets in the Moray Firth openly and with impunity', with the only response consisting of sending up 'a futile little patrol boat' to deter that behaviour. Finally, he criticises the government for the way they have 'no hesitation' in breaking off trading relations with Russia despite the fact that the fishing industry was 'more important to Scotland than it is to England'. As a result of this decision, 'the Russian market, that took 75 per cent of our total post-war curing, was denied us'.

He goes on to ask why this occurred: 'For whose benefit? Under what system?'

It is easy to criticise Gunn's words today. One could argue that he is being unfair on the government who put in price-guarantee schemes to help support the industry – for all that this only worked intermittently, making some years better than others. As a result of many factors, the high days and heyday of the herring were now largely in hindsight for those working in Scottish ports. The 'Scotch Cure', with its stamped barrels, might still have its market, but it was a diminishing one, with the size and scale of other producers increasing. Even in Great Yarmouth, the industry was receding. In 1925 it had 757 boats and 4,000 fisher women. By 1936 the numbers were about 460 and 2,000 respectively. This brought about an economic and cultural collapse that still continues to have an effect on many of these communities, which had prospered before the First World War; an effect every bit as bad as the one that occurred in the towns that depended on coal and steel.

Gunn was certainly naive, too, in the way he viewed the Soviet Union. What he saw as 'stupendous upheaval' and a great contrast with the 'spiritual sterility' of Scotland, we are now aware was a decade that ushered in the forced collectivisation of farms and brought about some ten to eleven million deaths, horrors unimaginable to a Highland writer. Given both the financial crisis and the penury of many of its citizens, it is unlikely that many would have been able to purchase any herring, even if this was open to them. Nevertheless, he was right in the way he notes the effect of the loss of the continental market on both Scotland's east and west coasts. The disappearance of the likes of the *Cailleach Ruiseanach* from the scene brought hardship in its wake – a by-product, too, of the way the likes of Winston Churchill declared war on the fledgling Soviet state, banning all trade with it. Many people emigrated from the once-busy herring ports at the edge of the country, their fishing nets folded as they packed up suitcases for their outward voyages to Canada and the United States.

For those who remained both at home and within the industry, hardships continued. Throughout the 1920s there were more strikes affecting the industry. Cairstìona Beaton from Back in Lewis, in an interview that took place in 2004, recalled how the herring girls in Yarmouth went on strike for sixpence a barrel. (She also stated how she arrived in Stornoway one year without enough money to travel a few short miles home on the bus.) In Castlebay in Barra, the gutters achieved some success, with the curers acceding to their demands for sixpence an hour to refill barrels. Yet little of this was reported in the press. In an economic depression, there were too many strikes and trade disputes going on for anyone to pay attention to one that involved a group of women laying down their gutting knives and refusing to lift herring for a time. There was one occasion in 1931 when for those employed in Yarmouth their arles was actually cut from 17/6 to 15/– (75p), the rate for a barrel reduced from a shilling to ten old pence – in decimal terms, 5p to 4p. Victory or even human justice is not always assured in hard times.

Yet there were exceptions to that. In 1930 the women, led by someone who styled herself 'Mrs Macleod, Aird a' Bhaigh', went to the Ministry of Labour in London to argue on behalf of the herring workers who had been refused unemployment benefit due to the seasonal nature of their work. How well she did was underlined by the 'promptness of their action thereafter', rectifying this injustice. On 24 October 1936, 3,000 girls in Yarmouth and 1,000 in Lowestoft went on strike for a pay increase of 2d a barrel. Their actions cost the industry tens of thousands of pounds, with a thousand drifters being tied up in harbour, their herring left ungutted. The time also brought a great deal of drama to the life of young Mairi Macdonald from Lewis. She remembered witnessing the police arriving on the scene, dragging two young women from a nearby village into the police van, the Black Maria.

'Now did two girls not land in prison. They arrested them, accusing them of being the ringleaders. They were no such thing. They were not doing a thing, not a thing, just like ourselves, shouting and laughing and all that.'

Mounted police also galloped through the herring troughs at some of the curing yards, chasing away the women who were attempting to prevent others working there. One building was besieged by the herring girls, too, chanting slogans and demanding fair pay, their 'tongues' gutting knife' – to quote the Gaelic poet, Ruaraidh MacThòmais, in his poem 'Clann-nighean an Sgadain' – 'cutting a strip' from those who opposed them. In the end, after two and a half days of striking, they won a victory. In mission halls and churches, they were provided with the good news, a hundred Gaelic-speaking fisher-girls hearing this from the lips of the Rev. Lachlann Macleod: 'Return to work tomorrow and the Herring Fishery Board guarantee that curers will pay you 1/- a barrel.'

There were other strikes later, especially in 1938, when the women from the Highlands and Islands walked out over the issue of working on the Sunday – alien to the Scottish Presbyterian tradition as a whole. It also, according to them, and with more than a little contradiction in their argument, gave the English fishermen an unfair advantage, as their northern equivalents never trailed their nets in the ocean on that day of the week.

Yet by that time the industry was already dwindling away, its demise hastened by the six years of war that followed. After the conflict there was little need for the nimbleness of women's fingers, the sharp and rhythmic cutting of a blade. Those who build and create machines had already found a way of fashioning a substitute, of mimicking the movement that had once been the preserve of the herring girl, the 'Knife point in/twist and rive/gills and gut/wan move' that had once been the sole preserve of the human hand.

Pl. XIII

Fig. 1.

Fig. 2.

Fig. 3.

Pesches de Mer. Sorretterie des Harengs et des Sardines. Duits Loup.

Previous page: *Sea fishing, herring and sardines, 1751–1777.* Illustrated in the middle of the print is a form of herring fence. Nowadays only the Ellenberger herring fence stretching across part of the river Schlei at Keppeln in Germany remains in place, the last survivor of a once common and traditional method of catching herring in Europe.

Below: Even at a glance, this map of Shetland by Herman Moll from 1725 shows that the discovery of the 'most plentiful' herring locations mentioned in his notes was far more important than any attempt to accurately represent the islands the herring shoaled around.

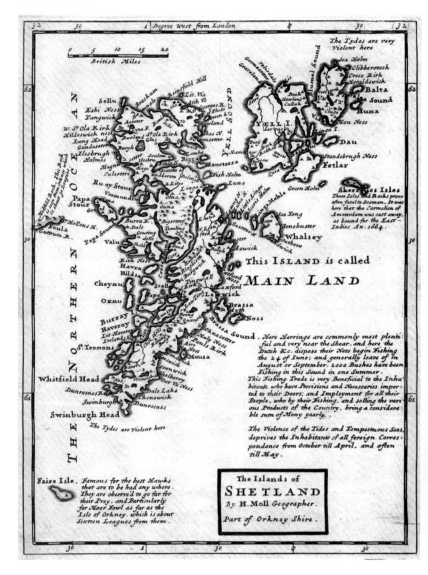

Published by THOMAS VARTY, 31, Strand, London.

FISH.

Above: This hand-coloured lithograph from the middle of the 18th century illustrates herring and other fish, and their importance to man.

Below: Stornoway Harbour, seen here with a forest of masts in the heyday of the herring industry, around the time of World War One. It was often said you could walk across the water without ever getting your feet wet.

Right: 'Dunna sit idle; tak dee sock'. Herring girls employed in the fishing industry kept their hands busy when they were not working, many knitting as they walked. Many of them were as quick with their knitting needles as they were with their gutting knives.

Below: The sturdiness of many of the herring girls tells its own story. In this photograph, they are engaged in 'filling up', typically a Monday morning job, draining off the pickle in which the catch had been kept.

Above: Another kind of dexterity was required of the women who worked at the farlans, the large wooden troughs full of herring: 'knife point in, twist and rive, gills and guts wan move'.

Below: A packer, holding up gutted herring, before packing them into a barrel.

Above: The Inverness-registered drifter, the *Whinnieknowe INS 149*, of Nairn, landing herring at Great Yarmouth. The two-handed creels – or sweels (anglicised as 'swills') – provide evidence of the location as these were distinctive to the port.

Below: Two gutters carrying a tub of gutted herring to the packer.

Above: The men 'freshing', packing the herring with ice at Great Yarmouth for consumption or processing in the next couple of days. Note the headgear.

Below: This photograph from 1934 shows a German fish-worker learning a new way of gutting herring by employing a machine to 'twist and rive'.

Above: Sporting the latest trend of the mid-thirties flowered overall and a headscarf – my Aunt Bella (second from left, back row) joins her older sister Aunt Agnes (far left, front row) and other members of an Isle of Lewis crew.

Below: *Is e 'n t-ionnsachadh òg an t-ionnsachadh bòidheach.* (Learning when young is lovely learning.) My cousin Murdo Angus Murray (far left) with some of his friends on Port of Ness Harbour in the early sixties.

CHAPTER FIVE

'Get Off of My Cloud'

Depending on where their music plays within northern Europe and beyond, the Rolling Stones clearly have a different effect on both herring and those who fish for them.

Their music was used to try and scare shoals of the fish out of the fjord at Kolgrafafjordur on the Snaefellsnes peninsula in the west of Iceland. Fifty thousand tons-worth of herring had been killed there both in 2012 and early the following year. The theories given for the causes of this event were almost as plentiful as the number of dead herring swept like tarnished silver dumped upon the shore. Some considered the loss of all these fish to have been due to a lack of oxygen, caused by landfill pollution after a new bridge had been built in 2012. Others pointed out the way shoals had crowded in huge numbers in the shallow fjord, recalling that a similar incident had occurred in 1941, when

British servicemen thrived for a long time on washed-up herring – long before the bridge had been created. Another individual put forward the idea that the underwater currents at this time of year were so cold that ice crystals might have formed inside the fish and killed them, particularly when they were this close to both the surface and shore.

Whatever the reason for the tragedy, however, the ill turn of that tide spilled a little good fortune into the lives of some nearby inhabitants. Large numbers of gannets, seals, orcas and dolphins gathered to enjoy the feast stretched out on the shoreline, tucking into the spread. Ravens pecked. A sea-eagle or two came to dine. Even the local mink grew fat, fed by schoolchildren who harvested the dead herring, bringing the gleaming corpses to a local farm. The remainder provided some rich and salty compost for the soil.

In order to stop this happening again, an Icelandic expert group called Star-Oddi tried a variety of techniques. They played low-frequency sounds and explosions underwater, as well as recordings of orcas and the Rolling Stones. Every tactic failed. Not even the chorus of 'Jumping Jack Flash' prevented silver flashing in and out of the fjord. Not even the veiled threats of 'Get Off of My Cloud' or 'Satisfaction'. One local wit suggested that, perhaps, they were using the wrong group from the 1960s. The Beatles' song 'I Am the Walrus' would work far better, particularly as the New York Aquarium advertises one of these creatures that somehow succeeds in sucking herring through the confines of a straw. Camels and needles come to mind.[*]

---

[*]These incidents are not unique. I heard of a number during the course of researching this book, including one in Irvine in Ayrshire in the early 1930s where a large shoal of herring became trapped in the harbour, probably due to the close attentions of a circling whale. The people of the town scooped up the large catch with baskets. Another occurred in the island and village of

The Rolling Stones clearly have a stronger appeal in the Dutch port of Scheveningen, one of eight districts of The Hague, the seat of government in the Netherlands. Throughout its streets, the band's logo – a set of thick crimson lips, a highly coloured version of those that greeted me in Florø – pointed the way to the local museum. An exhibition commemorating one of the band's first rock concerts outside the United Kingdom was being held there, one that had taken place in the town some fifty years before. Finally, my friend Roel and I reached the place. Upstairs were unmistakable images of that youthful-looking band. The youngsters of the Dutch town clambered to get near them, forcing back the constabulary while they tried to reach drummer Charlie Watts looking cool in sunglasses, Keith Richard much less cadaverous than he now appears, Old Fish Lips himself, Mick Jagger, slithering on stage in a similar pose to the one he adopts today, never – it seems for the present at any rate – to fade away.

And downstairs? That contained many images similar to those in fishing museums throughout northern Europe, for all that they had their own Dutch twist to them. There was the familiar trio of herring on the town crest, although this group wore crowns and had spawned its own political party, one that demanded greater autonomy for Scheveningen. There were photographs of herring girls with bright golden pins fixed into the tops of their scarves, a decoration they wore for high days, holidays and family photographs. (The statue of the Fisherman's Wife looking out over the fine white strand of Scheveningen beach

Continued from p. 98:
Lovund to the north of Norway in early 2014. A shoal swam too close to the shore and was frozen in place, unable to free itself from layers of ice and escape to deeper water. Locals expected the smell of rot to hang over their community for months afterwards. Fortunately, the tide is sometimes capable of cleansing the shoreline.

possessed similar headgear, her apron still and unmoving in the stiff breeze that greeted Roel and me when we walked there a short time later. We noted the wreaths that circled the base, a reminder of the frightening total of Dutch fishermen whose lives and boats had been swept away over the years, never returning to the families and ports that waited for them.) Some men wore black berets as they rolled out barrels; others possessed flat caps as they stood and shivered over – what George Mackay Brown called in his poem 'Hamnavoe' – a 'drift of herring'. Fish, too, were hung out to dry. So much, so familiar.

And then there was the painting that caught my eye: one of a fishing boat *LK 243*, the boat I knew as the *Swan*, making its way towards the Lodberries in my new hometown of Lerwick in Shetland. One of the Fifies, sailboats with vertical stern posts that measured 75 feet (23 metres), it was a familiar vessel. Originally launched in May 1900, it had been restored in 1996, having been discovered rotting in Hartlepool some six years earlier. Nowadays, it still sailed in and out of Lerwick, going as far as the fjords around Bergen or the far westerly island of St Kilda, its brown canvas sail reminding people of the heyday of the herring in these parts.

It was the exactness of the painting that impressed me. Each of the town's southern landmarks was perfectly in position. Robertson's Lodberry; Queen's Hotel; Yates' Lodberry; even the one that bore my own name, Murray's Lodberry. With so many back doors, gables and piers opening out to the sea, this area was reputedly a place where smugglers had once crept through darkness to deliver contraband to the merchants of the town. The name itself suggested that; the term derives from the Old Norse *hladberg* (loading rock), which within Shetland had come to mean a courtyard enclosed by a wall, its only opening provided by a door through which goods could be loaded or unloaded by a boat. I stopped before it, turning towards an old gentleman who was beside me in the museum.

'I stay here,' I informed him, indicating with my eyes the place depicted. 'Do you have any idea who painted it?'*

A strong-shouldered man with neat grey hair swept back from his forehead, he looked at me with the twinkle he had hitherto reserved for the young women who stepped into the museum. I had noticed him speaking to one earlier, his voice loud and cheery, movements as lithe and flowing as those of the elderly musician whose picture was on display upstairs.

'You are from Lerwick?'

'Yes . . . At least, that's where I stay now.'

His next response surprised me. 'That place is Sodom and Gomorrah,' he declared.

'Uh?'

'I used to go up there very often,' he said. 'When I was younger.'

'You were a fisherman?'

'Ja. Many years ago. I have left it long ago.' His eyes gleamed. 'Do you know that was where I learned my first words of English?'

'No.'

'I learned it for the young ladies. Those nights we went to the dances. Those times we washed ourselves for the first time in weeks.'

'What were they?'

'"Can I walk you home?" I learned to say it very well. What do you think?'

'Very well,' I smiled. 'They must have been impressed.'

'Very! In fact, do you know that when I went back there about ten years ago, I worried about how well I had pronounced them when I was young?'

---

*I discovered later it was by Dr Frank Robertson, a Shetland GP and artist.

'Why?'

'I was very frightened that when I was walking down the pier, some child would come up to me and say, "Hello, Grandad." I was nervous that might happen.'

He laughed, doubling up as he repeated the words:

'Hello, Grandad.'

After that introduction, we spoke for a short time about his fishing life, how many boats he had been on during his years at sea. Soon, however, my companion had spotted another young woman he recognised in a corner of the museum. His hand stretched out in greeting.

'Hello, darling,' he announced – or whatever is the nearest Dutch equivalent.

We were fortunate to meet another man in the courtyard outside the museum cafe. A quiet, thoughtful man, he sucked at his roll-your-own cigarette while, his words translated by Roel, he talked about his own life at sea. Proffering his tobacco tin, he offered his own brief verdict on some of the fishing ports he had encountered during these years.

'Lerwick?'

'A nice place but cold.'

'Stornoway?'

'A fine, sheltered bay.'

'The nicest place?'

'I liked Castletownbere in the south of Ireland. The people were friendly and the drink cheap.'

'And the wildest place? Where you were most scared?'

He drew in a mouthful of smoke before he replied. 'Near Fastnet. In the south-west of Ireland. There was one time when we were out there when the seas seemed to be walking upon the heavens. They rose up that high. I remember kneeling in front of them, my hand clasping the sole of my shoe, praying.'

From the mouth of such a quiet, reticent man, it sounded like poetry, a reminder, if any were needed, that fishing demanded the dearest rent of all trades, the lives of men lost

in its depths. This thought was coupled with a photograph
that was on display in a folder just beside the front door. It
was of a place that was familiar to me – the graveyard at the
top of the Knab, the sentinel of rock that stands guard over
Lerwick. Two men stood at its lower edge on a grey Shetland
day, one wearing the hat, coat, collar and tie most adult
males seemed to have been kitted out with in the mid to
late 1970s. The other was clearly speaking to a small, invisible
gathering, a poppy on the lapel of his dark suit, the crisp-
white cuffs of his sleeves showing as he brandished his arms
while addressing both them and the stiffness of the breeze.
They stood beside a newly erected white headstone which
had been set within a dark wooden frame. At its top, written
in Dutch, was an inscription I had once read. It was from
Psalm 65, verses 5 and 6.

> Therefore the ends of all the earth,
> and those afar that be
> Upon the sea, their confidence,
> O Lord, will place in thee.
> Who, being girt with pow'r, sets fast
> by his great strength the hills.
> Who noise of seas, noise of their waves,
> and people's tumult, stills.

Among the words carved – both in Dutch and English –
on the stone was the following: 'In Memory of the Dutch
Seamen who died at sea or in this country and who were
buried in this graveyard in the years 1875–1926.' There
were the names, too, of the fishing ports that had come
together to put up this small monument. They included
communities like Vlaardingen, Maassluis, Katwijk aan
Zee and Scheveningen – each cluster of vowels and
consonants alien and strange when read in the cold
November light of Shetland, Alongside them were a
number of other stones, often with the words 'Hier Rust'
inscribed on the crest; the names dated from the early years

of the twentieth century, winnowed and sometimes made illegible by the scour of wind and salt. Two of them are from Scheveningen: fifty-three-year-old Cornelis de Best, whose date of death is given as 19 July 1906, and Willem Dijkhuizen, who was only twenty when he perished on 5 June 2005.

And then there are the others who lie in the two main graveyards of Lerwick, the ones who are unnamed and possess no individual stones or markers to establish where exactly they might lie – a mingling of names and ages, ranging from sixteen to fifty-seven, each one dying for whatever reason, illness, mischance or accident, their corpses lying alongside a young woman from my own native island, who died while gutting herring away from home. In an article written to accompany the unveiling of the Lerwick memorial, I note their identities and ages – Martin Harteveld, aged seventeen, Klaar Pronk, sixteen, Hendrik Jacobus Johannes Oosterbaan at nineteen, paying particular attention to the younger ones, as if there is some greater, more overwhelming tragedy connected with their youth. It is as if we find it more difficult to imagine the others. Forty-six-year-old Machiel Vrolijk, whose absence from his home might have hurled a wife into a world of grief and darkness, set children on a path where the only possible destination was despair. Job Michiel Taal, who might have wondered, like his biblical namesake, why death and loss had come for him in his fifty-sixth year. Jacob Roeleveld . . . Cornelis den Heijer . . . Arie Knoster . . .

These names were recalled in a ceremony in Shetland on 18 June 2012 by Henk Grootveld, the chair of the committee that erected the memorial stone there, as well as a commemorative wall in Scheveningen. The Scheveningen memorial consisted of 25 metres of black granite slab on which 1,325 names of lost fishermen from the town had been engraved. Below it were the words *Niet teruggekeerd van zee, naam voor nam gegrift in steen* (Never returned from sea, name by name engraved in stone). In his speech in Lerwick, however, unveiling the stone there, Henk concentrated on both Shetland and the years 1880–1925, when these islands were visited by hundreds of booms and herring-luggers from Dutch villages such as his own, Katwijk, Vlaardingen and Maassluis. In May and June, they had sailed from Holland and assembled in places like Bressay Sound, which the Dutch termed 'De Baai van Lerwick', for the start of the herring season on 24 June (St John's Day or Johnsmas Day). In the weekends the fishermen anchored here for a rest and to get fresh water, provisions and souvenirs, such as the earthenware dogs they called the Shetland spaniels, which used to stand on the mantelpieces of households throughout much of northern Europe. The presence of these ornaments, otherwise known as Staffordshire dogs, was not always as innocent as it seemed. Prostitutes in England used to put these canine companions in their windows to show when they were available, if the dogs' noses were pressed together, or when they were entertaining one of their customers, when the dogs' tails were linked. (There was one in our home, until it was either smashed or thrown out sometime in my childhood. Perhaps someone found out.) Sometimes, too, the fishermen would die either within or on the edge of the island, on boats or in Lerwick's Gilbert Bain Hospital. Those who worked together on the headstone had traced twenty-five who were buried in the town cemetery. Perhaps, they acknowledged, there were more.

There is little doubt of that. They are not the only graves of Dutch seamen to be found in Shetland, both within the headstone's timespan and outside. There is, most unusually, a small memorial to what is known as Hollanders' Graves in Ronas Voe in Northmavine at the north end of the Shetland mainland. This marks the burial place of a number of Dutch sailors killed in 1674, during one of the three Anglo-Dutch wars of the seventeenth century. Their Dutch East Indian frigate *Wappen van Rotterdam* was captured while sheltering there by a number of Royal Navy vessels, the *Cambridge*,

Crown and *Newcastle*. In George Low's book *A Tour Through
the Islands of Orkney and Schetland*, a tour that took place in
1774, there is a reference to a black marble headstone with a
Dutch inscription on the island of Bressay. There will be
those, too, buried in other locations on the islands, unmarked
and unmourned and as far apart as Unst and Fair Isle, while
others lie in greater depths below the waves. More cheerfully,
there is also Hollanders Knowe near Scalloway where
Dutchmen and natives used to meet to do business at one
time, and a loch on Bressay formed when visitors from the
Netherlands hacked out a quarry for stone. In George Low's
book recording his visit in 1774, he notes that:

> The country folk are very smart in their bargains with the
> Dutch; they are now paid in money for everything, no such
> thing as formerly trucking one commodity for another; almost
> all of them speak as much Dutch, Danish, and Norwegian as
> serves the purpose of buying and selling, nay some of them
> speak these languages, especially the low Dutch, fluently.

All this is hardly surprising. Dutch vessels began visiting
places like Bressay sometime in the fifteenth century, drawn
there (largely) by the herring that flourished in their waters.
(It could also be argued that there were other attractions in
Lerwick during this time, some of which clearly lodged
in the mind and memory of at least one Scheveningen
fisherman. In its early days, a Bressay website notes
disdainfully, Lerwick 'started life as a shanty town used for
the debaucherous pursuits of Dutch fishermen'.) It was
clearly of great value to them. The Dutch were involved in
three wars there: the first in 1653 when Oliver Cromwell
was in power. The other occasions were during the Second
Dutch War in 1665 after the Stuarts had been restored, when
300 British men were temporarily stationed in Lerwick. In
1673 the Dutch took advantage of their absence. Their
sailors landed in Lerwick and – in behaviour worthy of

residents of certain twin towns that once stood near the River Jordan – set fire to the barracks and a number of houses that stood there. In 1720 the French, involved in their own conflicts in the War of the Spanish Succession with the Dutch, exacted their own revenge on their European neighbours – burning all the Dutch boats in the vicinity of Shetland.

It was herring that brought them there – a fish they had caught for some time before that, but mostly in their own coastal waters with their catch being hauled ashore, gutted and packed in brine.* They did this first of all in places like the Zuiderzee, now reclaimed land but at one time a shallow bay of the North Sea in the north-west of the Netherlands. At one time these waters contained their own variety of the species *Clupea harengus* – one that is now extinct. This was shorter and contained fewer vertebrae than other types of the fish. It was also more difficult to pickle or salt, giving it a shorter life-span than other kinds of herring. These fish have, too, long vanished, together with the waters in which they spawned. Some wonderful legacies of that lost sea still remain. They include the Dutch version of St Kilda, the former island of Schokland. For all that it was evacuated in 1859, it is still protected from an invisible rising sea by a retaining wall on its waterfront. At one time men and women used to perform a little dance when they passed each other on the wooden barrier, a strange kind of 'excuse-me-waltz' while the waves lashed around them, threatening their community's existence. Or there is Spakenburg, which I have also visited. Women with brightly shaded, often

---

*There were exceptions to this form of fishing 'close to shore'. In 1295, King Edward 1 of England issued an order decreeing that fishermen from Holland, Zeeland and Friesland should not be harassed while fishing near the Yarmouth coast where the herring arrived earlier than the fishing off Flanders. It is likely that they were coming there since the eleventh century.

flowery shoulder pads cycle up and down its canals, wearing lace caps on their heads and long, colourful dresses. It takes a moment to work out the purpose of these articles of clothing that makes them resemble softer, gentler versions of Sue-Ellen Ewing in the TV programme *Dallas* or the character played by Joan Collins in *Dynasty*. Perhaps it was a different form of power dressing, one that enabled women to carry heavy loads or to protect the remainder of their clothes from the gravity-borne attention of herring gull shit while they were gutting herring.

Even in retaining these traditional costumes for everyday use, these women show us a very different attitude to the herring trade and its legacy from the one that exists throughout much of the rest of northern Europe. They venerate and celebrate the fish in a way that is not done elsewhere on the Continent. This was not always the case. At one time the Dutch were like the majority of people throughout the north, following practices that had existed for centuries before. Largely they fished near to their own shores. Occasionally they bought herring from Denmark and Sweden. According to the twelfth-century Dutch chronicler Saxo Grammaticus, the Sound between the Danish island Zealand and Helsinborg in Scania, Sweden, contained so many herring that fishing boats would become stuck in their shoals and herring could be fished out with bare hands.

This may be a legend, just like another that is often told about the reasons for the rise of the Dutch herring industry. Historians have credited this to a Dutch discovery of how if pyloric caecae, the little pouches found in a herring's stomach, are kept entire and left in the brine mixture, the fish both possesses greater flavour and keeps for much longer. In a wonderful display of local chauvinism, different communities ascribe this invention to different individuals, all living within their own boundaries. Ostend puts forward Jacob Klein, Ouddorp on the isle of Goeree claims it was a gentleman called Jan Machiel Duffel, while elsewhere the favoured candidate was or is a gentleman with two small gutting knives chiselled on his headstone – Willem Beukels of Biervliet, a fishing village in northern Flanders in Zeeland province in the Netherlands. According to Dutch folklore, it was this discovery in the late fourteenth or early fifteenth century that permitted Dutch fishermen to move away from the coastline and fish in more distant stretches of shallow sea like Dogger Bank. There was silver there to be mined, herring to be brought back to feed hungry mouths ashore.

However attractive the myth might be, it is definitely false. Willem Beukels, a name that still appears among Lists of the Most Influential Dutchmen Who Ever Breathed or Walked the Earth, was not the inventor of this way of curing herring. Neither was any other Dutchman. Herring was treated in that way ashore long before the knife of any man from the Netherlands stumbled across the method. During the mid-thirteenth century, the method is recorded to have occurred in a number of locations, most notably near where Saxo Grammaticus wrote about, in Scania at the southern tip of Sweden, a place that was then a province of Denmark. In a variation on his words, it was claimed that the number of fish in these waters hindered the use of ship rudders. Under the control of merchants from the Baltic ports, particularly Lübeck, herring was exported from this area to much of the rest of Europe. What Beukels may have known as *kaken*, the 'Dutch' method of curing herring, was employed by them.

As a result, it was not this change that revolutionised Dutch herring fishing, though it undoubtedly contributed to it. There were other developments too. A succession of conflicts occurred, such as the war between the Hanseatic League and Denmark, which ended in 1370, and another that involved Lübeck and Holland, which occurred between 1437 and 1441. From 1388 to 1392, the Hanseatic merchants also caused themselves a great deal of commercial damage by boycotting the market in Bruges. This meant that the Dutch could no longer rely on a supply of herring from the north and were compelled to go out fishing further and further from their own shores. In this, they were aided by the creation of the *vleet*, a large net that combined several smaller drag nets. It was particularly necessary for fishing in English waters, where seventy-five nets might be required for one boat. As a result of this, a number of Dutch vessels kept becoming larger and larger; their local market, growing in number with the increasing population of the fifteenth century, became more and more dependent on their efforts to obtain food for their tables. They also needed to sail further in order both to increase their catch and to obtain it earlier in the season. Shetland loomed on the horizon. So did the Western Isles and the Irish Sea, where herring shoaled long before they arrived in any great number in the North Sea.

And as a result of this, someone, somewhere among the fishing fleet of the Netherlands performed a little experiment – attempting to cure the herring on board rather than waste both time and energy taking their vessel to shore. In the beginning they probably did this with only a small number of fish, the first and biggest ones, which they would sell as fresh herring on shore. The practice, however, spread, accompanied by the increasing use of the large *vleet* net. In turn, around the second decade of the fifteenth century this spawned the first herring buss, a large boat that was in itself a development of what had come before, likely to have been a modification of the standard Scandinavian cargo ship of the thirteenth century.* It was constructed with two goals in mind. It would need both to deal with the problems of using bigger nets and

---

*Or even before that. The 'buss-type' boat was already known in the Mediterranean as a cargo vessel during the Crusades and was used in Scandinavia as a development of the Viking longship, known as a 'buza'.

be able to tackle the rigours of the heavy seas herring fishermen would encounter around the coastline of islands like Shetland and the Western Isles. It would also require both the skills of shipbuilders and a great deal of money.

In essence, it was a factory ship – modified and altered to allow men to perform the process of gibbing, the technique of gutting and curing herring, while at sea for periods of five weeks or more. Its prototype was first built in Hoorn, near Amsterdam, in 1416. Like a cross between a Cunard liner and an aircraft carrier, it was a long, stout and seaworthy boat with bloated sides and a huge and spacious interior. It cut through the fiercest of waves, only returning home when its hull was crammed with barrels of cured herring, fish that even possessed the benefit of being a nicer-tasting variety than those that had been caught near to the shoreline for centuries before.

There were other changes that accompanied this. The buss needed a great deal of cooperation between different communities and interests. This was an attitude which the Dutch had succeeded in acquiring over many centuries, their constant struggle with the onslaught of the sea compelling them to work together, doing this in the building of dykes to protect their towns and villages and also in the draining of much of their flat, low-lying farmland to ensure it was both dry – mainly – and fertile. It was this history that they drew upon to help them revolutionise herring fishing. Instead of the smaller boats they had used before, where they could utilise and depend upon the skills of families, more hands now had to be on deck. They needed sawyers to cut the wood, carpenters to shape and fashion it, and ship chandlers to ensure these vessels were supplied with hemp, linen, tar, netting, tallow, barrels and salt.

They also required good government. Warships were sent out with guns bristling to protect these huge investments in both money and time, sailing nearby to guard the fleet from some of the more warlike traits to which an occasional fisherman has always been prone, especially that unfortunate tendency to see off any foreign invaders from 'their' waters. Government also defended the industry in other ways, creating a whole set of regulations that governed everything from the size of the nets fishermen were permitted to use to the processing and sale of herring. (In one of the first-ever conservation measures introduced by a central authority, they even laid down the size of the mesh in a fishing net. There were also only certain ports – Maassluis, Vlaardingen and Rotterdam – where fish could be bought and sold. Scheveningen was not among them till 1857.) The provincial government of Holland, at that time part of the Spanish Empire, was also innovative in other ways, introducing an early form of branding for the fish. The barrels had not only to be of a regulation size and quality, but also to be stamped as Holland herring. While many fishermen may have grumbled about the bureaucracy involved in all of this, they had less reason to complain about the result of all the care and attention to their product. It gave their catch a good reputation among those who purchased it. As a result, the cash kept on rolling in – just like the barrels, which they trundled up and down cobblestones, ensuring that the brine and herring were well mixed within.

The benefits of herring flowed in a much wider sense than this. It encouraged the construction of ships with timber imported from Germany and processed into planks that were exported to England, fostering a similar industry there. This process was assisted by a farmer from Uitgeest who patented a crankshaft, one that linked together the whirl of a windmill with the backwards and forwards movement of a saw. The herring, too, did much to widen the horizons of Dutch merchants, who learned not only to look north to places like Shetland, but also to gaze south to Mediterranean nations like Italy and Spain. They became gatherers of intelligence, chiefs of spy networks. Paying cash for any important information they received, they would send herring to countries where they had been told the harvest had failed, aware that people will pay high prices when hunger and starvation haunt their existence. They supplied their population not only with fish, but also with grain, rye, wheat, wine, beer and other commodities.

As a means to this end, the Dutch and their neighbours became some of the pioneers in the art of cartography, following in the footsteps of the Portuguese, who were early practitioners in this craft. In 1570, for instance, the Flemish map engraver Abraham Ortelius, an associate of the great Gerardus Mercator, started to produce what was termed *Theatrum Orbis Terrarum* (Theatre of the Earth). An extremely insightful individual, he was the first to suggest that the continents of the world were at one time connected together before drifting far apart. He travelled widely and had many contacts in his field throughout Europe. He journeyed in England, Ireland, Italy and France, yet his efforts included a vague map of South America – which he later improved upon – and Scotia tabula, or a specific map of Scotland. This is interesting in the way he manages to get details of the inland parts of the country wrong, placing the Grampian mountains between the Forth and Clyde, yet succeeds in being more accurate about, say, the Inner Hebrides, its broken coastlines edged and laced with water – the knowledge of this part of the world based, perhaps, on the observations of fishermen from the Low Countries. Over the decades his successors become more and more accurate in undertaking this task. By 1592, the well-known Dutch cartographer Lucas Janszoon Waghenaer was creating what have been termed both vivid and functional maps, ideal for those setting out to sea in the late sixteenth century and afterwards. Some of the detail must have been a boon to the Dutch herring fishermen working around the coastline of northern Europe. His charts include much essential for the trade, including the results of depth measurements, courses of navigation channels, and beacons and other landmarks, such as church spires and houses that are visible from the sea. A cluster of depth figures is included next to most ports, essential when sailing into and out of harbours and rivers. He does all this, too, in a more systematic way than his predecessors, trying his utmost to ensure that it is all done to a uniform scale, seeking to produce his 'Mariner's Mirrour' in a way that would befit his life as a naval chief officer. His *Thresoor de Zeevaert* (Treasure of Navigation) even incorporates accurate representations of the distant archipelago known as St Kilda into his charts. It was a place where fishermen could shelter from storm-ridden seas and also obtain fresh water, both essential for the catchers of herring and other fish if they were blown west by fierce and unexpected winds.

Another cartographer, albeit one operating out of London, was Herman Moll, whose map of 1725 of, for instance, Shetland, is very clear in its purpose. (Unlike his family origins: he may have been Dutch; he also could have been from Bremen in Germany.) In the notes inscribed on the map are the words: 'Here herrings are commonly most plentiful and very near the Shoar; and here the Dutch & c. dispose their Nets begin fishing the 24 of June and generally leave of in August or September. 2000 Bushes have been Fishing In this Sound in one Summer.'

All this was part of what made Dutch townships and the fishermen they spawned different. Unlike in cities like Ghent and Bruges in what is now modern Belgium, the trade of Amsterdam and other locations in the Netherlands was not connected with the finer, fancier stuff of life, such as spices or rare fabrics. Its foundations were built on herring bones; its early houses reeking, perhaps, of fish guts and stale beer. Within this locality, a new form of capitalism began to develop and grow. Unlike for the family boats that existed before, the construction of the busses required large financial investment. Stocks and shares were sold to allow the making of these floating fortresses to ensure that they could leave their home harbours and set out to sea. In doing this, it sparked a habit of mind that would eventually lead to the creation of ventures like the Dutch East Indies Company before it spread elsewhere to the far corners of the world. It was a vision, too, that as time went on came to be formed and flavoured by Dutch Calvinism. Investing in stocks and shares was a respectable way for a dour burgher to use his money, an acceptable form of gambling when compared to the more frivolous ways others frittered it away – on women, drink or parties in some of the Sodoms and Gomorrahs found elsewhere in the world. To use the words of historian R. H. Tawney, the attitudes they displayed were those of 'an earnest, zealous, godly generation, punctual in labour, constant in prayer, thrifty and thriving, filled with a decent pride in themselves and their calling, assured that strenuous toil is acceptable in Heaven, a people like those Dutch Calvinists whose economic triumphs were as famous as their iron Protestantism'.

Or perhaps not. As Michael Pye points out in his book *The Edge of the World*, capitalism may have been coming into existence anyway at this time. In the markets found in the Low Countries during this period there was a great mingling of cultures, always conducive to both creativity and change. Many working there spoke Italian, passed on part of their profits to a Spanish overlord and traded continually with both the Portuguese and every other Catholic power in Europe. (One can even see how, in terms of mapmaking and other skills, they learned from the Portuguese.) There were similar changes emerging in, say, the Antwerp wool trade, where those involved had to know the value of wool or grain before investing in different commodities. Capitalism may have emerged out of this situation long before the religious differences arrived to cloud the scene, for all that its rise might have coincided with the emergence of Dutch Calvinism. Contributing to it were the bad relationships the Dutch had with their neighbours in Catholic France. The young men had little choice but to go north for the herring. The English Channel was 'off limits' to them.

There is, however, little doubt that it was Dutch patriotism that defined much of the substance of that particular faith. It originated partly in reaction to the Spanish brand of Catholicism, more intense and fervent during that period than most. Unlike that society and its church's opulence and ostentation, Calvinism characterized itself by simplicity and plainness, a description that even applied to the food placed upon the table. Not for the Calvinists the richness and vulgarity of, say, game or other meats. Not for them excess and plenty – as countless pictures from the period demonstrate, providing little moral lectures on the dangers of greed within their frames. Instead, both rich and poor often plumped for the simplicity of herring, a food that the good Lord had provided for them not only on their own coastline but further from their shores. It was even provided as the main meal on Dutch ships, both commercial and naval, unlike for the British and French, who preferred salt cod. Eating herring flesh was a sign that you shared Dutch faith and values, practising humility and restraint even in terms of your appetite, and showing that you placed more emphasis on your future heavenly comforts than those found upon the dining tables of either sea or land.

One more reason why herring is seen as important can be found in a comic book that belongs to the same tradition as Hergé's famous character, Tintin. Willy Vandersteen's two creations, *Suske en Wiske*, are a boy and girl who run amok in a surreal version of the Low Countries, one that involves time travel, talking insects and spaceships. The titles reflect their absurdity. The buzzing egg. The tyrannic beetle. The singing mushrooms. The Zincshrinker. They even tackle what might be the most overgrown herring in existence – the monster of Loch Ness. And then there is an issue of the comic that reflects yet another reason why the herring might be venerated by the people of the Netherlands. Entitled *Suske en Wiske Het Lijdende Lieden*, it tells of an episode in the history of Lieden, the important university town in the south of the country.

In 1574, during the long Dutch struggle for independence from the Habsburg Empire, the city of Leiden was besieged by Spanish troops from May to September. Prayer is all that sustains the city's people; the populace is so hungry that, according to legend, one of its number, burgomaster Van der Werff, offered his own flesh to eat. (The people refuse, choosing, or so the chronicles tell us, to swallow dogs, cats, grass and roots.) It is at this point that the leader of the Dutch forces, William of Orange, comes up with a plan to put an end to the siege. His forces breach the Ijsseldijk as well as other river defences, the waters surrounding and cutting off large communities like Gouda and Rotterdam. Yet this is not enough. In order for the population of Leiden to be rescued, the water has to be sufficiently deep both to stop Spanish troops moving and to allow the Dutch ships to come close to the city walls. The pages of Suske and Wiske's comic book remind us how this occurred in mid-September, Suske splashing through puddles as the rain slashes down, storm clouds stacked high above his spiked hairstyle. Drenched, the Spaniards retreat, shouting, '*Dit is hooploos! Retiren! Terugtrekken!*' as they flee the flood of battle. And then, a providential meal arrives. The Dutch forces – those known rather insultingly by the Spanish as the Sea Beggars – bring this to the starving. In its simplicity, it reminds all who gather around with empty mouths and open, outstretched hands of how Jesus fed the multitude who gathered around to hear Him preach. Simple bread and herring – the food of salvation – are shared among the hungry of the town.

It is an event that is not simply recorded in Suske and Wiske's adventures. It was dramatised in a propaganda play by the seventeenth-century rhetorician Jacob Duym, who even portrayed the seas and wind as bearing arms along with the righteous citizens of Leiden against their imperial masters. It is recorded in countless paintings, a number completed after the Belgian revolution of 1830, when the Dutch looked to console themselves for the loss of – what they considered to be – part of their country. Some artists, like Pieter van Veen, recorded the feeding of the liberated people of Leiden. Others, like Joris van Schooten, were commissioned to portray how Van der Werff offered his naked chest to those looking for food. He points a sword at himself, as if he is trying to persuade those around him to end their hunger and plunge it within, this cannibalistic treat satisfying their need for food. There is also the Lancaere Tapestry stitched in 1587 by the Delft Tapestry weaver Joost Jansz Lanckeart to mark the role the university town played in the Dutch Wars of Independence. That example of a traditional Dutch craft hangs in the Stedelijk Museum alongside a much more contemporary depiction of the Siege – the work of photographer Erwin Olaf in 2011. Haunted faces stare out of these photographs, their costumes torn to reveal the thin, naked bodies dying from want and need. It possesses a dramatic urgency that the painters of another age would not have been able to display, the scruples of the time demanding that both flesh and the full horror of their hunger be buttoned up and hidden. There is also a modern celebration which takes place each year on 3 October where the (comparatively well-fed) citizens of the modern city of Leiden take to the streets to toast and recall the ending of the siege. Along with the obligatory rock music and disco lights, they recall that moment by feasting on *hutspot*, a meal of boiled potatoes, carrots and turnips, and the patriotic sacrament, a herring sandwich, one sprinkled with chopped onions, served as it had been centuries before.

All this does much to explain the Dutch attitude to herring. It reveals to us why Scheveningen celebrates the beginning of the herring season with a *Vlaggetjesdag* (Flag Day), where thousands throng the streets and the fishing boats are all bright and beautiful, bedecked with colourful flags. The first barrel of new herring is also auctioned, the proceedings given to various charities. It shows why there are advertising pictures of Dutch football fans resplendent with orange wigs and T-shirts, their country's flags painted on their cheeks, their mouths open as they slip a *maatje*, a raw virgin herring, down their throats. It gives us the reason why there are similar posters of Dutch maidens, complete with clogs and lace caps, with the fish dangling just beyond their lips. It provides us with what lay behind their purpose and motivation to sail to Shetland and beyond in search of herring.

It is a similar reason as to why so many Norwegians chewed wind-dried herring in a tent in Florø. Or why my fellow Hebrideans picked their way through salt herring when they gathered together in Glasgow or Edinburgh.

Or to use the words of the Chinese writer Lin Yutang: 'What is patriotism but a love of the food one ate as a child.'

Sometimes we eat to remind us who we are.

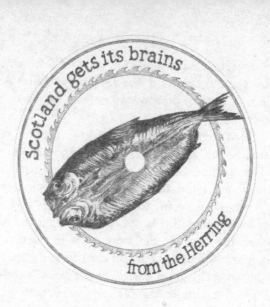

CHAPTER SIX

'Starman'

It was both the percussion and precision that impressed me most about the men who worked at the Speyside Cooperage near the small township of Craigellachie in the north-east of Scotland. On the concrete floor in front of the viewing gallery where we stood they spun wooden barrels as children once rolled a hoopla or tyre, twirling them round and round in the direction of their own separate desks and workspaces. Employing tools their predecessors had gripped and held for generations on the nation's quays and harbours, they hammered and pounded, working to a rhythm of which a rock drummer might have been proud, building up to a crescendo of wood and metal as they set hoop and stave perfectly in place. I watched them as they laboured, the generations working near one another in this task that is almost timeless, going back to prehistoric times over

8,000 years ago. It is mentioned in the Old Testament Book of Kings where we are told that the prophet Elijah defeated the priests of Baal by pouring water from barrels over their burnt offerings.

The older men stood directly below us; their younger counterparts, the apprentices, at the opposite end of the room. Despite the way they all wore uniform red T-shirts with the logo of the company – an oak leaf, acorn and barrel – on their front, some individuals stood out. A strongly built man with a barrel chest, ponytail and bandana dominated the stage at the front as if he were a circus acrobat, his power and athleticism clear from the speed with which he wheeled out a barrel. At the back, a red-haired youth looked intent, serving the early years, perhaps, of the four in which he was expected to learn the basis of the trade. We watched them do much that was surprising and unexpected. Alongside them, the tops of barrels lay on their sides like full moons: some dark, as if lined and marked by cloud; others bright and clear. Long, dry reeds – apparently from the banks of the River Ouse in Cambridgeshire – were stretched out like circus whips on their workspace. These were used to loop around the barrel tops, one way of ensuring that they were watertight, that the lids were firmly in place. We watched the men pound them, a succession of staccato sounds accompanying their every movement. By our side our guide Ronnie Grant told us that, in fact, the noise was much less than it had been centuries before. No longer was it all adjusted and riveted by hand. Modern machines – such as the windlass or even the laser beam, ensuring the lid was cut in a perfect circle – assisted in the process, making sure the barrels were firm and tight.

We were pleased to have Ronnie with us. While this clamour went on, he explained all the booming and banging beneath our feet, casting light on its mysteries. A lithe and fit man with dark hair and glasses, he would gesture and point towards the work floor as he spoke, telling us what was going on, the techniques and tools they were using. Among the information he provided was the type of wood they were utilising. 'White oak from the Mississippi–Missouri, ideal for the whisky trade,' he told us, reminding us of the sheer number of distilleries we had seen on our drive to the cooperage, the vast majority being concentrated in this part of Scotland. The shavings from their work were collected and sent out for other purposes, including the smoking of fish. I smiled wryly at the thought of this new connection with the herring industry I had trekked across Europe to discover. There might no longer be around 1,500 coopers producing over a million barrels, as there were in the herring industry's heyday back in 1915, but that fish – together with trout or salmon – could still be flavoured by the remnants of their labours in smoking houses on Scotland's coastline today.

Together with the posters that decorated the walls of the Speyside cooperage, Ronnie also provided us with the details of how the work was being done. He spoke of how the barrel is just one kind of cask made by the cooper. They range in size from the butt and puncheon – both designed to hold 110 gallons or 500 litres, for all they are of different shapes – to the hogshead of 54 gallons or 245 litres. One of the smallest of these was the barrel, created to contain 40 gallons or 180 litres. It was casks of this size – made from cheaper woods like spruce (mainly), fir or birch – which were once seen in their thousands around the country's coastline. They would bear not only the stamp of the firm or individual who made them – just as in the Speyside Cooperage today – but also the name of the company that had employed the girls salting and packing the herring.[*]

[*]One moving story that centres on the branding of barrels by companies involved in the herring trade is about a man from Stornoway, who often played in a yard operated by a firm called Clydesdale when he was young – that mark imprinted upon the

And then there were the foundations of the trade. Ronnie spoke of how the casks were raised up; how the cooper first selected properly seasoned oak of the right length and thickness to create the staves, using terms like 'listing' to describe how there is an angled taper cut at each end of the stave, or 'backing' to tell how it is shaped to form the rounded side of the cask, with the inside face hollowed out. There is also 'jointing', when the edge of the stave is cut to make sure it fits well. After this, a 'raising-up hoop' is used to defy gravity and hold them together. (I must confess my cowardice at not attempting this, aware that each stave would scuttle across the floor like a strike in a tenpin bowling alley.) A 'steel truss hoop' would then be hammered down over the staves to hold the wood together.

Watching it all was an alien experience. Each single manoeuvre seemed part of a different time, a separate era from that to which we as onlookers belonged, feeling as much in awe at its mysteries as we did when faced with the latest technological products from our own age. The same was true when we encountered both the names and looks of some of the tools that were involved in the process. The 'adze' that was wielded to shape the angled taper at the end of the stave. The 'croze' that cuts a groove into staves. The 'crumb knife'. The 'skillop'. The 'head vice'. (The last one conjured up some painful thoughts. One imagined it – wrongly – pressing on a skull.) These lost words seemed almost unable to be translated into our vocabulary, as if the world they belong to has been stacked and put aside like the

Continued from p. 123:

barrels he scrambled among. During the latter years of the Second World War, he was in a prisoner-of-war camp in Poland. Allowed by his guards to forage for food outside the barbed wire, he discovered himself in a ruined warehouse. Among its contents he found an old barrel engraved with this trademark. Much to his disappointment, it was empty. He often spoke of this moment as being his lowest point in the war.

last remnants of the herring industry, never to be employed any more.

And that even applied to some of the movements we saw. There was one of the older men, his hands clutching a metal compass, making it dance around the rim of the barrel. His ability to find the centre of a barrel lid, using finger and thumb, appeared to belong as much to magic as mathematics, the exactness of this instinct a part of an earlier experience which has slipped away from our modern world.

It's all part of another Scotland, part of our collective past and one that the Glasgow eccentric and comedian Ivor Cutler once declared 'gets its brains from the herring'. To make sure his grandchildren were blessed with intelligence, Ivor Cutler said his grandfather had resorted to a number of extreme measures. He made certain that the children occasionally had herring heads to play with (good for gleaming in the dark) or that he mainly fished for herring on a river estuary. To ensure that he captured only bright and educated fish, he posted a notice on the waterline that informed 'herring red-eyed through reading' to swim 'this way'. He would catch them while their red eyes 'peered' at these words, bringing them home to cook. It was a treat they always prepared with porridge, waiting 'twenty-five minutes' until the surface of a pan containing *Clupea harengus* and oats cracked and the 'juice steamed through with a glad fizz'. After that, we are informed, 'we ate the batter first to take the edge of our appetite so that we could eat the herring with respect, which we did – including the bones'.

For all that Ivor Cutler's approach to the herring might be deliciously eccentric, it only slightly parodies a viewpoint that is in existence throughout Scotland and even further afield. It is one that asserts the role of eating fish in the development of human intelligence. This belongs to the school of thought among a minority of biologists that mankind was descended from 'acquatic apes'. This notion was first put forward in 1960 by Sir Alister Hardy, who held the view that an early population of humans was left isolated during a time of seismic instability, living within a flooded forest environment not at all dissimilar to parts of the Amazon rainforest. If they were not to perish, they either had to adjust to water or take to the trees. This brought about certain changes, allowing them to swim and dive more easily than other kinds of ape, which were both then and are now averse to water. Some scientists have argued that those aspects that are unique to humans among the ape family, such as a descended larynx, walking upright and fat beneath the skin, could be accounted for as a way of adapting for lengthy periods to a watery environment.

And also an extremely large brain. The basis for growing this, according to Professor Michael Crawford from Imperial College London, is to be found in fish. 'DHA, or Docosa-hexaenoic Acid,' he has argued, 'is essential for developing brain tissue, and in order for our brains to grow to the size we have now, our ancestors must have had to eat a lot of fish.' This has resulted in the pleasure that so many of us find in walking by the sea or any large body of water. Humans feel at home there. The most expensive houses are often found in places like riverbanks – providing they don't flood – or shorelines, if the ocean does not wash up right to your door. The rich like to have swimming pools beside their properties, dipping into their depths whenever the need takes them. The poor traditionally made do by taking day trips to seaside towns like Blackpool, Brighton or Ayr, seeing the ocean stretch out before them as they whirled around on Ferris wheels and dodgems and rode the Big Dipper, watching the gleam of saltwater in the distance.

Of course, all this is simply a theory. (One could equally well argue that the longing to go to space is a sign that the original humans came from Jupiter or Mars.) However, there is no doubt that the people of these islands ate considerable quantities of fish. In the beginning these were largely freshwater fish obtained from a river or lake in the vicinity. However, a quick sift through household middens reveals that something altered around AD 1000 in England. Archaeologists have noted the existence of fish bones from saltwater fish within them around that time. These included herring, which in their vast quantities often swam inland and upstream during that period. A few centuries later and herring was being traded on the Continent. In modern-day Belgium, it arrived in the middle of the tenth century. In inland areas of Poland, it was being sold in the eleventh century. In France, it began to be more common by the thirteenth century. As Michael Pye declares in his work on the North Sea, 'fishing at sea was, for the first time [during these years] also feeding the land'.

In these early years, there is no doubt that there was less of a role for herring's main and later 'rival', cod. As a result, cod was considerably less important in the feeding of the poor before the tenth century. (The Anglo-Saxon language, for instance, had no word for this fish. It lived too far from land for it ever to swim into either the nets or vocabulary of the Anglo-Saxons.) The Picts, in Scotland's earlier times, only caught fish from shore, using rod and line; the gleam and turmoil in water a sign that shoals were present near land. The search for cod, in contrast, required larger boats, greater investment and a measure of centring of political power, as found among the merchants of the Hanseatic League on the Baltic coast from the thirteenth century onwards. Herring fishing was, in terms of its beginnings, a much more spontaneous affair. A crofter or small-time farmer could go out with others on a boat after his spring-time seed had been planted, much like those in my home village, who would form an improvised group whenever the urge to go fishing occurred to them. They only required a beach where they could drag their boat, or a row of rafters, perhaps, where they could dry out their nets after use. (Sometimes they did not even have this. A roughly hewn rope could be stretched out between two posts for the purpose, the nets draped like a household's weekly wash upon the line.*) It is true that in some areas there were restrictions to these practices. They may not have been allowed to possess nets that might scoop up young or other fish lying on the sea bottom. They would have to be acutely aware of the presence of monks, clan chieftains or royal officials keeping a beady eye out for their share.

While one might not go so far as to claim, along with Ivor Cutler, that any country or area 'gets its brains from the herring', it may be the case that, as Arstein Svihus informed me – with his tongue embedded in his cheek – during my time in Bergen, the dynamic and unpredictable nature of herring fishing created a very particular form of intelligence. The sheer scale of herring shoals and sometimes, too, the fluctuations in the size of the catch made it necessary for communities to work closely together. This engendered flexibility, especially in terms of working hours and, perhaps, even in gender roles. The gutting and cleaning of fish required the mobilisation of a large workforce. It was one where physical strength and stamina was very important. This even influenced fishing men in the physical shape of the women they chose for their wives. Not for them the slim, small, lithe companions some prefer in the contemporary world. The women's main attraction lay in the breadth of their shoulders and the strength of their backs – in short, their ability to bear and carry heavy loads. This emphasis on bulk and strength is not something readily understood by those with a modern mentality. There is a story I heard while

---

*An Applecross storyteller told me of a winter's night when a high tide and a strong northerly combined to create its own brand of havoc for the locality. In the storm, the sea lashed over the pier with some of the herring drift nets being washed half over the edge. When the men went down the following morning to sort them out, there were so many herring swimming right up to the shore that some of these nets, just hanging by their edges, were heavy with a harvest of fish.

travelling around the north-east of Scotland about a committee in one of its small towns that had been formed to create the statue of a 'herring girl' in its harbour. Its chair – a young, fit woman with a lithe, slim body, one engineered through countless hours of jogging in both gym and street – had seen the opportunity for immortality, offering herself as model for the sculpture. No amount of persuasion would convince her that she was not perfect for the role. It was worse later when she tried to insist that the statue's head should be uncovered in the sculpture, her locks on public display; her sense of vanity was clearly more important than any kind of historical authenticity.

The difference between cod and herring fishing in, say, the west of Norway has also led to a little verbal jousting between the two communities. It would be the view of the cod-fishing community that the sheer monotony of a diet of bread or potatoes with herring every day has created a certain sluggishness of mind, one that causes people to be restricted and unimaginative in their thinking. (If herring-based communities had any real insight into the restricted nature of their lives or the undependable nature of the fish they try to catch, they would surely go out to seek some other kind of harvest, one that would sustain them in their lives.) They compare this with the more adventurous nature of cod fishing, where both men and boats tend to be away from their home shoreline for longer periods, coming across new and different locations as they follow their catch. They would also argue that there is greater certainty in cod. Unlike the more flighty herring, the presence of the fish they seek is more dependable, occupying the same stretch of water year upon unchanging year.

'Nonsense', those in herring communities might counter and claim. The sheer unpredictability of the herring made those who sought it more quick and innovative than those who sought cod in the waters of the North Atlantic. They had to be more adaptable, depending sometimes on grain or potatoes from their own fields to keep body and soul together. They also possessed a little more time to take on the role of husband or father than their far-flung brethren overseas.

On the Isle of Man, they go further than this. For centuries on that island the herring was seen as the symbol of wisdom and justice. In its traditional law, the oath taken by the Deemster or judge on appointment to office required them 'to execute the laws of the Isle justly,' acting 'betwixt party and party as indifferently as the herring backbone doth lie in the midst of the fish'. On the wall of the entrance to the island's main court, the Deemsters, there is a sculpture manufactured in Cor-ten steel by Bryan Kneale, who came from the island and originally studied at Douglas School of Art. Its dark brown shape shows the fish both inside and out, clear and transparent; the form showing how evenly its bones are distributed, like the good it represents. It is, too, both flexible and resilient, as both justice and the herring should always be. With even its shade resembling that of the traditional Manx kipper, one has a sense of an artist scrutinising the fish's structure for both its form and the idea it represents.

Yet the appearance of the herring is not always as rational, fair or predictable as one at least hopes the law aspires to be. There is no doubt that their irregular habits may have generated an awareness of the existence of luck in those who searched for herring shoals. This emphasis on fortune is apparent in some of the stories that come from fishing communities everywhere, perhaps inspired by the observation that the sea itself is not always predictable or just in its dealings with men. One has always to guard oneself against its caprice and trickery. We see this in Neil Gunn's great novel about the beginning of the Scottish herring industry, *The Silver Darlings*. The central character Finn objects to being wished 'good luck', as this is seen to invite the volatility of fate. The mention of the word 'God' has to be met and responded to with the expression 'Cold iron'. The presence of a clergyman is regarded as a harbinger of trouble and woe. This superstition in particular seems to me to be based upon a kernel of sense. If you were paying a tithe to the clergy, as many fishermen did throughout the centuries, one can understand why you wanted to avoid seeing them – or even mentioning their names – while either heading out to sea or being on a boat. It would be in your economic interest to avoid all sight of a dark cassock or white collar – and to make sure that those who wore these items of clothing never saw you.

Local areas, too, had their own distinct and different superstitions. In the case of Finn, it would seem to be permissible to purse his lips and 'whistle up the wind' when the sea is calm near Duncansby Head in the north-east of Scotland. If a young fisherman did this on a boat sailing from the Isle of Man, he would be reprimanded for it. For Manx fishermen, whistling was deemed to be 'troubling the wind', and even on quiet, peaceful days was never done. Apparently, a knife was stuck in the side of the mast in the direction you wished a gust or breeze to blow.

This is even more noticeable on Scotland's east coast. A religious publication bemoaned the following behaviour when it was noted in its pages:

> Some of the fishermen of Buckie on Wednesday last dressed a cooper in a flannel shirt, with burs stuck all over it, and in this condition he was carried in procession through the town in a hand-barrow. This was done to bring better luck to the fishing. In some of the fishing towns on the north-east coast of Scotland a mode of securing luck in the herring fishery is to 'draw blood', an act which must be performed on the first day of the year.[*]

In St Monan's in Fife, there was no church bell; there was one hanging from a tree in the churchyard, though

[*] *Toilers of the Deep*, MDSF, 1888, p. 83

even this was moved away during the herring-fishing season. This was because the community believed that the peal of the bell scared away the shoals that might be swimming around the coast. Friday was believed to be an unlucky day of the week to start fishing, a view that was not uncommon throughout much of the rest of the country. This was because it was believed that St Monan died on that day of the week after a confrontation with demonic forces. Hares – or *maukens* – were regarded as unlucky, with the sight of a dead one seen as especially so, in ports like Buckhaven, where fishermen are reputed to tremble at the sight.

Yet just as odd and distinctive as the superstitions related to herring fishing at sea are the ones connected with the fish on land. There is, for instance, the custom of the Herring Queen, which once existed in many of the old herring ports in Scotland. A young girl, traditionally the most beautiful in the town, was crowned near the harbour, often with colourfully gowned attendants by her side. It is a custom that still survives in Eyemouth in the Scottish borders, where it was introduced to celebrate the end of the First World War, marking both the coming of peace and the everyday concerns and affairs of a fishing community. (As a result of this, it is also called either the 'Peace Picnic' or the 'Fisherman's Picnic'.) The Herring Queen and her court of six, all girls from the local High School, are brought by a fishing boat some time during the month of July from the nearby port of St Abbs. Once she arrives, she is crowned by her predecessor and required to present prizes and awards throughout the year.

There are other signs of the importance of the ceremony to this small town. Travel through its streets and it is easy to spot where the current Herring Queen lives. Posters and placards – complete with the reminder that seventy years have passed since the first ceremony – decorate the gates to her home. A drawing of a herring, painted a distinct shade of red, floats upstairs on white walls. A pink garland adorns the front door. For much of the year, an exhibition featuring photographs of the young lady's sixty-nine predecessors dominates the town's museum – an interesting and well-run establishment, among the best of all in the small towns I visited. It displays the vast range of hairstyles and dresses that the nation's fashion designers and advisers have considered necessary and desirable to enhance female beauty over much of the last century and beyond.

In other areas, it is not beauty queens who are clothed in finery but the fish itself. Mention 'dressed herring' in Russia, and that country's citizens will think of a meal they also call either 'herring under a fur coat' or a 'fur coat'. It involves a salad which comprises layers of diced salt herring, chopped onions, mayonnaise and grated, boiled vegetables. They will think, too, of the herring that makes a typical *zakuski* – an appetiser served with a glass of iced vodka or some other alcoholic drink. At Christmas and New Year, too, the table is filled with other delicacies, such as canapés with sprats, sauerkraut salad and brined herring – the fish seasoned with sunflower oil and onions.

Together with the serving of alcohol, it is only the season that has much in common with how 'dressed herring' was once known in Dundee and its nearby towns in Scotland. The festivities that involved the fish were once associated with Hogmanay, or the first day in January, when locals would vie for the honour of becoming the 'first foot' stepping over the threshold of a relative or friend's house. It might also be accompanied by alcohol – a half-bottle of whisky, perhaps – clutched within a neighbour or relative's hand when they came to the door of their host's home. In addition, there might be other gifts. A lump of coal could be handed over, a way of ensuring there would be warmth in the house they were visiting, or perhaps some black bun – a fruit cake wrapped in pastry traditionally associated with Hogmanay and the Scottish way of celebrating New Year. It was provided as a means of guaranteeing that those called upon would have enough food to eat over the coming year.

The coal, whisky and black bun are standard fare throughout Scotland. What is unique to this one area is the 'dressed herring', which up until the early 1970s was brought delicately to people's doors shortly after the bells had chimed the beginning of the New Year in the city of Dundee and the nearby port of Arbroath. It was a tradition I first heard about when I journeyed to the Thai Teak Coffee shop in Fife in summer 2014, where I met the artists Derek Robertson and his wife Deirdre. Within its walls, I heard a pair of stories more strange and otherworldly than even that building's existence – a structure brought back in its entirety from Thailand. It sits upon a platform, a fine and alien place with an array of cartwheels and wooden furniture around its entrance. At the other side of the car park there is a shop selling carved goods, harvested by the family that owns the surrounding farm on its annual visit to South-east Asia. Occasionally Derek would look up, glancing at the birds landing on the fields and nearby trees. Derek is one of Scotland's best wildlife artists, and I had long been impressed by his meticulous drawings of the country's birds and other animals. Whether fish, flesh or fowl, they possess a wonderful and vivid exactitude, much like the Gaelic he has learned to speak over the years. His wife Deirdre's artwork draws upon another way of observing the world. She has a great interest in the history of her native city, Dundee, using its often forgotten landscape and landmarks as a way of inspiring not only herself but her fellow citizens into uncovering the world that surrounds them.

Over a meal of fishcakes, hot soup and a plate of sandwiches, Deirdre began to tell her story. It was about her mother Rena Gillespie, who used to give 'dressed herrings' to her family, parents and in-laws. In this, she was not unusual. Dundonians in their late seventies and older still vividly remember the tradition, stating that this surreal fashion was one that everybody followed at that time.

'Ideally, it would be a tall, dark, handsome man who would present the herring,' Deirdre said, smiling. 'If he were the "first foot" over the threshold, he would hand over the fish in its full, flowing dress to the man or woman in charge of the household, wishing good luck to everybody in the home. The fish would then be placed above the inside of the front door for the entire year until it was replaced by the next year's herring. That would usually be dressed in a different colour from the previous year's. A whole new glamorous outfit.'

Deirdre went on to explain where the dressed herrings had been obtained till the early 1970s, when the tradition started to disappear.

'They were even in the cartoon *The Broons* before then, dangling in the fingers of the younger children, the Bairn and the Twins, in the pages of Dundee and Scotland's *Sunday Post*. And for good reason. It was easy to buy them in Dundee – in fishmongers, as you left the rail station, and on stalls or barrows in the centre of town, where the Overgate shopping centre now stands.' She was referring to the shopping mall with its stores, shops and cafes that now dominates the middle of the city, taller than the church that is one of Dundee's oldest buildings. 'The dressed herrings were kitted out in all the colours of the rainbow – blowing in the wind, dressed like little fishwives or perhaps Victorian ladies – in full crinoline skirts made of gathered crêpe paper, with white dolly aprons and bonnets, cottonwood hair and finished, fastened ribbons. Some had sequins for eyes, peering out at you. Occasionally there were matching male fish done too: dwarf, fish-faced princes to escort those in gowns.'

Then came the changes, reflected, too, in the city's architecture and buildings, its sense, perhaps, of itself. By 1972 the warren of eighteenth- and nineteenth-century streets where the dressed herrings had been sold had been demolished, making way eventually for the new Overgate shopping centre, all polished glass and cut prices. With them, too, the 'buster stalls' found within their shadows disappeared, together with some of the odder purchases to be found on their counters. Deirdre pointed out that this also coincided with the increase in fridges and freezers. This brought an end to the days when it was commonplace to have a large barrel of salted fish in the household, part of the annual source of sustenance for the family living there.

'Adding one more herring into a house already reeking of fish would not have been a big deal.' Deirdre grinned. 'Only a slight increase in the all-pervasive aroma.'

We talked for a while about how this custom started. I told Derek and Deirdre of a tale I heard in the Netherlands, that the Catholic population in the country's south used to hang a single herring above the inside doorway during Lent, allowing people to take a bite out of it whenever hunger threatened to overwhelm them. There was also the possibility, perhaps, that dressed herring might be linked to the corn dolly, the doll-like figure that was plaited and shaped from the last sheaf of oats made from the harvest, ploughed into the ground in the following year. It was a custom I was aware of existing throughout Europe, especially in the Celtic parts of Scotland and Ireland.

'No one knows for sure where this notion of dressing herring came from,' Deirdre declared. 'Some of the local newspapers suggest that it might be a superstition related to hygiene. At that time, it wasn't that unusual to get a large delivery of fish for your table, enough to fill a barrel or so. People would encourage feasting to clear the bottom of the barrel before the new batch arrived. Otherwise, the bottom layer was left for several years, spoiling the rest of the barrel in the process. The giving of a dressed herring might have been a sign that you had cleared the barrel some time around the turn of the year. You handed over the last one to your neighbour as a symbol of good luck.'

It was a tradition that hung on in Deirdre's family longer than most – for all that the present Lady Dundee stepped out with a herring in 1991 when the city celebrated its eight-hundredth birthday. (For those interested in such matters, the fish wore a matching ball gown created by her personal high-fashion designer.) At another level in society, however, even by 1973 Deirdre's mother Rena was unable to buy dressed herring – whether in 'haute couture' or not – and, instead, began to make her own. It was a smelly, unpleasant task which took both time and precision. It began with stripping off the herring's flesh. One slip of a small, sharp knife and the spine might be broken, forcing her to start again. Eventually, though, she succeeded, leaving a head, skeleton and tail; these parts were dipped in lemon juice and varnish. Despite this, it was not an experience she enjoyed or relished. That year, she declared she would never repeat the exercise again.

It was a vow she only kept for one year. The following one, 1974, brought its own measure of tragedy. Rena's mother was diagnosed with cancer, dying in August. For all that Rena was an intelligent, rational individual, having even obtained a degree in Logic and Metaphysics at the University of St Andrews, she took on the notion that her mother had passed away as a result of her failure to give her relatives a dressed herring in January that year. As a result, the process started again: the flesh stripped away slowly and exactly with a keen, sharp knife; the children – like Deirdre – creating the dresses to cover their skeletons once again. Unlike their predecessors, however, they did not put the herring on public display, a sign of the changing times.

'My mother Rena kept hers hidden in the large freezer chest in the garage before it was thrown out the following New Year. My gran, Dad's mother, used to hang them up above the door, stuck inside a plastic bag. I don't think the sight was seen as quite so respectable by that time. It was 1995, when the old woman died, that my mother stopped making them.' Deirdre smiled, looking out of the window at a teak bench she had noticed a short time before, wanting it, perhaps, for the family's own garden. 'The fact that so few were doing it was probably one reason for that.'

Over the last few years, however, Deirdre has taken on the role of reviving the tradition – not for her home on this occasion but as part of an art exhibition that she and her husband have devised. Dressed herring float and hover, all in silver, purple and scarlet, a range of sparkling sequins, as they hang from the ceiling on an invisible stretch of string. Behind them, looking almost as unworldly, is a portrait of Cathel, a fisherman from north-west Sutherland in Scotland, whom Derek painted a number of years ago. The story of this painting is in itself moving and dramatic, connected with a similar strangeness to the dressed herring.*

The herring and those who seek to catch them are marked in a different way in the art found on the mainland of continental Europe. A sign on one of the traditional, rainbow-shaded stores on Bryggen Wharf, the waterfront of Bergen, reminds us of the importance that once attached to the herring. 'Sild – Fisk', it reads, before providing the name of the merchant who occupied its walls: Alfred Skulstad. Nearby, the gaze of a gargantuan-headed fish follows you as you step around one of the wharf's hidden courtyards. Whittled from a tree-trunk, it fixes all its camera-snapping visitors with its stare, haunting their dreams as they go through their snapshots later. On a wooden wall, a faded poster informs those who come here of the different words

---

*Derek painted this figure after receiving news of Cathel's drowning – together with another man – near Handa Island in Scourie, Sutherland in August 1987. It was an event that occurred a short time after Cathel had saved Derek's life in a similar incident. Derek sold the painting a short time after completing it. It was a sale he came to regret, trying to find its purchaser for years. Unbeknownst to him, Richard Barrett, the man who had bought the artwork, had also been trying to find Derek, the painting having inspired him to compose a song and write a novel. Around twenty-seven years after he had first completed it, Derek and *Cathel* were once again united.

for herring – as well as many other fish – found among the tongues of Europe and beyond.

> German – *Hering*
> Danish – *Sild*
> Italian – *Aringa*
> Finnish – *Silli*
> Estonian – *Heeringas*
> Czech – *Sleea*
> Spanish and Portuguese – *Arenque*
> Dutch – *Haring*
> Japanese – *Kadoiwaski*
> Turkish – *Ringa* . . .

Even this, however, does not show the full complexity of how the fish is described in certain European tongues. Several of the populations living in countries bordering the Baltic have different words for the smaller, leaner Baltic variety than the ones caught in the Atlantic. In Sweden, for instance, the Atlantic herring is called a *sill* while the Baltic fish is a *stromming*. The Russians call those fished in the Atlantic a *sel'd* while the other version is a *salaka*.

Herring – or *pennog* (Welsh), *sald* (Icelandic), *scadán* (Irish) – is one of the fish on offer at Bergen's fish market on the quay, where buckling (hot smoked herring) with the heads and insides removed is sold, alongside dark cuts of whalemeat and catfish, monkfish, shrimp, the full variety of crops harvested from the sea. Those who served meals here, whether at downmarket fish-stalls or an upmarket glass-fronted restaurant, seemed also to be netted from many different shores. A woman from Russia served me at one point; on another occasion, young men and women from Spain and Greece prepared food, doling out fish soup to the tourists who gathered around them, as adept in their mastery of languages as in their culinary skills. For all that Mount Floyen with its giddy heights and funicular railway might have shadowed the city in a physical sense, it was the sea that dominated it, the ebb and flow not only of its waters but also of both history and people, providing the community that had settled there with much of its identity.

This was true even of the city itself. A statue of one of its most famous citizens, the playwright Henrik Ibsen, stands furled up in a grey coat outside the theatre, braced for its winter wind. A bronze sculpture of composer Edvard Grieg – just outside the city – looks outwards, strutting like one of the town's dandies. There are even a few figures – the Danish girl, the Crying Boy, the Lying Poet (are there any other kind?) – braving the elements in various green parks. Yet in a country which seems more than most to embody its achievements in stone, it is the Seafarers Monument on Torgallmenningen, one of the main streets, that defines Bergen almost as much as the 'seven mountains' which reputedly form an arc around it, the peninsula spreading its splintered fingers into different fjords and bays, stretching out towards the islands that shelter it from the full-blown fury of the waves.

This tall, seven-metre-high sculpture, created at two separate heights, with its four reliefs and twelve statues, are reflected these days in all the paraphernalia of a modern city, such as the windows of a department store or the red, enticing signs of a Chinese restaurant, for all that they attempt to sum up the community's maritime past. The merchant statue, complete with waistcoat and top hat, stares outwards as if in disbelief at how his modern counterparts reap their profits, how the descendants of his former customers earn and spend their cash. By his side, a bare-armed fisherman slouches, hands perched in pockets. Elsewhere, a sea captain stands, his greatcoat fastened almost to its neck, a pair of binoculars hanging ready to examine a horizon that another figure, garbed in traditional Viking clothing, might once have explored. A Christian monk is among them, a carved reminder of Christ's injunction that they should be 'fishers of men'.

The reliefs above the heads of the statues tell their stories in more detail. A Viking ship in full sail plunges through stormy waters. A whale is lanced by a harpoon. The news of Christ's crucifixion is brought by a small boat to these shores. The grey outline of a submarine sinks within dark depths. Each scene sums up an aspect of the ocean the people of Bergen have both feared and savoured over the lifetime of their city, exploring its hidden inlets, lengths and stretches, and the heavy price they sometimes pay for herring and other kinds of fish.

Yet of all the art I came across during my travels around Europe, it was the print work of a German–Norwegian artist, Rolf Nesch, that seemed to sum up best both the excitement and danger of being involved in fishing for herring. An expressionist artist who fled from Nazi rule in Germany in 1933, Nesch travelled north to the Lofoten islands to experience the winter fishing in that harsh, remote environment. It was a journey that brought about his discarding of paintbrush and canvas in favour of other materials. One of the results of his exile, the work *Sildefiske* (Fishing for Herring) is a turmoil of waves, boats and men. There is a vibrancy to both movement and expression as jagged, frenetic figures haul on board nets laden down with herring in what he termed 'material pictures', barely confined within the borders of his artwork. It is a work suggesting both the abundance of shoals and the speedy, slithery quality of their movement, each fish merging with others. A similar work is *Herring Catch* (1938), which can be seen in the British Museum in London. A colour metal print in six parts, he said that it was inspired by 'an immense experience that I shall never forget. I have made a series of prints, six coloured sheets that go together .... It is my best graphic work so far. Under no circumstances whatsoever would I leave this country without having seen the herring catch.'

A similar, fantastical approach is seen in much of the rest of Nesch's output. Fishermen cut fish over barrels, their faces as spiked and sharp as their blades. His odd 'catches' of fish possess surreal and vivid shapes and colours, sprawling in the dark commotion of the sea off that far northern coastline. In doing this, he captures the dramatic nature of the industry, the way that even human life can slip from hand or grip when men and boats are caught at its centre.

It especially forms a great contrast with much of the art I saw within the galleries of the Netherlands. Much of it seemed tranquil and reflective. This even applies to the boats that go out to seek and catch herring. In the work of Willem van de Velde the Younger, the fishing vessels often sail in a perpetual calm, their sails billowing in a gentle breeze. It is a description that applies to his *Two Smalschips off the End of a Pier* (1710), where a group of men look on as a pair of vessels goes out to sea, for all that occasionally a gust of wind drives them onwards, as in his 1672 work entitled *Ships on a Stormy Sea*. The later painter Hendrik Willem Mesdag shows a similar fascination with those who catch the fish in his marine paintings, his boats often seen at either sunrise or sunset. His *Pinks in the Breakers* – painted between 1875 and 1885 – portrays women waiting on the shoreline before a wind-trammelled sea. One is even seen wading through the waves with her creel taut upon her back. Even Vermeer – not traditionally linked with such subjects – paints a herring buss under repair beside the town's harbour in his splendid *View of Delft*.

The herring itself seems to be even more placid, featuring in much of Dutch still-life painting of the period. Van Gogh created at least two artworks with herring at their centre – both *Two Red Herring* and *Still Life with Two Herrings, a Cloth and a Glass* (1886). The seventeenth-century artist Pieter Claesz, one of the leading exponents of the *banketjestuk* (breakfast piece), was part, too, of a tradition the Dutch invented. This involved painting, both exactly and in subdued light, the ingredients of a simple meal, not necessarily breakfast for all the title of the genre might declare it so. In the case of Claesz, this might be a wedge of cheese, a loaf of bread or even a lobster. His *Still Life with Herring, Roemer and Stone Jug* is one example of this, with the art historian and critic Simon Schama claiming that his 'herring offer just the merest glint of scaly light to offset the pewter monochrome of their background'. In a painting by Anthonius Leemans created in 1655, the herring seem to be acquiring all the virtues of Dutch patriotism. Bearing the splendid title *Still Life with a Copy of De Waere Mercurius*, a broadsheet with the news of Tromp's victory over three English ships on 28 June 1639, and a poem telling the story of Apelles and the cobbler, a rather succulent fish lies somewhat incongruously alongside not only these objects but the top of a suit of armour – a gorget, in other words – and a violin. Its patriotic credentials were underlined in the preacher Jacob Westerbaen's verse '*Lof Des Pekelhareng*' ('In Praise of Pickled Herring') where, after all the delights of the fish's appearance and taste were outlined, the reader was informed that if you consume too much of it, its flesh 'will make you apt to piss/And you will not fail/(With pardon) to shit/And ceaselessly fart ...' Despite this rather dubious message, the poem – together with a collection of other items such as herring, bread and onions – was the subject of a popular painting by Josephus de Bray. Clearly the prospect of severe internal disruption did not deter the lovers of either art or poetry from appreciating the quality of the fish.

Yet far from always subjecting both stomach and spirit to disorder, the herring could take on religious overtones too. Good, well-ordered households were pictured praying over meals of simple, frugal herring, as opposed to the chaos found in various paintings called *The Fat Kitchen* by Hendrick de Kempenaer and Jan Steen, where table, lips and waistline spill over with the results of too much meat or drink. In Pieter Bruegel's painting of *The Battle Between Carnival and Lent* (1559), a fight goes on between the rotund Carnival perched upon a cask, trying to impale his skeletal opponent, Lent, with a spear of bound capons. The figure resisting him has only one weapon to brandish against his foe – a herring fastened to a bread peel.

And so it goes on. When Adriaen van de Venne in the early seventeenth century paints his *De Zielenvisserij* (Fishing For Souls), he draws upon images from herring fishing to create his satirical portrait of the struggle between Protestant and Catholic clergymen for the souls of the populace. Colourfully robed bishops and dark-suited clergymen struggle with nets as they seek to save those foundering in the waters that surround their boats. On the shoreline their congregations look on, the arc of a rainbow stretching in the sky above them, as if promising deliverance from the chaos that is occurring.

There are times, though, when the presence of a herring in someone's hand seems either to invite or mark that disorder. In one of Gerrit Dou's paintings, an old woman rebukes a young boy with a herring between her fingers, giving him a scolding (or what is known euphemistically as a 'herring') for some mischief he has done. The broken-toothed smile of a number of Hendrick ter Brugghen's merry drinkers shows us those who have surrendered to life's pleasures. They raise a tankard to their lips while squeezing a herring in the grip of their hands, soiling their fingers and souls with their greed and gluttony. Female herring sellers emerge from the shadows with heightened colouring, open lips and eyes, offering – one might imagine – more than the silver-scaled fish they display in their hands.

This might be connected to another way of looking at the herring which also appears in Dutch art, especially in the work of Jan Steen, who painted a number of paintings on the theme of 'The Doctor's Visit'. In some of them, it is clear what ails the young lady whom the medic comes to see. A statuette of Cupid twinkles down at her. A painting of young lovers, clasped in one another's arms, hangs upon the wall. Finally, there is a dish containing a herring – complete with two onions – on a small table by her side, lying untouched as a result of her illness. In another work, an unshaved man with a lewd, crude expression even dangles one above her head. It is clear from a glance what the doctor's diagnosis has to be. The young woman is suffering from love-sickness – or, to put it more crudely, the need for a man.

This connection between herring and manhood is not only found in Dutch art. It is present even in Shakespeare, where Romeo, thought to be pining for Rosaline in Act IV of the play (in fact he has met Juliet by then, though his friends don't know), is described by Mercutio as being:

'Without his roe, like a dried herring. O flesh, flesh, how art thou fishified!'

Falstaff also declares in *King Henry IV*:

'If manhood, good manhood, be not forgotten upon the face of the earth, then am I a shotten herring' [a herring that has spawned].

However, it is most clearly seen in work like that of Christiaen van Couwenbergh's *Man with Herring*, painted in 1655. As he holds both a knife and herring upright in his fingers, a mischievous expression on his face, it is clear that, like the man who hovers with the same fish over one of Jan Steen's female patients, there is only one subject on his mind.

CHAPTER SEVEN

'Celebration of the Lizard'

For some people, the herring has always been one of Nature's more comical creations.

This view is apparent in the painting I mentioned earlier, Christiaen van Couwenbergh's *Man with Herring*. He holds the fish upright, its tail flicked upwards. The fish's head and one side of its skin hang downwards, where he has clearly just used the knife on it. It has been suggested that there is a sexual reference here, with the lower part representing an impotent, spent penis. It provides the reason why the drunken figures in Dutch art sometimes squeeze a herring in their hand, soiling their fingers, spilling seed. It is why Dutch fishermen, too, traditionally made jokes about their neighbours, the fishermen of Normandy. Due to the movement of the herring catch around their shoreline, the Normans frequently netted the herring after it had spawned, limp and possessing less flavour than its northern counterpart. The men of Scheveningen nudged each other when they talked about the more southerly rivals to their fishing grounds, suggesting that they were not unlike the fish that was their quarry, somewhat lacking in manhood, neither as virile nor as courageous as they were. The French are probably returning this insult when they declare: *La caque sent toujours le hareng* (The barrel always smells of the herring) – a way of declaring that, no matter what the circumstances, breeding will tell.

It is perhaps for this reason that the fish is the subject of so many jokes. One can see this especially in the work of Woody Allen, the American comedian, who uses the fish as raw – and sometimes boiled or pickled – material time and time again in his writings and film work. The impotent old man, Voskovec, whom Diane Keaton marries in Allen's film *Love and Death* about Russia during the Napoleonic wars, is a herring merchant. Obsessed with his work, he is blissfully unaware that Diane Keaton's character, Sonja, is carrying on affairs not only behind his back but also directly in front of him, employing – it seems – most of St Petersburg's available males for that purpose. Again and again, Allen tells jokes about him and the herring he sells. Voskovec's love affair with the fish is such that he even buys his young wife 'herring-scented cologne', providing the reason why cats follow her around everywhere. He talks obsessively about the subject (a little like me while researching this book): 'What people don't understand is that there are hundreds of types of herring, each with its own interesting character.'

Talking about how the French are blockading Russian ports, preventing the import of his favourite fish, he utters an ominous threat: 'When something hurts herring, it hurts me.'

And so it goes on, little jibes and jokes, found not only in Woody Allen's film but elsewhere too, like these much repeated Jewish jests:

> 'A doctor prescribes sea air for a patient, supplying him, too, with the means to obtain this. A herring and a fan.'

Two little old ladies, Gertrude and Zelda, were sitting on a park bench near Golders Green having a serious conversation.

'Gertrude,' said Zelda, 'I don't understand something. I simply have no appetite lately. No matter how much I try to eat, I have no appetite.'

Gertrude said, 'Listen, Zelda, my doctor, the lovely Doctor Myers, once told me that if I didn't have an appetite I should take a little piece of herring before meals and I would soon get an appetite. So I tried it and it was true. So take my advice, Zelda, and try a little piece of herring before lunch and you'll see, you'll develop an appetite.'

A few days later the two meet again in the park.

'Nu, Zelda, how do you feel now? Did the herring give you an appetite?'

Zelda sighed. 'I took your advice. First I had a little piece of herring. Then I had a whole herring. I really wanted to give it a chance, so I ate six herrings. But Gertrude, your advice didn't work for me. Would you believe, when lunch time came, I had absolutely no appetite!'

Then there is *Bottom of the Barrel*, a collection of verse by David R. Slavitt. He parodies Louis MacNeice, Percy Bysshe Shelley, even William Shakespeare, mentioning herring in many of his lines. His efforts are such that one can imagine 'My love is like a red, red herring' in their midst.

It is at this point that I feel like taking on the character of Voskovec, the herring merchant, pounding my chest and trumpeting my own version of his words, 'Whatever hurts the herring hurts me.' There are many reasons for my defensiveness, particularly the way that over the last few years we have seen a succession of nature books featuring some of the more 'noble' creatures of land, sea and air. These have included the whale, wolf and goshawk. Even the corvids – both rook and crow – have enjoyed their moment of rehabilitation, transformed from the dark, brooding presences they were known as in the past to smarter and more sociable creatures, able to share the lives and homes of men and women, as mentioned in Esther Woolfson's book, *Corvid*. So far, though, it seems to me that it is our view of both flesh and fowl, once seen as 'Nature red in tooth and claw', that has been altered. We have learned to see more clearly what we have half perceived for centuries – the nobility of these birds and beasts, which we once saw as predators or even, as in the case of whales, our rivals in terms of domination of the sea.

It is for this reason that we understand one side of what Barry Lopez in his writing about wolves called 'the conversation of death', where both potential prey and predator size up one another in a wordless calculation of which will be the hunter and which the hunted. We have still to learn what it must be like to be one of Nature's victims, the powerless creature in this exchange. We continue to identify with the hawk and not the starling or rabbit, the shark or whale, and not the humble herring. This must explain a little about how man continues to see the planet on which he lives. Even when we identify with birds or other animals, we still see ourselves as among those who reveal their mastery and not their victimhood.

In her book *H is for Hawk*, the writer Helen Macdonald goes deeply into these questions. She refers to an anthropologist, Rane Willerslev, who once lived for a year with the Yukaghir tribe in the north-east of Siberia. In his research, he noted how the hunters have to learn to think like, say, elk, attempting to perceive the world in the way they might see it, noting where they might go in particular winds and weathers, guessing how they would react in certain situations. This brings with it its own dangers. It has its effect on the hunters' human relationships, making it harder for them to relate to their partners and children.

This is clearly the way, too, a herring fisherman has traditionally had to respond to his environment, acquiring learning of the kind the herring merchant, Voskovec, longs for in his death scene in Woody Allen's film – what it must be like to be 'swimming out in the open sea, like the great wild herring'. He must be able to know how the sky swims above the water, watching how its light and shadow show where fish both shoal and settle. He must be able to 'think' like the herring he hunts. Again, there is probably some difficulty when he has to step away from cabin and deck, and learn to live in a family kitchen again.

There is, however, a difference in the herring fishermen's prey compared to that of those who might seek out the wolf or bear, or learn to live with a falcon perched on their arm. Unlike the shark or the whale, herring do not in themselves signify any danger for those who approach them – for all that the conditions in which they exist might be hazardous to life and limb. They also do not suggest any nobility of spirit. Their faces are placid and mysterious. No harsh, unblinking stare ever crosses their expression in the manner of, say, a hawk or a big cat. No 'conversation of death' ever occurs between the herring and prey. (Very difficult to do when your life is sustained by the marine equivalent of grass.) Instead, this fish would seem to be a commoner, a peasant, one of the hoi polloi.

Or as the nineteenth-century English Romantic poet Leigh Hunt might have put it as he stared into the face of a herring, writing the poem 'The Fish, the Man, and the Spirit', interrogating the 'angle-faced, dreary mouthed, gaping' creature in front of him:

> O scaly, slippery, wet, swift, staring wights,
> What is't ye do? what life lead? eh, dull goggles?
> How do ye vary your vile days and nights?
> How pass your Sundays? Are ye still but joggles
> In ceaseless wash? Still nought but gapes, and bites,
> And drinks, and stares, diversified with boggles? . . .

And yet fishermen have not always seen the herring that way. Instead, they have attempted to convince us that it possesses a little nobility, as can be seen in the folklore below, derived from a Manx legend.

How the herring became King of the Sea

It was the Shark that proposed the whole idea. He had surveyed the chaos and disagreement all around him and decided enough was enough.

'We must have a government,' he said.

'A king,' Bollan the Pollock added.

'Someone to lay down the law if there are disagreements between us.' The shark nodded.

The others looked at him suspiciously, aware that he had himself in mind for the role.

'Well, we'd better elect our king then,' Captain Jiarg the Red Mullet said.

'That's not a bad idea,' Brae Gorm the Mackerel smiled.

The others looked in the direction of the pair of them too, aware that they had their own plans worked out in advance. Captain Jiarg thought he might win because his entire body was a flash and dash of scarlet. Brae Gorm presumed he would succeed because there was a multitude of colours decorating his skin.

'We'll wait till this evening for the vote. That'll give us time both to think and prepare ourselves.'

'Good idea.'

When the time came, they had all done much to smarten their appearance. Athag the Haddock had tried to scrub clean the black marks the devil had been reputed to have left behind on his skin. The shark had polished himself so much that his coat possessed the polished sheen of a fine, grey horse. Fluke, too, had gone to get ready, dotting herself with little red marks. She spent so long doing this that she wasn't around when the voting took place.

'We want someone who's humble enough not to lord it over us,' Dirty Peggy the Cuttlefish decided.

'We want someone who's far travelled. Seen the world,' Bollan declared.

'And someone who's small and quick enough to slip from the mouth of a whale,' Scarrag the Skate said.

In the end, it was Skeddan the Herring that won the contest, a little crown being placed on his head. His power and majesty was recognised not only by the other fish, but also by those Manxmen who knew that his royal court lay just off the shoulder of the island. They would honour him by never placing his bones in the fire when they were finished eating, in case this caused the herring pain. A song would also come to their lips when they were out fishing, its chorus booming out from their vessels as they sailed in these waters, spreading out their nets.

Oh! The herring, boys, the herring.
Oh! The herring, boys, for me!
Red or kippered, fresh or pickled,
Oh, the herring is king of the sea.

There is at least one change I have made to the original story. For instance, Fluke is given a good, hard smack by Captain Jiarg for her failure to turn up for the vote, the reason for the peculiar twist that is present in that fish's mouth even today.

The notion that the herring possessed great power is not only seen in this piece of folklore. It is present, too, in the belief among Manx fishermen that herring bones should never be thrown and burnt in an open fire. Their crackling might be overheard by herring swimming near the island's shores, which might be offended by this action, staying away from island waters and boats in future. This idea is echoed in a piece of Lowland Scots verse that has the fish utter the following threat:

Beat me or bury me but dinna burn ma banes
Or Ah'll cam roond to yer hoose and do the same tae yer ain.

The idea that herring is royalty is not only present in the folklore of the Isle of Man. One finds it in some of the French coastal ports, such as Etaples-Sur-Mer and Boulogne-Sur-Mer, where the Hareng Roi or King Herring festival is held each November. (The latter town apparently possesses the largest fish tank in Europe, including even sharks. One wonders whether the grilled, marinated or smoked herring left over after the music and dancing have died away are gulped down by the sharks in an attempt to recycle.) There is a similar approach on the northern side of the English Channel where the Lowestoft-born writer Thomas Nashe had a version of a tale not unlike the one told by Manxmen among his writings. (One of Shakespeare's near contemporaries, alive at the end of the sixteenth century, he seems to me one of the best writers about herring. Even his words imitate the way they shoal, flowing in endless sentences, circling continually, offering gleams and sparks of light, avoiding sometimes any kind of net a reader might cast over them, reining in sense and structure.) Go to the Time and Tide Museum in Great Yarmouth, based within a former herring curing yard, and you will see pictures of the fish there, all wrapped in ermine and with a gold crown perched on his head. He can also be seen that way on the signs of fishmongers, fish and chip shops, and even on the wrapping of a sweet packet or two.

There is also the odd notion that there is a king of herrings, a fish that governs the shoals that sweep around the shallows and skerries that are found throughout the world. This appears in a wonderfully eccentric book called the *Visboek* (Fish Book) by Adriaen Coenen, a fisherman, fish auctioneer and, finally, wreckmaster of Holland, who lived in Scheveningen at the end of the sixteenth century. Some 800 pages long, it seems to me the visual equivalent of Thomas Nashe's writing. Its pages brim over with much more than the average Dutch seaman's fishing net, containing in its haul a collection of fish and other creatures associated with the ocean. They include the 'tunnyfish', its scales marked with images of ships it had glimpsed while circling the Mediterranean. Alongside this was the 'zeebischop', a creature that clutched a hat, wand, slippers and a chasuble as it prayed and led other fish in worship through the channels of the sea. This ecclesiastical figure was believed by Nashe to be clinching proof of the existence of God, so much so that he was inspired to write a poem about this 'unnatural' wonder. Equally divine were the 'tree geese'. They came to life in the far north and were somehow both plant and animal, flapping from the branches of an unknown forest before they hovered over the rest of Europe. (This is different from the barnacle goose, which hatches, as we all know, from the confines of a certain shellfish clutching rocks and the undersides of boats.) And, of course, there were mermen and mermaids, figures glimpsed through the dim, maritime light of the coastline, though the writer concedes at one point, 'I cannot find a man this day who with his own eye in the year 1579 has seen one.'

All gloriously and astoundingly mad, yet all the more impressive when we realise Mr Coenen did not begin this venture until he reached the age of sixty-three, collecting his material from other sources, including the work of Swedish chronicler Olaus Magnus, who claimed that the people of the far north built their homes from the ribcages of whales. It appears that the authorities in Scheveningen share my awe at the compiler's genius. Pages from the book are spread out and displayed on the benches near the sea front, not far from where the statue of the Fisherman's Wife peers out over the stretch of sand. From there I learned that whales could be enticed into shallow waters by fishermen playing flutes before being harpooned as a result of their musical taste. Dolphins loved the strumming of a harp. (Unfortunately, this had an important side effect. They thrashed their tales against the water in appreciation, summoning a storm.) The tinkling of bells had a similar effect on certain fish, their fondness for a carillon or even, perhaps, the tambourine ensuring they ended up as part of a fisherman's catch.

And then there were the sections about the herring – or what Coenen terms 'our big golden mountain in Holland'. The writer has a two-page spread where he details where the fish can be found, the map and its locations based on tales he has heard from the lips of fishermen coming to the port. On another page, he reveals the fish that he believes to be 'king of the herring'. From a casual glance, this appears to resemble a delicacy found in the waters of the Mediterranean, once reared and kept by the Romans, who apparently loved to fondle and caress them, the Latin writer Juvenal satirising them as the 'emperor's fish'.

It is, in fact, a red mullet.

There are other pretenders to the throne. One that possesses a 'crown' of sorts, even if it is only the long red wisps of its dorsal fin, is the giant oarfish. The longest bony fish in the world, sometimes reaching 36 feet (11 metres), its silver, unscaled body snakes around the black depths of the ocean, rarely coming to the surface except when it is disorientated or in the throes of death. For all their fierce appearance, giant oarfish are utterly harmless, possessing small mouths and no teeth. They live by straining seawater, consuming the krill found within. Occasionally giant oarfish have been seen swimming near herring shoals, giving rise to the notion that the smaller fish are paying court to them. It has been rumoured, too, that they are the sea serpents that reside within the confines of Loch Ness and other mystical locations, sometimes showing part of their curving, twisting bodies for visitors to snap. Their undulating movements certainly resemble these creatures of myth.

Sometimes, too, this 'king of the herring' is seen to have great power. In Japan, two appeared on the ocean's surface shortly before a major earthquake on 25 October 2013. According to that country's legends, the oarfish is meant to be a messenger of the Sea God's Palace and a harbinger of natural disaster. In Norse mythology its appearance seems to be linked to Ragnarok, the end of the world or the 'Doom of the Gods', when among other events 'the Midgard Serpent, named Jormungand, shall free itself from its tail and rise up from the ocean'.

No doubt it will take revenge then on all those who made jokes about its smaller silver counterpart.

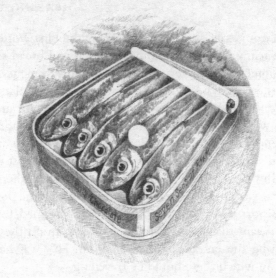

CHAPTER EIGHT

'Seven Seas of Rhye'

It was the name that drew me to the place.

'Holm' was a word with which I had grown up, part of the vocabulary of my childhood. It was the name of the small village I could glimpse from the ferry deck each time I return to my home port of Stornoway: a succession of crofthouses and bungalows not far from the island shoreline, with green croftland stretched behind it, a glimmer of street lights lining its road. For all that it looked like many of the other villages on Lewis, there was a part of its history that sparked our imaginations, distinguishing it from the rest. Invariably coupled with the phrase 'the Beasts of', its location formed a dark and fierce part of the mythology of the island. It had been on the rocks nearby that the vessel the *Iolaire* was washed up on the night of 1 January 1919. Over 200 men had been lost there: the final end of their return from exile over the four years of the First World War, where many had navigated the channels and broad seas of the conflict or else served within narrow trenches. And then there had been this. A cramped ship. A dark and stormy night. A sense, perhaps, that their captain did not know what he was doing, their unease growing from the moment the side of the ship had been scraped when it arrived at Kyle of Lochalsh on the north-west coast of the Scottish mainland. The suspicion, too, of some of them that the boat was going in the wrong direction, that the position of the port and starboard lights as they steamed towards town meant that they were about to end up on the rocks bordering the entrance to the harbour. This was not the route on which they should be travelling.

But this 'Holm' looked very different – though its place name shared the same origin. It too was a low-lying place that was liable to flooding, like so many locations – from Denmark to Sweden, England to Shetland – which possessed the same title, sometimes as a suffix like 'Stockholm' or 'Bjornholm', sometimes as a word standing on its own. This Holm lay near Schleswig on the Schlei, a twenty-mile inlet of the Baltic Sea in Schleswig-Holstein in southern Jutland in Germany. There were no jagged rocks nearby, no unpredictable surges of the ocean with the difference between high and low tide being as great as five metres on occasion, as in my home port of Stornoway. In contrast, the Schlei – and the Baltic nearby – are still and placid stretches of water, barely rising or falling when high or low tide comes. Looking out across its waters, I could see green rushes, wild birds flapping up and down, and a wall of green trees of a kind that always seems a little alien to me, used as I have been throughout much of my life to bare shoreline or moorland.

And then there was, too, the town in its vicinity. It dwarfed Stornoway not only in scale but also in historical importance. Long ago, it had been the home of the Dukes of

Schleswig-Holstein-Gottorp, one of many small states that now make up modern Germany. Schleswig Cathedral towers above its streets; King Frederick II of Denmark is entombed within the now alien ground where the building's foundations have been dug. In the sixteenth century, Frederick I of both Denmark and Norway set up his main royal palace there. Nowadays, Gottorp castle houses the state art gallery and museum. There are even one or two Danish shop signs that remind the passer-by this town had not always been part of Germany, and a museum featuring teddy bears that belies the brutality of much of this area's history. Until the middle of the nineteenth century and the Schleswig-Holstein question had been addressed and settled by conflict for the final time, this city had been part of Denmark. It was some of the population here that the current Queen of Denmark was thinking about when she spoke to the Danes 'across the border' in her annual Christmas broadcast. These people were still part of the 'Danish' population even as far away as Hamburg, a Danish diaspora still in existence, for all their voices were dwindling and hushed. As a result of the Treaty of Vienna in 1864, Denmark lost 40 per cent of its land mass and a million inhabitants, much of the means to catch the fabled Baltic herring and feed its population with their flesh. Only 1.6 million people now lived under Danish rule. Some of them even crossed the border into Germany at weekends, taking advantage of the lower prices found in the shops and stores of towns like Flensburg to the north of Schleswig.

The Schleswig wars were not the only ones that affected places like Holm. Near the gateway to the whitewashed church that forms the centre of the town, two small stone monuments can be seen. One bears an iron cross and an inscription to the fallen of the Second World War 'Unseren Gefallenen 1939 – 1945 Die Holmer Beliebung'. Another slightly larger memorial with similar wording stands on the other side of the pathway, dedicated to the dead of the First World War. Beside them both is a collection of other stones. German names – such as 'Karl Wolff 22.12.83 – 19.8.15' and 'Carl Reincke 9.5.97 – 2.7.18' – are carved on stones that cluster all around them, a reminder that, unlike the northern part of Schleswig-Holstein, the people here were predominantly German.[*] After examining these for a short time on my visit there, I began to wander around the cemetery, one that had been in place since 1650, noting the names of those who were buried there. Among the 'Fischers', 'Wolffs' and 'Hallmans', I began to notice a number of headstones bearing the surname 'Ross'. There was an 'Adolf Ross' and his wife 'Christa', a 'Wilhelm Ross' and his wife 'Emma'; the last-named's memorial bearing a design that was quite familiar within the churchyard. The outline of a full-sailed fishing boat was etched above their names.

In the beginning I took little notice of this. The village was both charming and picturesque. A cobblestone road curved around it; red-roofed, brightly coloured, painted buildings, largely white, dominated its streets. Some had dates on their gable ends – '1760', '1738'. As in houses in the Netherlands, there were often examples of lace craftwork on display, neat white stars in some windows; others had curtains made of similar materials shadowing the rooms. More unusually, there was a great deal of ironwork. A weathervane – in the form of a sailed fishing boat – decorated one roof. A black herring ornamented the panel of someone's front door. Another curved to form a door handle, its fins and tails allowing people to gain access to both this village's history and someone's private home. A window was designed like a ship's porthole, a tiny anchor hanging above. In some ways it resembled some of the villages of the East Neuk of Fife, Pittenween or Crail, perhaps. The red pantiles that covered the roofs there looked

[*]Over 6,000 people of Danish descent served in the Imperial German army during the First World War – a source of much resentment among the Danish descendents.

like the pantiles Dutch and Belgian captains used as ballast when they were trading with the east coast of Scotland and England. The locals had employed them, finding them excellent roofing material. There was also the same sense – from windows displaying craftwork I had noticed in some of the fishing villages in the Netherlands, too – of a community having moved out, allowing artists to move in. And then, finally, was this doorway with the nameplate 'Ross'. A small family crest hung above it. Its presence intrigued me – the Scottish name coupled with an awareness of the past.

I found the family a short time afterwards – not those who belonged to this house but another one a short distance away. A pair of young men were stepping out in the waters of the Schlei on that Sunday afternoon, untying their small boat from its place beside a low wooden pier, one that was decorated with blue plastic barrels, bright yellow barrels and a tangle of old nets. I took a few photos of them, noting how, with their orange waders and dark caps, they looked so much like their contemporaries in places like Mallaig or Kyle of Lochalsh, for all that the boats required for such places were so much stronger and sturdier than these. The same could be said for the older man who stepped towards me as I sat there, speaking German rapidly. A broad-shouldered individual, he too had the grey stubble and yellow waders fashionable among fishermen everywhere. As he stood beside me, I questioned him about the fish that both he and his sons caught with their nets. His answer was indecipherable to me apart from one word: 'Herring.'

'Where are you from?' he asked me.

'Scotland.'

· He pressed his chest with his thumbs. 'I . . . I am Scottish too. My name is Ross.'

It was then I obtained – with the help of both his sister and daughter-in-law – the family story. The Ross family had arrived in Holm in 1719. 'We worked for the Spanish in Scotland,' I was told. 'As messengers between them and some Scots people. We fled there after some battle we had lost.'

By chance, I knew exactly to which incident they were referring – the Battle of Glensheil in Wester Ross in 1719, where the Jacobite forces had been defeated by the Hanoverian army. I returned to my hotel to research the event more, discovering that there was more than a little truth in the family legend. Clan Ross – a family largely centred in the locality of towns like Alness, Invergordon and Dingwall on the edge of Scotland's north-eastern Highlands – had been involved in what was called the Nineteen. However, they had fought on the 'British' side, opposing the soldiers of the Regiment Galicia from Spain. One could only wonder why the fisherman's ancestors had fled the scene After all, they were likely to have been employed by the winning side. There seemed, however, to be good reason why the Rosses might have chosen Denmark as their destination. King Frederick IV of Denmark was involved in the Great Northern War with his neighbours in Sweden. Swords were required for hire. There were rewards for those who wielded them. In 1721, after the coalition of which his forces had been part had won the Great Northern War, the King of Denmark was given control of Schleswig-Holstein. He had need of those who might be loyal to him. Members of a clan that – even back then – probably had some experience of fishing for herring in Scottish waters fitted this description. No doubt they provided some of their catch for the banquets that might have been held in Gottorp castle, providing fish for the fare.

If so, they were not alone. This area of the Baltic Sea was at one time famous for its herring. For all that its main shoals seem to have veered away in or around 1425, as I have noted before, there were still a few of the *Clupea harengus* species loitering around its waters. During my time in Germany, I visited a number of ports that were traditionally associated with them. They included Flensburg, some ten miles from the Danish border. While there, I stood on the bridge of the new *Loch Seaforth*, the ferry being built in its dockyard for my native Isle of Lewis, speaking Gaelic to a man from a few miles away from my old home – and encountering, too, a young man who came from Cunnings-burgh in Shetland, one of the nearest villages to my new one. An hour or so later and I was walking along the harbour, seeing all the historic boats that were tied up there, eating Bismarck herring bought from one of the small booths I found all over Germany. These offered *matjes*, cups of hot seafood soup and other varieties of fish designed to warm up an individual when they strolled around the vessels tied up on the waterfront. On the dull, dark, cloudy day in late summer that I strolled there, the title of one particular group seemed to be an utter misnomer – the Jolly Boats Collection. It strained at its moorings alongside Commercial Sailing Vessels, Classic Yachts, the Steamer Collection, the Museum Boatyard and the Maritime Museum. It was to this last place that, finding that the fortification of neither hot steaming soup nor pickled gherkins was quite enough, I ran for shelter. There is good reason why fierce, cold winds are referred to as 'Baltic'.

Far from concentrating much on Flensburg's fishing past, the exhibitions focused on other aspects of its life as a seaport. Paintings of huge steel hulls, products of the shipbuilders I had visited, hung on its walls. In another room there were a number of barrels. None, however, had ever contained herring. Instead, they had brimmed over once upon a time with rum, a product of the long years in which the Danes had owned the US Virgin Islands of St Thomas, St John and St Croix. Part of the display read like stepping into a confessional, where the Danes apologised for their long involvement in the crime of slavery. Downstairs, in the museum shop, there was a little more. Guy de Maupassant's famous trawling story – in which a fisherman cuts off his brother's arm rather than lose a valuable net – was translated into German and there upon the shelves. Carsten Jensen's seaborne novel *We, the Drowned* sat alongside, its opening section drawn from the aftermath of the first Schleswig War. A short distance away, and in the confectionery section, stood a small selection of glass jars crammed with black and white sweets. The product of a firm in Hamburg, they had the cheerful image of a chortling fish ringed with the words 'Salz Heringe'.

I discovered that they are not the only ones of their kind. Another kind of *salzheringe* sparkle in their sugar coatings in a bright blue bag. One more comes with its stablemate – 'Zombie Smiles' – in clear packaging, wrapped with a scarlet ribbon. In Gluckstadt, another former herring port in Schleswig-Holstein, can be found Herr Hai Mac Heringe – a salt liquorice version. One of the strangest aspects of the northern European taste in confectionery is *sockersaltad*, a Swedish term for the combination of sugar and salt in which one ingredient brings out the taste of the other. Bread can have sugar laced through it; cake a sprinkling of salt. Each time I have tasted anything of that kind, it has only succeeded in twisting my lips into a gigantic zombie smile.

Together with this there can be found large chocolate herrings, which grin from inside the port's shop windows with all the studied intensity of resurrected zombies, daring the customer to join the undead and swallow a treat that looks like a charcoal-coated kipper. Then there are the scores of little chocolates wrapped to look like sardines. To quote the words of French writer Jules Michelet in *La Mer* in his description of herring, looking at these confectionery displays it might seem as if 'a whole living world has just risen from the depths to the surface, following the call of warmth, desire and the light'.

One can only wonder what is the purpose of this – to prepare children for a grown-up menu? An attempt to fool them? To tell kids that they are about to eat *salzheringe*, the sweet, before they plunge a spoonful of the most bitter, briny morsels they can find into their tiny mouths? Is this counterpart of Zombie Smiles in itself a false form of comfort, something that sweetens both mind and mouth before it tastes adult despair? The thought gives me something to chew over as I wander around Kappeln, another town on the Schlei. Its innovations are, at least, original. Its harbour appears busy with fishboxes from 'Bornholm', 'Klintholm' – both in Denmark – and 'Władysławowo' in Poland bright upon its quay. Bronze herring shoal the pavement, each with the name of a firm or individual inscribed upon it. Around the base of the cross in St Nicholas church is the shape of a boat, lined and illuminated by candles. The two-hundredth anniversary of the community is under way and St Christopher wades across a stretch of water with a child straddling his back, a reference, it seems, to a time before bridges were built. Six herring – three on each side – gobble air and look at his actions with some amazement. In some ways, this is very similar to the way I feel when I wander through the town and hear the strains of Dougie MacLean's 'Caledonia'. The words reverberate through the air, sung by a group currently on the stage that – without a trace of irony – calls itself Drumchapel Mist. I find myself longing for the presence of 'MerQury – best of Queen' who will appear a few hours later on the same stage. Anything would be better than a Scottish folk group that intends to summon up the ghosts of a Glasgow housing estate and set them loose upon a crowd of unsuspecting German tourists.

Yet it is none of these things – not 'Seven Seas of Rhye', not 'Flower of Scotland', which I hear a short time later – that lies behind Kappeln's claim to be a unique location. Instead, it is the Ellenberger Heringszaun (herring fence) which stretches across part of the Schlei at Kappeln. In the brochures it is described as a 'thicket', woven between 3-metre posts that form a wall impenetrable to fish. Its wide throat becomes tighter and tighter the closer it comes towards the main bridge in Kappeln, ending in *reusen* (fish traps), which can be taken out, their catch weighed and measured. Once common throughout Europe, it is now the last such fence remaining, standing in its current location since 1482, the only one left out of thirty-eight counted on the Schlei in 1648. Their existence was once based on the sheer quantity of fish that streamed upriver throughout the Continent. The decline in these shoals brought about the herring fences' end. This one only comes into existence again on one of the interminable religious holidays that bedeck the German calendar during May, a date rejoicing under the amusing – to an English-speaker's ears – title of Himmelfahrt. (The more religiously informed might know it instead as 'Ascension Thursday'.) This occurs forty days after Easter when Jesus ascended to heaven after spending that length of time in the desert. For some strange reason, this day is when odds are laid on the 'herring bet'. Guests are asked to guess the size of the haul found within the *reusen*. The one who comes closest to the exact result will be proclaimed – in shades of Eyemouth – Herring Queen or King for one year. It is not known whether or not their homes are also decorated with illustrations of herring or if there are any pink garlands upon their door as in Eyemouth.

Canada possesses similar herring fences, however, with one being in place since before history was recorded. The Mnjikaning fish weirs are one of the oldest human developments in that country, built by the First Nations people so far back that it is believed they have been in place before some of the Egyptian pyramids. And then there were those in England and elsewhere, mentioned even in the Magna Carta of 1215, which includes a clause embodying the barons' demands for the removal of the king's weirs and others: 'All fish-weirs shall be removed from the Thames, the Medway, and throughout the whole of England, except on the sea coast.'

One can understand the reasons for this demand – not only how the more rapacious aspects of human nature must have denuded these rivers of fish, but also the difficulties of navigating when they are encountered en route. This was especially the case on the coast where a clutch of stones might be gathered to form a boundary to a rock pool, preventing the herring or any other fish from escaping to the sea.

I spent a short time musing on all this before I went on my way in Kappeln, navigating the wonderful labyrinth of both land and water that is this part of Germany. It was a place which I was vaguely familiar with from literature. As a young man I had read a number of the novels of Siegfried Lenz, whose work includes *The Lightship*, set upon a vessel of that description in the Baltic Sea. (The film based on the book shifts its location, for some reason best known to those whose senses have long been swirled away by being in the proximity of the Hollywood sign, to somewhere off the coast of Carolina, USA.) The novel that impressed me most was called *The German Lesson*. For all its foreign subject matter, about a boy's relationship with his policeman father, loyal to the Nazi cause, its setting was one to which I could relate. Taking place in Schleswig-Holstein, not far from the Danish border, its salt-sharp winds were with me each time I walked the shoreline or even crossed the moorland that was such a feature of both Lenz's work and my life. It was the first time I became truly aware that peat-cutting was a feature of German life, too. I pictured the book's characters in the kind of postures into which my body was contorted every summer – bending down to lift the peat sod from the bank, crouching to lift the half-dried slabs off the heather, dodging the badly aimed ones some of my neighbours launched towards the tractor-trailer, nursing the wounds that were inflicted by either their throws or the midges that plagued my skin with their tiny bites.

And there were other books too. There was Günter Grass, whose books like *The Flounder* and *The Tin Drum* somehow reeked of sea life, whether of the Baltic or North Sea coast. Eels writhed through the pages of *The Tin Drum*, even snaking from the underskirts of one of the female characters. The flounder – definitely a more acquired taste than the herring in both a literary and culinary sense – whispered into the ears of men, emerging from one of Grimms' fairy tales about the fish. (In the Grimms' original, it is an anti-feminist fable.) Leaf through Grass's books and one could gain the sense of the smells of the grocer's shop in Danzig (Gdansk) in which he spent many of his childhood years – the stockfish and pickled herring among the many odoriferous items, sour and salt, on its shelves. In later years he wrote in his autobiography, *Peeling the Onion*, that he recalls his years in Berlin where he used to serve 'green herrings rolled in flour and fried on a hot plate'; the meal became such a staple of his diet that his neighbour used to object to the smell of the dish wafting in continually from the next-door studio. In *The Flounder*, he also provided the fourteenth-century mystic and Catholic saint, Dorothea Van Mantau, with a good helping of herring – as well as tripe, cod, potato soup, kidneys in mushroom sauce, and potato soup for some of his other characters.

Günter Grass Haus now stands in Lübeck, not far from a museum dedicated to the memory of a man who was an even greater hero of mine, Willy Brandt, the former Chancellor of Germany. (He too has a 'fishy' connection, as escaping Nazi rule, he went on a fishing boat from Lübeck to Denmark, and from there to Norway, in 1933, continuing his resistance work there.) Among his paintings and sculptures, there are some of cods' heads and flounders. Chickens, too, glare at you from the wall. The fish are, of course, not out of place in Lübeck. Like Bergen, Hamburg, Tallinn, Riga and many other ports throughout Europe, Lübeck was part of the Hanseatic League, a loose association of merchants in these and other cities that lasted from the fourteenth century till the seventeenth. In fact, one could argue that it was

Lübeck's alliance with Hamburg that provided the foundation for this trading league in the first place.

Salt played a major part in this trading confederation. Much of it came to the city from Lüneburg, where there were huge saltworks; the produce was initially brought to Lübeck overland by means of the Old Salt Route, one of many similar tracks that were used for trade across Europe. This was not the safest or most efficient means of travel. Sometimes the unsurfaced route was wet and sandy. Often it was dangerous. Robbers and brigands lingered nearby to steal the 'white gold' that was being brought to Lübeck and beyond, conscious that there were many merchants elsewhere who would pay a high sum for its savour. Among the purposes for which the grains were employed was to salt and preserve the herring men had netted in ports as far apart as Bergen and Visby.

In 1398 the Stecknitz Canal, one of the first man-made canals in Europe, was built. This made the transportation of salt both safer and swifter. By the sixteenth century, for example, about 19,000 tons were being carried from Lüneburg to Lübeck each year, its movement less hindered by thieves or weather than ever before. This is not to say that, by our standards, the journeys were all that quick. Even by water, it still took about twenty days to complete each trip. There was also, from the fifteenth century onwards, high-quality Setúbal white salt from Portugal coming to these shores, the low prices and low taxes imposed on the substance making its transportation worthwhile. When the boats arrived in Lübeck, their cargo was put away and stored in buildings that were the predecessors of the Salzspeicher, a row of historic buildings close to the Holstentor gate that forms the entrance to the city. These well-preserved gabled buildings were built as warehouses to store salt and date from the sixteenth to the eighteenth century. They were located alongside the canal to allow barges to easily bring the precious salt to the city, permitting them, too, to travel the ring of water that surrounds the city. It is still – from the Niederegger marzipan sold in its shops to the cathedral at its centre – a very impressive place. From the little devil perched outside St Mary's Church to the faces of the characters gazing down at you from the balcony of the *Rathaus* (town hall), Lübeck is an endearing mixture of the eccentric and efficient.

It also lies at a crossroads. For much of the post-war period, it sat a short distance away from the East German border; its guards looked out over the twists and turns of the river nearby, trying to stop the passage of people making their way to the West. (On the banks of the river, I became involved in a long, multinational discussion with Russians, Swedes and Germans. One of the Germans started talking about his longing for the simple clarities of his early life in the East. Even the water on the river's shoreline apparently was purer and clearer, not like the murky grimness of that found on the other side.) Earlier, though, the city formed a junction in other ways. Though its main interest was cod, a more easily preserved product than herring, it also took catches from places such as Visby in Gotland, Sweden, and Bergen in Norway, added a dash or two of salt, and exported this fish both west and east, the central fulcrum of an endless swirl of trade.

The success of this city – and the Hanseatic League more generally – was based partly on ensuring that the methods of processing herring were standardised, a way of making certain of its quality, in terms of both flavour and longevity. This extended throughout the range of its control. There is, for instance, a document which survives from 1474 that describes the situation in two fishing villages, Falsterbo and Skanör in the south of Sweden, showing how mass production was organised there. In both locations, around 5,000 people were employed in the herring trade. These included the 3,500 men employed in 762 small fishing boats; 700 others who worked transferring the hauls from twenty-six larger barges to either boats or carts to take them elsewhere; 174 women who worked gutting and placing the catch in barrels long before the Dutch 'invented' the process; the numerous coopers who made and repaired barrels; 200 merchants; and the journeymen and apprentices who were also involved, working away in the dappled light and foam of these harbours, grains of salt and scales of herring colouring their hands. For much of the year these small ports expanded, becoming almost, briefly, medieval cities when the trade was at its height. It was in bays and inlets like these that, contrary to certain Dutch claims and even a statue of the fish-gutter of myths Willem Beukels of Biervliet, unveiled in his hometown of Biervliet by Tsar Nicholas II of Russia in 1856, the technique of gutting and laying the fish in brine was first developed.

Before the arrival of the Hanseatic League, rotten herring was frequently sold to people. The quality of the salt used to preserve them was variable. Frequently, this was peat salt, drenched by the ocean and found in places like southern Denmark and the north of Holland. When this was free from soil it would produce a white, fine-grained salt, but all too often it was laced with white ash derived from the peat from which it had been burned away, a way of bulking up the product but not necessarily improving its value or flavour. The Hanseatic League would fine anyone caught doing this, or disguising a barrel of poor fish with a layer or two of high-quality, fine, round-backed herring. The League would even burn herring of a lower standard instead of throwing them back into the sea, fearful that other fish might swallow them and become fouled and polluted with their taste.

Yet for all this control, the Hanseatic League was always a loose organisation in terms of its structure, more an opportunistic, adaptable alliance of tradesmen than anything like a nation state. In some ways it was more like the European Union without that body's tiers of bureaucrats and regulations. It possessed no constitution and no permanent army, navy or governing body, except for periodic assemblies or diets. Even these were convened less and less frequently from the early fifteenth century, as the towns' separate and individual interests began to outweigh their common concerns. By the middle of the sixteenth century, Lübeck had declined in importance. Part of this was caused by the growing role that the New World played in global trade, one that involved the countries bordering the Baltic and Mediterranean seas. Sweden was becoming the most important economic power in the Baltic. Dutch ships also carried goods from the Baltic to the west, with the English emerging as their chief rivals. By 1669 the diet of the Hanseatic League had met for the last time.

Yet it left its legacy. A fondness for herring – and salt cod! – unites much of northern Europe. While travelling around Hamburg, Bremen and the Baltic coast, I dined again and again on the fish. Sometimes I ate rollmops; on other occasions Bismarck herring was my culinary choice, bought from both harbour booths and fast-food establishments in railway stations. The rollmop is known throughout the world. Often stored in jars or tubs, the fish is rolled around a filling of onion, pickled gherkin or green olive and pimento, and held together by two wooden skewers. Its marinade contains white vinegar, water and salt, though sometimes a little sugar, onion rings and mustard seed can be added. Bismarck herring are similar, marinated in vinegar, oil, onions, mustard seed and bay leaf, often contained within a bread roll. They were not my favourite dish, curdling in my stomach as I swallowed them, an effect Dutch *maatje* never had on me. And then there was *labskaus*, where the main ingredients are salted meat or corned beef, potatoes and onion. Some recipes put beetroot, pickled gherkin or even a dash of herring in the dish. All this allowed me to sympathise with another Woody Allen joke I came across on my travels:

A man who could not marry off his ugly daughter visited Rabbi Shimmel of Cracow. 'My heart is heavy,' he told the rabbi, 'because God has given me an ugly daughter.'

'How ugly?' the seer asked.

'If she were lying on a plate with a herring, you wouldn't be able to tell the difference.'

The Seer of Cracow thought for a long time and finally asked, 'What kind of herring?'

The man, taken aback by the query, thought quickly and said, 'Er – Bismarck.'

'Too bad,' the seer said. 'If it was Maatjes, she'd have a better chance.'

Then there are the other German varieties. One such is *brathering*, which is marinated and fried. It has one great advantage over the Scottish version, which is coated with oatmeal and fried, and that is that after being marinated for some time, one has to spit out few of the troublesome bones that plague the meal with which I had been long familiar.

In other countries bordering both the North Atlantic and the Baltic Sea, there are yet more tastes. The Swedish *smörgåsbord* provides one of them. This involves a tableful of herring and smoked fish spread out on a table for a social gathering, a notion also found in the Jewish feast of *forshpeis*. This can have its own local innovations. In a similar way to the ceremony I encountered in Florø in Norway, the Swedes and Danes often drink aquavit or *nubbe* with their *sill* (herring), forms of schnapps that possess distinctive and different national flavours. (The Norwegians boast that theirs has the deepest, darkest colour and the strongest taste. They also have the odd tradition of the *Linje Aquavits*, where aquavit is stored in barrels which are then sent to Australia and back again. Apparently, rolling it up and down a warehouse floor for the length of time a voyage takes does not have the same effect.) Aquavit is also consumed in Schleswig-Holstein, where so many people of Danish descent can be found; this yellow-shaded drink obtains its characteristic flavour from dill or caraway. It serves, according to legend, to flush the fish that accompanies it down someone's throat all the way to the stomach, aiding the digestion. It is not, however, the only accompaniment provided for the herring. Danes, Swedes and Swedish-speaking Finns – some 5 per cent of Finland's population – also wash fish down with a *snapsvisa* (drinking song) or two. These songs are odes in praise of drinking schnapps and dozens of them can serenade, among other meals, herring or crayfish* at parties. By the end of the meal, it is not only fish that are slithering and slipping.

In the Middle Ages, as well as being preserved by wind-drying, herring was sometimes preserved by being given a light covering of salt, perhaps together with flour or malt barley, wrapped in the bark of birch or other trees, then buried in the earth. In the cool soil of Scandinavia, the fish preserved this way was transformed eventually into *sursild* (sour herring). In the fifteenth century, according to the Swedish *Karls' Kronike* (Karl's Chronicle), this was the most important form of sustenance for the Norwegian military, eaten along with thin, hard flatbread. In Alan Davidson's work *Food in Motion: The Migration of Foodstuffs and Cooking*, he notes: 'The famous Norwegian clergyman and author, Peter Dass, writes in 1739 about the mountain farmer from the fjords who travels to the coast in the autumn to buy the herring he needs during the winter and how he prefers the strongest smelling barrel.'

Some clearly favoured the sourer, sharper taste when they were eaten, which must have been not unlike the taste of shark that is still sometimes buried in the manure heaps of Iceland,

*August Strindberg, the nineteenth-century father of Swedish literature, was clearly an aficionado of both herring and crayfish. His novel *By the Open Sea* must be the only major work in any language to feature a herring inspector as its central character. His descriptions of eating crayfish have what can only be termed an erotic quality, such is the relish with which he portrays the experience. After reading the book, I will never look at that fish in quite the same way again.

fermenting within the different layers of cow dung, household ash and straw that are left there. In itself, this practice was not unusual. Skate used to be buried within similar structures on my native island. One can imagine that its reek even after it had been cooked did little to improve the romantic prospects of the bachelors in the area. For the women considering the prospect of becoming entangled with these stalwart men, it must have been a case of 'once kissed, twice shy'.

There is an obvious reason why such a method of storing herring caught on. It is more common in, for instance, northern and eastern Norway than it is on the western coast, and increases in frequency the closer one comes to polar areas. In these places, the winters are both colder and longer than they are elsewhere. Even on a rare warm day, this technique is still effective. A layer of soil prevents the sun's rays from hastening the decay of the fish, especially when the local inhabitants have had to obtain their haul some distance from home and in an area where there were few roads till recent decades. This is also a part of the country where salt, and perhaps even barrels, are less easily obtained. More prosperous householders may even have dug cellars below their homes in which to store their herring catch and its more upmarket equivalents, the gravadlax (salmon) and gravad trout.

There are other unusual ways of eating or using the fish. Some people even concentrate specifically on the herring's head. An old Estonian tradition involved that country's noblemen eating fried heads, accompanied by beer. Sometimes the heads were boiled in water and drunk as a hangover cure. (The Germans see the consumption of Bismarck herring in a similar way, often eating them the morning after.) Another is the rare Finnish tradition of *kalakukko*, which occured in Savonia, part of eastern Finland. This involved the cooking of fish, traditionally freshwater fish such as a form of perch, inside a loaf of rye bread, which people took with them to work. In times of want, herring heads might be placed within the dough, giving the food some of the flavour of that fish. Before eating the bread, each fish was carefully, tentatively removed.

It would also appear that the further people lived from the ocean, the more unusually the herring was cooked. While in Aberdeen on a day when the wind seemed to blow in from the Baltic, I wandered into La Lombarda, a little Italian restaurant that stands just beside the Mercat Cross at the eastern end of Union Street. Looking out of the window, I watched the storm billow plastic bags across the pavement, its force making even the hardiest of its inhabitants cower and shiver. It occurred to me – not for the first time – how much the city had changed from the days when men like David Farquharson had painted *The Herring Fleet Leaving the Dee*, the sails of the boats puffing out in that same wind; even how much it has changed since my own father's generation. The townscape now is one dominated by the high towers and higher profits of the oil industry.

La Lombarda had been there in my father's time, opened way back in the year of his birth – 1922 – by Joe and Nan Birnie, a family that came from the region in north-east Italy that gives the venue its name. As I sat there, I felt reassured by the fact that at least one thing about the city had not altered. I was being served by a man called Luca Bettoni, who originally came from a village on the shores of Lake Iseo in Lombardy. While we talked, he tried to sell this place to me as a tourist destination, mentioning the lake, the village squares, the vibrant colours of the location – such a contrast to the grey shades of wintry, wind-bruised Aberdeen. While I waited a short time for my order to be served, I thought about some of the material I had discovered on my travels. *The Fish Book* given to me in Bergen by my Norwegian friend Einar Sandal. The display in the Time and Tide Museum in Great Yarmouth, which told me that herring from that port has been sent to Italy, specifically from the Tower Curing Works in the town. It was a custom

Left: Standing beside the peat stack near his home on the isle of Lewis, Uncle John shows off his *taigh-thàbhaidh* and – to my Aunt Joan's chagrin – dirty dungarees. Using these large spoon-shaped nets as a means of fishing, by baiting and reaching them into the water from a standing point on the rocks at the edge of croftland, is probably one of the most ancient methods of catching fish in Europe.

Below: Having exchanged her flowered overall for a more practical oilskin apron, my Aunt Bella (second from right) joins another group of *clann-nighean an sgadain*, island women employed to gut herring.

Above: Three generations of the Spaans family from Dutch herring port Scheveningen.

Below: Scheveningen's herring girls wore bright golden pins fixed into the tops of their scarves, a decoration they retained for high days, holidays and family portraits. Even on wedding days, like Lena Spaan's in April 1941, links with their community and the town's fishing trade were not forgotten.

Above: Here two Scheveningen women can be seen wearing the distinctive, traditional costume of their herring port in 1990 while chatting over their garden fence.

Below: A very different kind of traditional seaside headgear can be seen here: a group of Dundee women wear Kiss Me Quick hats as they admire a couple of dressed herring in all their finery.

Above: A group of Dutch men and women show how they enjoy their herring.

Below: A moment of grace; a plain and simple form of the Protestant faith was often associated with those who went fishing, as these Dutch fisherman remind us.

Left: One of the many small fishing boats I saw on my trip to Kappeln on the Schlei. It was moored a short distance from the last remaining herring fence, which stretches across a section of the Schlei where herring once streamed upriver in huge numbers. The decline of those shoals brought about the demise of this method of fishing. Boats, however, still fish in the river or off the nearby coastline.

Left: The view across the fjord from the town of Siglufjörður. In the background you can see the icy slope that unleashed an avalanche of snow in 1911, crushing Iceland's first fishmeal factory and killing nine people.

Left: Grána is one of the three main buildings that form the centre of Siglufjörður's Herring Era Museum, which is the largest maritime museum in Iceland and the world's only herring museum. Grána includes a unique exhibition about the history of the herring industry.

Above: From herring paste to kipper snacks, these are just a few of the fishy treats on display in the Herring Era Museum in Siglufjörður.

Below: Anyone for herring? This is a small selection of the herring fare that arrived in many forms and flavours in Florø during my visit to the Norwegian town in June 2014.

Above: Visitors and residents tucking into as much as they can of the huge variety of dishes on offer in Florø during its herring festival.

Below: School's out! Seen here wearing the authentic cap and clothing of the town's fishermen, one of Florø's many residents serving the hordes that flock to the town in June each year to sit at the 'Longest Herring Table in the World'.

Above: A view of almost all 350 metres of the legendary 'Longest Herring Table in the World' that is set up in June each year in Florø's streets. Just a few hours after this photograph was taken, and after enormous amounts of herring had been consumed, plates and tables were cleared away to allow residents and visitors to dance in the streets to Legend, a Bob Marley tribute band from England.

gained at the expense of the Scots, who had first sold herring there in the 1860s, the Yarmouth merchants having the advantage that the product caught off their shores at the end of the season was less oily than its northern counterparts. (This display went on to inform me that the package was particularly important where this market was concerned. The Italian housewife apparently set great store by style.) Yet any time I mentioned this to Italians I knew, there was a shake of a head. There was even one who was brought up in Stornoway for whom *sgadan* was still not part of the (almost) daily diet. This time I turned to Luca with my question.

'Did you ever eat herring when you were growing up?'

'Yes . . . yes . . . all the time. We used to have it fried – just like fish and chips – when there was a market day in the village square. Sometimes it was sold there smoked. Like a type of kipper. And then there were other ways.'

He went on to list them, describing them in much the same way as those in Einar's informative book.

'When it was cold, we used to have them with polenta. Sometimes it was freshwater fish from the lakes. Sometimes herring. In wartime, they used to just smear the polenta with the juices from the herring rather than use the whole fish. Sometimes they used the oil after cooking it to flavour the polenta. Just to give people the taste. And then sometimes we used to wrap up the herring in buttery paper and burn it in the flames of the fire. After that was done, we used to serve it with onions and a little oil.'

I nodded, having heard of this before. A friend of mine had informed me that once he had wrapped a herring in layers of damp newspaper, cramming it behind an old-fashioned radiator. ('It was delicious,' he said. 'But the room honked afterwards for weeks.') In the novel *The Credit Draper* by another friend, J. David Symons, there is a scene where one of his Glaswegian characters does the same in a household fire, finding a good use for his copy, perhaps, of the *Daily Express*, cooking the fish on the edge of the flames.

'Was the herring eaten all over Italy?'

Luca shakes his head. 'No. No. No. Only in the more selective parts. Like Lombardy and Venice. There is a good reason for that. The Adriatic is very poor for sea fish. Not very good quality. The herring is much nicer than that. The king of fish.'

I discovered later that it was slightly wider than that. By the 1780s, red herring was being sent to not only Venice but also Florence and Palermo in the south of Italy, where it was eaten and enjoyed. The Greeks also relished its taste, importing the fish in vast numbers. There is little doubt that those further north in the colder parts of Europe also savoured the wines and fruit that were sent back by return.

Of all the ways of preparing herring, however, there are a number that compete for the title of most eccentric. One of these is the frying of fresh river herring (alewife) that is extremely popular in eastern North Carolina in the United States. The herring was at one time fished using weirs, hooks, nets, traps and sometimes bow and arrow by the Algonquian tribe, who had settled both in and near Roanoke Island, the location where Sir Walter Raleigh established the first English colony in the New World. Since then, the river herring has been enjoyed by people there for centuries, caught by a large variety of different nets. These include the large, expensive seine net, as well as the smaller Dutch or pound net. In order to deal with the perennial problem of its long, thin bones, they fry the fish to such an extent that all of it except the central backbone can be eaten. This process makes the dish resemble 'cracklins' (pork scratchings) more than fish, earning it the title 'Roanoke River bacon' in some parts of the county. It is then eaten as one might consume corn on the cob, nibbling away at its edges, and served with boiled potatoes, coleslaw and hush puppies – tiny pieces of deep-fried cornmeal that were sometimes thrown as scraps to quieten the dog. Another comparison that is made about the way it is eaten is it that it is like 'playing a harmonica'.

In Europe, however, there is little doubt that the most individual and odd preparation method is the one that made the knees of my good friend Kenny Maciver buckle and bend – the *surströmming*. It is a dish about which a thousand legends have been conjured. Some argue that it was invented to repel invaders, including over-inquisitive tourists and Norwegian neighbours, pointing out that Sweden is one of the few countries in northern Europe not to have been invaded by either Genghis Khan or Adolf Hitler. It is believed, too, to draw flies in its direction, cleansing the air of mites and insects that go out of their way to bite sweaty individuals emerging from saunas. In the cold of northern Sweden, it was claimed to double as a means of prompting people to exercise, especially during the winter months. They ran half-marathons, ploughing onwards through blizzards and snowstorms in a desperate attempt to escape the smell.

There is also the common myth that alleges the dish started with Swedish sailors in the sixteenth century. Only having half the quantity of salt needed to keep their fish fresh, their store of herring started to rot. They solved this problem by playing a confidence trick on some Finnish islanders they came across on their voyage, selling them the rotten herring. A year later the Swedish sailors returned to the island. Expecting an angry reaction, they were surprised when those they had visited said how much they had enjoyed their treat, wondering if they had any more. It was at this point that the sailors decided to taste it themselves. Relishing the flavour, they decided they would make some more. It was an innovation that proved popular throughout northern Sweden. *Surströmming* was even supplied as army rations to troops from that region in the Thirty Years War in the sixteenth century, though foreign conscripts and soldiers from the south responded to it in the way their descendants still (largely) do to this day – refusing to let it pass their lips. For the rare exceptions living in, say, Stockholm or

Gothenburg who enjoyed the dish, it wasn't until the nineteenth century that they obtained the option of satisfying their appetites. Instead of being stored in barrels, *surströmming* then started to be canned, becoming the food that is now sometimes banned from planes, blamed for gas leaks and used as the legal justification for German landlords to ban tenants who consume it from their rented homes.

Those who defend the dish, however, would point out that the way it was prepared for Kenny Maciver and me that day outside the BBC studio in Stornoway was totally wrong. We should apparently have split the herring, removing the roe. Its rose-tinted flesh should have been placed on a buttered, crisp Swedish cracker beside some mashed potatoes. Onions could have been added, too, though this is apparently a matter of personal taste. One man I spoke to who savoured the dish very much despite living in the southern, sheltered climes of downtown Stockholm was the sunglass-sporting, piano-playing maestro Adrian Holmstrom. Defending his strange way of consuming the fish, he told me:

'As my father is from the north of Sweden, they ate *surströmming* a lot there. When I was a child, I tried and liked it even though I knew the smell was strange. It is very important, though, to eat it with all the other stuff such as thin bread, butter, potatoes and onion. The strong alcoholic *nubbe* makes the whole thing taste wonderful. The best thing is the salty rich taste of the fish that makes a perfect contrast to the other ingredients. There's a tingle in my mouth as I await its arrival.'

And so we come to another strange manner in which the herring was once celebrated. Between 1888 and 1905, when their union was finally dissolved, the flag that marked the combined kingdom of Norway and Sweden was known mockingly by all and sundry as the 'herring salad'. Its mix of red, white, blue and yellow was said to resemble a Norwegian dish: one that mingled herring with chopped egg salad, egg whites, beetroot and parsley in a psychedelic range of shades that would blind any guests if they encountered it on the dining table.

One would hope no one would take it amiss if I suggested that it might be resurrected – to mark and celebrate the kingdom of which the herring is the monarch, its domain the North Sea and the broad Atlantic, the Minch and Irish Sea, the Pentland Firth, the Baltic, the English Channel, all the way to Iceland . . .

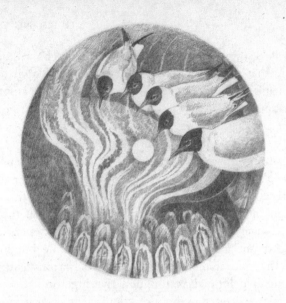

CHAPTER NINE

'Blowin' in the Wind'

Seagulls inform those in kipper yards when to start work for the day. In places like Seahouses in Northumberland, Mallaig on Scotland's west coast and Peel on the Isle of Man, their employees watch out for the way the birds' feathers are ruffled, in what direction their beaks are pointing, or even how their wings are pulled and pushed by the breeze, before deciding whether or not to begin the process of smoking the fish. In their own way, they offer proof of Bob Dylan's old adage about the weatherman: you don't always need to have one around. And then when the workers have decided that the gusts and omens are good, they start their labours for the day, gathering the oak shavings they require to transform the fish that have been soaked in brine into kippers for somebody's breakfast, somebody's plate.

In Peel, those employed at Moore's Kipper Yards always ensure that the smoke from their labours is blown to the west bank of the river Neb, its swirl clouding the emptiness of that part of their city rather than the east side, where most of the population lives and works. It is a habit born from long experience, the crimson sign fixed to its white walls proclaiming the fact that it is 'Still Smoking the Same Way As 1862' – and presumably in the same directions, for all that it might have had a change of owner or two in that time. Within the smokehouse, there is evidence of all the soot that has accrued in its years of existence. Black encrusts the inside of the kiln, contrasting with the white building. It licks the door panels that stand at its various entrances, looking like little dark tongues, layering too the rods or 'speets' that stretch across the kiln as if it is slavering over them with a dark coating of tar. It is from these that the herring – or ham, salmon or other seafood – hangs, ready and waiting for the smoke to curl around and cure it.

And then Oleg, complete with baseball cap and sweatshirt, picks up his spade, opens up the door panels and creates six mounds of damp oak shavings, spacing them neatly around the base of the kiln. Moments later, he adds a smattering of dry oak shavings. These are not sherry or whisky flavoured as, courtesy of old barrels from the Speyside Cooperage, some of the shavings used in Buckie or ports in the north-east of Scotland are. These are wisps of the coldest, purest smoke. Oleg watches them carefully after he lights them, making certain that each pile 'takes', making sure, too, that it does not 'take' too readily, catching flame. What he wants is for the mounds to glow and smoulder, imbuing the fish with flavour, never scorching tail or fin with too much heat or allowing the flame to extinguish and die, providing the herring with no taste at all. It is a fine balancing act and one which this young Lithuanian performs with the same agility as he masters the English language, each word pronounced accurately and exactly, displaying the same kind of warmth as he does when he greets his young son, being taken on his morning stroll a short time later.

Later still and I am outside the building, watching the smoke waft out from the narrow vents on its black-slated roof. It coils around the edge of the town, its smell summoning up a spirit that this small harbour does its level best to preserve. One can see this in the neat signs that decorate the walls of many of the buildings on the waterfront. 'Thos. Joshua Graves. Estd 1857. Flax and Hemp Herring Nets For Sale. Sixteen Jeebins. Four In Depth. 9s 8d' reads one. Another advertises the firm of 'William Moore & Son Estd Sailmakers and Barkers of All Kinds Of Nets'. (This gentleman is also a 'Shipping Agent' who requires 'Ladies and Gentlemen to sail with the Peggy Lucy To The Colonies. Apply to Captain Jamie'.) Most charming of all, a red Victoria Regina postbox advertises the fact that 'The Postmaster General of Peel begs to inform the Good Inhabitants of This Fair City That Collections From This Box Are Made Monday to Saturday 7.30am and 6.30pm'. And then there is the sign which gives rise to the thought that you might be back in Roman times – 'John & Caesar Corris Est'd 1883' are apparently still trading as 'Traditional Rule Of Thumb Boat Builders' in the town.

The illusion does not last long. Even the air itself is too pristine to convince anyone that they are back in Victorian times or earlier. Fish do not reek in its harbour. Neither do many seagulls cluster there. Oleg has an easy task keeping an eye on them all. There are no 'Jeebins' – the Manx word for fishing nets – spread out to dry on Peel Hill to the west of the city as there were for generations before with the tang of the sea still caught within their mesh. The bay in front of St Patrick's Isle where Peel Castle stands is almost empty of boats. There is also none of the smell of tar that was once almost ubiquitous in fishing harbours throughout the country. Not only was it used to protect the hulls of fishing boats, it was also employed for the oddest of purposes. They used it, mingled with linseed oil, to make their leather boots last for around thirty years. They employed warm tar at sea to heal wounds, as the substance was already sterile. My friend Maggie Smith has told me of a man from Uig on the west coast of the Isle of Lewis who lost part of his leg in the First World War. The remainder was smeared in that nautical necessity, Archangel Tar, and he was sent home. Apparently, the cure worked. He limped around for years afterwards. She also pointed me in the direction of a Gaelic book which tells of the way certain people were so desperate for a smoke that: '*Dh'fheuch iad pìosan de lìon-sgadain a bha air an gearradh nan criomagan a smocadh ann am pìob. Thuirt e gur e rop-teàrrta rud cho uabhasach 's a chuir e riamh ann am pìob airson a smocadh.*' In short, an occasional aroma might have drifted in the direction of a passer-by from a fisherman's pipe, packed with fragments of herring nets and tarred rope.

Then there was 'the barking yard', a feature of many former herring ports throughout the country. There is a particularly good example of this in the old fisher town of Nairn in the north-east of Scotland. Dated '1220–1975' and bearing the insignia and name of the 'Royal Burgh of Nairn', its notice reads: 'This was the tannery of the fishertown where boat crews barked their nets and sails. Owned by the fishermen's society, there were three boilers and kettles, fired by wood. Deepwater nets were boiled with a tree resin called Burmese cutch to preserve them, resulting in a distinctive brown stain. Inshore nets were paler with steeping in alum. The yard was last used in 1968.'

Three chimneys also stand beside the building, one to mark each brew: a task that was performed in copper cauldrons once a month. After being dried in open fields or locations like Peel Hill, it was believed that the nets would – barring accident – last around five years. Oilskins were also boiled either there or elsewhere in the port, as a means of waterproofing them and getting them ready for the whip of salt and wild weather. Another reek to add to the many that swirled around the port.

There was also the smell of red herring. The Isle of Man – Douglas, Derbyhaven, Port St Mary and Peel – was one of the locations that specialised in this product, after the means of preserving herring was introduced from Yarmouth in 1777. By 1838, however, the red-herring houses on the island had begun to close. The plantation owners in America no longer required preserved herring for the slaves that had been freed during the course of that momentous year. Those in the Caribbean who had consumed them no longer wished to eat a product that had been long associated with their condition, turning from the fish in distaste. Or, perhaps, they could not afford them, many suffering hunger in their early years of freedom. The dish only became acceptable later if it was transformed into a paste, mixed with chilli pepper and served on a cracker. Other than that, 'dem bellies' were 'full'.

Peel is not the only town on the west coast of these islands that was known for its kippers. There is Campbeltown on Loch Fyne, my native town of Stornoway and the port of Mallaig, a place in which everyday existence can sometimes seem like an extraordinary miracle. Step down the slope that sweeps from its high school to the harbour and you gain a sense of how great a challenge it must have been to build homes here. The soil is thin. Rocks guard the road at odd angles. Buildings – like the school hostel on the edge of cliff and shore – seem on the verge of surrendering to the landscape that surrounds them, part of the roof having been swept away shortly before the day I visited. There is not one structure of great note; all that has been put in place by the hands of men here seemingly frail and insubstantial.

And yet with a setting like this, how can men compete? Of all the places I have encountered during my travels, this is one of the few that can truly compare with the likes of Bergen and Florø. It isn't only altitude that takes people's breath away when they visit places like these. There is the view across the Sound of Sleat to Skye; the sight of An Sgurr, the grey, barren ridge that dominates the isle of Eigg a short distance away; even the hills that surround and clasp this small township. Above all, there is the question that comes to mind: 'Why did people ever come to live here?' The road to reach it – much improved over the last few years – still swerves and curls. The railway from Fort William required the creation of that vast structure the Glenfinnan Viaduct, which the train curves around, suspending its passengers for a short time over what seems an unimaginable and giddy height. Built from a mixture of faith, Victorian self-belief and concrete, it seems to belong quite firmly to the world of Harry Potter, in which films it sometimes appears.

The answer to that question is the same one that applied to Florø. For all that neither ring of herring nor a statue of Mick Jagger's jagged toothed lips appear in its streets, Mallaig owes its existence to precisely the same fish. (There is a statue in the harbour – a bearded fisherman who points to the ocean with one hand while clutching a young girl's fingers with the other. It's not quite up to the same standard as the Rolling Stones logo but . . .) The Glenfinnan Viaduct also came into being for precisely the same reason. One of its earlier acts of wizardry was to keep the 'kipper train' aloft every morning as its carriages shoaled in the direction of Glasgow and the markets further south.

The impressive heritage centre curated by Malcolm Poole provides me with some enlightenment about Mallaig's beginnings. It stands near the railway station, not far from a cluster of shops and restaurants. (Mallaig is not unlike Peel in the way the town tries to entice tourists and visitors into its net these days.) On its walls and within small booklets it tells the story of the origins of that community. It was not founded until the 1840s, when Lord Lovat, who at that time owned North Morar Estate, divided up the farm that was there, encouraging his tenants to travel west and begin to fish for a living.

In the lateness of its creation, it was not unique. The British Fisheries Society was formed in 1786, with one of its primary roles to create new harbours where the displaced people of the Highlands could both fish and flourish. There were a number of such communities, some succeeding, others failing. In the latter group was Lochbay in Skye, founded in 1790. Both the remarkable figure of George Dempster and the architect Thomas Telford were involved in this project, creating whitewashed terraces that still exist today. Ironically, one of the reasons why the creation of this community failed was because of the good quality of the land there. Man could live by croft alone. Why risk limb and line when one could have a good life on shore? It was an issue that was raised – from the opposite perspective – by a Shetland fisherman I met, who pointed out that the men from places like Whalsay and the Skerries had retained their traditional way of life, while those in the more fertile South Mainland of Shetland had been in 'a hurry to let go their boats'.

'And all just to grow some watery potatoes.' He had shaken his head and smiled.

Yet, as a landlubber, this response also seems to me to be understandable, and goes some way to explain the success of Shetland boats over, say, their counterparts in my own native Isle of Lewis. Many men, especially after they have a family, do not want to go to sea. They are aware of the estrangement that sometimes comes with the lifestyle – from their wives and partners, from the everyday business of their communities, even from the earth itself and its change of seasons, that cycle of seed, growth and harvest that is all but hidden from them while they are on the Minch or North Sea. They are conscious, too, that they are in the world of men, with all its brisk bluntness, and may somehow lose the sureness of touch required to deal with both the young and the opposite gender. With a few, notable exceptions, it is only the young and adventurous who describe being at sea in the same glowing terms as Finn in Gunn's *The Silver Darlings*: 'Pleasant it was to see the land slipping by and the headland of home slowly closing on the stores, the yards, the beach, the river-mouth, like a gate closing in a dream until all their kindred were shut off, leaving them to adventure in the great expanse of the world.'

At the time when communities like Mallaig and Lochbay were being created, there was also the dramatic change that moving to such locations often entailed. It was not just a new environment but a new way of thinking, one often brought into being by the very authority – the landlord – whom both Highlander and islander had good, historical reason to distrust. As Jean Dunlop puts it in *The British Fisheries Society*: 'The Highlander had always been self-supporting, growing his own oats, catching his own fish and supplying his own clothing and household goods, and this economy was in his nature rather than the Lowland one of earning money at a single trade to pay for other necessities.'

In contrast to Lochbay, Ullapool, on the shores of Loch Broom, was a reasonable success for the opposite reason. Founded in 1788 by the same society, its neat houses, designed by David Aitken, with later amendments by Thomas Telford, were rooted in the poorer soil of Wester Ross, a good reason for those who settled there to set aside the plough and lift the net and line instead. And so we could go on – to the port on the Isle of Mull that inspired the children's television programme *Balamory*. The colourful community of Tobermory, founded in the late eighteenth century, also owes much to Thomas Telford, the British Fisheries Society and the herring. In the period of the Highland Clearances in the 18th and 19th centuries, when so many people were evicted from their homes in the north of Scotland, it was often the fish alone that provided a good economic reason to cling to these shores, for all that it meant a huge change in the mindset of the inhabitants.

And so it was with Mallaig, where Lovat imitated the work that the British Fisheries Society had done elsewhere, for all that he lacked the inclination to provide such good housing. As Neil Gunn points out when he writes in *The Silver Darlings* about the imagined community of Dunster, based on Dunbeath at the north-eastern edge of the Highlands, it was the profit motive that inspired Lovat and many other landlords at that time – what he might make out of 'the buildings and curing stations and boats' dues' and all the other developments that 'would pay him out of the rents alone. Think of what ten shillings added to each croft rent would mean, in total, from Dunster itself.' This was mitigated to some extent by the fact that Lovat helped out considerably in the early days of the community, helping to pay for the damage that high winds and tides had done to people's homes and boats in 1881. A few years later, in 1885, 1886 and 1887, the herring were their fey and fickle selves, failing to call in vast numbers near their shores.

During the last decades of the nineteenth century, there were other, busier ports on the west coast. These included Stornoway and Castlebay, the latter even possessing a large – and now crumbling – Church of Scotland, built around the same time as the Church of Our Lady of the Sea in 1888. One catered for the large number of visiting Protestant fishermen; the other for the largely Catholic population of the island, which had moved to Castlebay for work during this period. (The small port has an impressive 'herring walk' on its shoreline, recalling the drama and industry of these days, noting too the landmarks of the days when – in an expression of *sgadanostalgia* – 'you could walk from one end of the bay to the other on the fishing boats clustered there'.) And then there was Tobermory, its catches going through Oban – in itself an important fishing port – which had gained its own railway in 1880. Oban provided the route for boats from Campbeltown and Lochgilphead to send their fish to market.

It was not until 1899 that life began to alter for the people of Mallaig. In that year the bill for building the West Highland Railway to Fort William was presented to Parliament. This was followed by a campaign to persuade the Treasury to provide some form of financial guarantee for the extension of the line to Mallaig. When this was successful, it brought about an immediate change in the fortunes of the west-coast town. The foundations of the first slate-roofed building in Mallaig were dug even before the first railway sleeper was put in place, in itself a sign of confidence that the community was about to change. In 1901 the railway was finally in place, allowing the small port to become the leading one of its kind in the Fort William area some four years later. It was a development that encouraged people from the east coast to move there. Soon, those with surnames like Aitchison, Martin and Johnston arrived from Berwickshire; the Mansons and Macleans from the Moray coast. At the railway station near the harbour, one could hear English spoken along with Gaelic, Scots accents combining with the more musical voices of the people of the Highlands to create a symphony as they worked.

This did not mean that it was not without its problems. Some persist till this day. Robert MacMillan, the port manager, spoke about them when he welcomed me into his office one warm afternoon in May. He spoke about how the harbour was sometimes inaccessible when the wind blew in a northerly direction, how it needed a breakwater to protect it from the wind and whiplash of the waves from time to time. There was also the huge tidal range found within the waters rolling in and out of Mallaig. During spring tide the tidal range could be as much as 5 metres. In neap tide or autumn it might be 3.5 metres. I contrasted all this with what I knew of Lerwick in Shetland. There the tidal range was only 3 feet (around 1 metre) at neap tide and 5 feet (less than 2 metres) at spring tide. These figures clearly made a difference to the running costs involved in maintaining a harbour; a huge disparity between places like Mallaig and Lerwick in the expense of maintaining man's barricades and bulwarks against the full force of the sea. A thought sneaked into my head – one expressed by others in my company. These late Victorians might have been better building their main harbour at nearby Arisaig. That township's pier on Loch nan Ceall is not the most attractive a visitor can find in Scotland, but it is both functional and effective, mainly protected from the storms that often affect boats going in and out of Mallaig. Still, there was little doubt that the people of Mallaig were making the best of their situation. Lorries crammed with farmed salmon were winding their way out of the harbour, heading to Fort William and restaurants and supermarkets beyond. A yachting marina was being built. Visitors looking for a whiff, perhaps, of the magic of Harry Potter were wandering around its quays.

The fierce challenge of the sea was not the only quarrel the people of Mallaig had with the world around them. Sometimes they had difficulties with those from other seafaring communities, such as the men of Loch Fyne to their south, praised by the Scottish poet George Campbell Hay in *Seeker, Reaper*. It is a work in which the mixed cultural inheritance of the west coast of Scotland can be seen, the language of the Norse invaders alongside Gaelic, English and Scots in this fine poem which includes the lines:

> She's a solan, she's a tramper, she's a sea-shaker,
> she's a hawk, she's a hammer, she's a big sea-breaker,
> she's a falcon, she's a kestrel, she's a wide-night-seeker,
> she's a river, she's a render, she's a foam-spray-waker.

Sometimes that tension between communities possessing different outlooks and attitudes may have emerged in other ways. There was, for instance, friction between north and south, Hebridean and mainlander, one coastal port and the next, over the introduction by some fishing populations of developments like the ring-net. The historian and poet from Campbeltown in Scotland's south-west, Angus Martin, told me a little about this one day, writing the following note:

> The ring-net, Kintyre's unique contribution to world fishing technology, was nothing special to begin with: a small seine-net, little different from beach-nets the world over. But the coming of motor power, in the early 20th century, allowed nets to be lengthened and deepened and adapted for deep water. That is when the 'trawl', as it was earlier and confusingly known, became the ring-net. Yet, the modern ring-net was short-lived on the west of Scotland, where it evolved – it lasted no longer than the span of an old man's life.
>
> Before the 'trawl' appeared in the mid-nineteenth century, there had been one dominant method of herring fishing, the drift net, and its adherents abhorred the innovation. The outcry was partly motivated by economic self-interest, but there were also what would now be described as environmental issues involved – the trawl-fishermen were accused of indiscriminate destruction of massive quantities of immature herring and spawn in their small-meshed nets. With hindsight, the warnings were prescient, and were replicated almost everywhere the ring-net was taken, notably on the Donegal coast and in the Minches and Firth of Forth.
>
> 'Trawling' was adopted in Tarbert and Ardrishaig, but the pioneers were at first isolated. The other fishing communities of Loch Fyne and Kintyre opposed the trawlers and created so much trouble that the new method was outlawed from 1851 until 1867, during which period hardship and violence were rife. Trawl crews were harassed ashore by fishery officers and by a special police force recruited in 1860. There were battles on land and sea, between opposing factions of fishermen and between the trawlers and the enforcement agencies, which periodically included gunboat

crews. In 1853, a 28-year-old Tarbert trawl-fisherman, Colin MacKeich, was shot and wounded off Skipness by crew-members of HMS *Porcupine*, and in 1861 a teenage Ardrishaig fisherman, Peter MacDougall, was shot dead at East Otter, on Loch Fyne. An officer and marine from HMS *Jackal* were tried at the High Court, Edinburgh, on charges of culpable homicide, but were acquitted.

Until I began researching my first book, *The Ring-Net Fishermen*, in 1974, I was entirely unaware that my own family had also suffered in the birth pains of ring-netting. In April 1861, my great-great-grandfather, John Martin, and five of his Dalintober crew, including a son, Duncan, were jailed for illegal fishing with a trawl-net. It was a big story at the time. In the local newspaper, the *Argyllshire Herald*, it eclipsed even an American Civil War report ('Troops Attacked by Mob') and the death of seven thousand people ('Dreadful Earthquake at Mendoza'), and the *Glasgow Herald* devoted eight column inches and an editorial to the case. Other Dalintober and neighbouring Campbeltown fishermen were also jailed, but, remarkably, there was no record of these troubled years in oral tradition, not even among elderly relatives of my own who were born a mere generation after the trials and convictions. In Tarbert, by contrast, I collected dozens of stories, told with relish, about the trawl fishermen's dodges to outwit the fishery police and gunboat crews, and the riots ashore, women-folk often to the fore. Why the one community concealed its law-breaking and the other preserved and celebrated it, is unclear to me, and I'll never find answers now.

In my former life as a teacher, the last sentiment was something I often pondered, noting how one community seemed to spawn rebels while another a few miles away bred natural conformists, those who sometimes over-respected and rarely challenged those in authority. Sometimes, though, it is difficult to tell one from the other. It can take the smallest of incidents to turn the most quiet and law-abiding of people into the opposite. (Again, my classroom experience told me this repeatedly.) For a quarter of a century, for instance, what was once the largest herring port in Europe, Wick in Caithness at the north-eastern tip of Scotland, was a calm and peaceful place. (It was said that the smell of herring was so powerful there that, even at some miles distant, your nose could 'pick up Wick'.) In 1859 this sense of tranquillity altered – after tensions within that town of six thousand, which each season more than doubled its population with fishermen, herring girls and those who followed other related trades, spun out of control. It all began when an orange rolled out of the fingers of a young Hebridean fisherman who had arrived, like so many others, in the town.

Purchased as a rare treat, the fruit rolled across the cobblestones, towards the feet of one of the Wick men standing among the crowd. The older man snatched it in his grasp, rotating it in his fingers as he waved it towards the boy, taunting the younger man, perhaps, with a mockery of the sounds of his Gaelic language.

'Give it back,' the Lewis youngster probably said in faltering English. 'It's mine.'

'No.'

'Give it back.'

'No.'

It was all that was needed. A few moments later and the boy, fired by this injustice, was shouting to his friends for help. According to hearsay, the orange was returned to its rightful owner but not before the one who had first lifted it had been assaulted. A Lewisman whose spirits had been affected by a glass or more of spirits pounded his fist into the face of the Wick man who had teased the youngster. Serious trouble ensued; a fight broke out across the cobblestones of Market Square, punches and feet flailing, pushing aside both the citizens and stallholders who had gathered there. It was this that forced the police to take action. They waded in, arresting a few of the men who had been trading fury and fisticuffs in the centre of that major fishing port. Included among them was a Highlander, believed to be a ringleader. He was taken to the jail in the town's Bridge Street, not far away from the church with its tall spire, hoping that this would make the action settle and subside.

It did nothing of the kind. Instead, the opposite took place. The gentlemen of what passed for the most northerly constabulary in Scotland discovered they had a riot going on.* First of all, the Highlanders waved fists; a number of the locals – transformed into special constables for the day – brandished batons. A short time later some of the visitors had even gone down to the local harbour and obtained the mast of their boat for use as a battering ram on the prison door. Soon, however, those who clutched police batons held sway. They swung their weapons back and forth among the crowd, beating the Highlanders back, breaking their skin as though it were orange peel, the blood draining from the open wounds.

The trouble seeped away that Saturday night. The following day remained calm. The kirks were probably full as usual, though there were many in the congregation who had little forgiveness in either their minds or prayers. It was on Monday, however, that a price was paid for the way that – as the harbourmaster suggested – the police had armed 'many of the thoughtless lads of the place' with batons. There had been too many blows exchanged, too many insults aimed at the Gaelic-speaking fishermen from outside Wick and Caithness. The cuts and bruises were not forgotten. The time of reckoning for them came on Monday, with numbers of the Highlanders thronging Bridge Street and threatening vengeance against the parties using the batons on Saturday evening. By 6 p.m., 'upwards of 22 persons' had been 'struck and abused' with 'no available force able in any way to check the violence offered'. As the day trailed away, much of the passion and dislike did too. The Highlanders, having tasted

*There was no properly constituted police force in Wick at that time.

revenge, were 'now willing to enter upon armistices', for all that one or two still wielded weapons – albeit only in the dark flash and hatred of their eyes.

It was probably this that prompted the authorities to send for the army – a task made unnecessary by the fact that with the fishing season being over, many of the fishermen from the Highlands and islands had already headed home. Next Saturday one hundred soldiers arrived by steamer in the town; a response that would normally have meant that trouble had finally come to an end. However, later that night the Wick youths took it as a signal to behave in quite another way. They went once more on the rampage, running through the streets with knives and stabbing any Highlanders they found outside. The military were called out. It took them two hours to 'scatter the rebels'. By this time, eleven people had been stabbed, some badly wounded, though luckily no one died from their wounds.

The Wick harbourmaster made the following observation in his diary next day, Monday, 5 September 1859: 'The Highlanders leaving the town in great numbers, others making ready, the men have no confidence after the usages to which they have been subjected, in terror of their lives for several nights past.' Clearly it took several years for the ill-feeling generated by this incident to seep away. Highlanders who were there would mention the name of the town – *Inbhir Ùige* in Gaelic – with a shudder. The native people of Wick would regard the presence of fishing boats from the islands and their neighbouring counties with distrust. As someone who spent some time in the town, especially in my adolescence, I can say, however, that the inhabitants of Wick have always made me welcome, though some strange attitudes still persist. Never was a place more proud of being monoglot and monocultural than Wick in Caithness – an anachronism in a modern age where most people recognise that human creativity and progress come from a mingling of cultures. It is an odd and mistaken legacy that remains with 'many of the thoughtless lads' of that town and county even today.

Yet more often than not, the sea-going communities have shown solidarity with each other, and not division, especially in times of grief and loss. This can be seen through countless incidents; some, like the fishing disaster of August 1848, even involved the town of Wick. Eighteen boats from the north of Scotland port were lost on the rocks; thirty boats from throughout the north of Scotland. Ninety-seven men drowned, thirty-four of them from the Caithness port. One of the most moving, however, was the Eyemouth disaster, which occurred long after the herring season had ended, on 14 October 1881. By the close of that day, 189 fishermen from the small ports of that part of the east coast, such as Burnmouth, Newhaven, Cove, Fisherrow and St Abbs, had drowned; 129 of them from Eyemouth itself. Each one had been a victim of a terrible windstorm that blew up that day, one that lasted for twenty-five hours. The little vessels were caught within its swells and tumbles, troughs and summits. Remarkably, some men and boats survived the storm when both sail and wood were torn like paper, masts tossed from decks and smashed, ropes, men and rigging swept away by the ocean's weight, the waves folding over and concealing those who had slipped and fallen. In contrast to this, the *Pilgrim*, for instance, was lifted up by gigantic waves which knitted together like a blanket, throwing her first on to rocks and later safely to shore. The *Ariel Gazelle* hobbled into harbour after her crew had spent forty-five terrifying hours at sea, their limbs bruised and broken by the fury of the encounter.

It left a terrifying legacy in its wake, similar to the one that afflicted my hometown of Stornoway after it lost 200 men following the end of the First World War.[*] It lost much of its fishing fleet, the means of sustenance for its

[*]The ship *Iolaire* sank near Stornoway harbour on 1 January 1919 and over 200 returning seamen were drowned.

people. Its population, a little short of 3,000 at the time of the tragedy, dipped and fell. It is only in the last few years that it has stopped declining. As someone informed me when I visited Eyemouth, 'It takes around a century for a community to heal its wounds.' I thought of my own home place of Stornoway and nodded in understanding and agreement.

The trick, it seems to me, is in not forgetting. A monument, in the form of a broken mast, stands in the middle of Eyemouth, a constant reminder of the tragedy for the people. Go into the town's museum and you can see a 5-metre-long tapestry, first displayed in October 1981, one hundred years after the disaster. Designed by the high school's art teacher, Alistair I. Scott, its nine panels, covering the small port and its disaster and the names of the boats that were lost, were stitched together by some of the women of Eyemouth, five of them descendants of those involved. It was a task that fitted the events. Some of their ancestors undoubtedly knitted and sewed, using the skills with which their fingers had been blessed to ward off all thought of the dangers their men must sometimes have experienced at sea. It is an extension of the advice that Shetland women and others must have been given when they stood on shore during the years their fathers, husbands and sons were out hunting the herring and other fish at sea:

'Dunna sit idle; tak dee sock.'

Even today it is art and craft that continues to nurture the communities of the coastline. It can be seen in the tiny sculptures that stand in places like the visitor centre in St Abbs. Some take the form of a group of women looking out to sea with their scarves and skirts flapping on the day of the Eyemouth disaster, trying to catch a glimpse of their men out on their boats. The artistry reminded me of a scene in another of my favourite Neil Gunn novels, *Morning Tide*, where the women, too, stand on a hilltop, and use their cleavages to restore warmth to the feet and hands of the fishermen who had been snatched from death among the waves. The image of women waiting on the shoreline is present, too, in *Get Up and Tie Your Fingers*, a play by Ann Coburn. Part of a production by Customs House Theatre in South Shields, this recently toured much of the east coast of both the south of Scotland and much of England, visiting Berwick, Hartlepool, Grimsby, Hull, Great Yarmouth, Folkestone . . .

And on its route, it spurred people to song and to sewing. There was the lilt and lift of voices in many of these ports, recalling the times when herring girls and fishermen visited them in great numbers, singing both sea shanties and psalms in their harbours. In a linked project, organised by Essen Kaya, the descendants of these women whose fingers were never still knitted once again, creating starfish and seagulls, shells and stones, a shoal of a thousand herring. A giant wave, woven from wool, accompanied the tour, acting as a net for the fish that had been fashioned within that area. There was, too, a full-scale knitted fishing vessel, a *Coat for a Boat*, at the centre, stitching people together through both conversations and centuries, recalling and recreating the days when women's hands moved quickly, following a rhythm that took them out, far beyond the narrow limits of themselves, recalling the common humanity of those who worked together on the nation's piers.

The image shows fish hanging down with tags reading: "Brazilian Coffee", "190,000 Crates of Oranges", "8000 tons of Prunes", "2000 Moskvitch", "Australian Apples".

CHAPTER TEN

'Dweller on the Threshold'

As most decent, well-meaning people might do, Jon Winding-Sørensen objects to being called 'the Norwegian Jeremy Clarkson'. He has none of the swagger of the erstwhile British presenter of *Top Gear*, little of the arrogance of that celebrity figure who loves to court controversy wherever he steers and swerves. What he does, however, share with that preposterous figure is a love of cars. Now approaching his mid-seventies, the Oslo–based engineer and journalist has written about them for a long time, beginning work for *Car* magazine during the pioneering years of popular reporting about the subject in the 1960s, and founding and editing Norway's first independent motoring paper, *BIL*, in 1975. His presence is still to be found on its premises and in its pages, work he combines with writing about music, fashion, design and technology for other papers.

For all the range of his talents, however, he has rarely been asked about herring, a subject I raised with him by phone. It was easy to sense the twinkle in his eye when he was asked about the fish, my question transporting him back to a very different kind of Norway from the nation in which he lives and works today.

It was one in which the country had not yet shaken off the effects of either poverty or the Second World War. In the late 1940s and throughout the 1950s, a great deal of privation still existed within Norway's borders. The government kept a tight control on the economy. There was a lack of foreign currencies and imports were kept down to the minimum. This had an effect on those who wanted to travel the length and breadth of the country's roads. People had to rely on buses, trucks and a few taxis to take them from place to place.

'There were very few cars around,' Jon declared. 'And then those that existed belonged to doctors, lawyers. Professional people.'

But then the possibility of change appeared. Trade with the Eastern European countries had a long tradition in Norway, but during the post-war years the east European currencies – the złoty, koruna, the East German mark – were of no value. This meant that the Norwegians had little alternative but to start real trading, bartering for items they required in their country.

'Goods exported meant goods imported,' Jon mused. 'And not only with the East Europeans, by the way. In 1948, we traded stockfish or dried cod with coffee from Brazil. We got 190,000 crates of oranges from Italy and loads of apples from Australia, all thanks to dried fish. From Canada we had 8,000 tons of prunes in return for 80,000 fox furs.'

One of the first deals involving salt herring was with Bulgaria in 1954, when the Norwegians gained grapes and dried fruit in exchange for their catch. The first agreement that centred on cars was in the autumn of 1953. Herring was not singled out on this occasion but it was part of a consignment of fish sent to Russia in a swap that saw 2,000 cars coming west. Nine hundred were supposed to be Pobedas, ordered by a taxi-owners' cooperative in Norway.

'But they were doomed to disappointment,' Jon declared. 'The first 400 that arrived in the early winter were all Moskvitch. Two hundred and twenty-five were sold the first week. You didn't need any kind of permission to buy these, you see. Import of cars from the West was still restricted and they could be acquired only with special permits. Restrictions like that lasted till the end of 1960.'

Their appearances in the country created an angry reaction among the traditional car importers, seeing their hold on the market broken. Despite the importers' doubts and arguments, the sale of East European cars was freed completely by the Norwegian government in June 1954. The first six months of 1955 saw Moskvitch, Pobeda, Skoda and IFA among the top sellers in Norway, with vehicles from Czechoslovakia, East Germany and the Soviet Union beginning to be seen on the country's roads. A shoal of Polish cars followed when the Warszawa was added to the Norwegian car population in 1956. This was followed by curiosities like the Kaiser and Henry J, products of a Willy's factory in Haifa, Israel. This was yet another country with no currency that had any real value at the exchange, one more that proved a welcome recipient for the strange new Norwegian currency of not the krone but herring, paper and pulp.

This way of making business kept rolling on, becoming more and more complex over time. Jon told me that it became possible to make similar switch-deals with other countries. For instance, Norwegian herring went to Russia, resulting in wheat and silver that was sold on to the Federal Republic of Germany. 'From there we received motor cars back,' Jon said. 'In May 1954, 803 Opel Olympias arrived, but they were sold with stricter control than cars coming from the East. In 1957 we also had 300 cars from Vauxhall and a hundred coming from Rootes in Great Britain. These were in exchange for sardines. But the resistance to this deal was great. The British canning industry complained about the price. The Norwegian motor industry wanted a bigger part of these transactions, as a deal with Volvo for 3,000 cars had been recently signed. But the deal went through, followed by another hundred Hillmans from Rootes. The whole thing became so popular that a Norwegian newspaper proposed, tongue in cheek, that the British motor industry should put up big posters in the car-production centres of Birmingham and Coventry, encouraging people to "Eat more Herring. Support your Local Motor Industry".'

Perhaps it is just as well that the suggestion of this campaign was a shade whimsical. In 1957, 1,500 Renaults were part of a deal for exchange with the French company, but this never happened. Fishing was so bad during that particular spring that Norway could not meet its part of the bargain. After this, trade started to return to normal. More people could buy Western cars until finally all restrictions were removed. By then, most of the East European cars had disappeared through natural causes, unable to withstand the whip of wind and salt in the same way as the herring had done through centuries. Only the Czech car Skoda has survived to the present day, though there was an attempt to import Polski Fiats in the mid-1970s.

'They were imported using currency, and not fish.' Jon twinkles. 'Though this wasn't a great success either.'

Jon's tale is not the only one I have heard involving cars, herring and the countries of the Eastern Bloc. One I was told when I visited Iceland, where a similar barter was done. Another came from the lips of two men I have met with connections in the Ullapool area, folk singer and telecommunications engineer Andy Mitchell, who lived there for many years but is now staying in Skye, and exiled Harrisman Donald John MacDonald, who worked in a variety of capacities at fishing ports around the coast of Britain, from Lerwick in Shetland to Falmouth in Cornwall. Both told of the night an armada of unlicensed Lada cars and vans made its way from Inverness to the west Highland fishing port, snaking through the suburbs of Contin, the broad streets of Garve, the high-life and highlights of Aultguish.

Its final destination? A fleet of East European 'factory ships' that were anchored in Loch Broom, the sea loch that provides sheltered entrance to Ullapool harbour, during much of the late 1970s and '80s. They came in the wake of vessels which, in the late 1960s to early '70s, I used to see in Stornoway, low-draft Scandinavian cargo ships arriving to buy herring,* employing many local men to ice those caught by the east-coast boats, which were then taken to parts of the world like Norway, Africa, the Canary islands and the Faroes. These boats would then sometimes return filled with fruit for the home markets.

Symbols such as the hammer and sickle of the Soviet Union, or the hammer, compass and ring of rye of the DDR, clung on to what seemed to be the flaking layers of rust and grey steel of the factory ships. I watched them, fascinated, as I travelled home for Christmas to Stornoway on the ferry during these years, great, hulking boats with steep bows and sterns that looked as if they had been corroded by centuries of salt and sleet, bashed, too, by the very hammers they sported. As grim and mysterious as the letters of the Cyrillic alphabet that were sometimes emblazoned on their sides, they somehow rivalled the mountains that shadowed the

---

*And sometimes sheep's heads, which they used to sugar and salt and send to the Faroe Islands, a phenomenon I recall from my teenage years.

small port, dominating the houses that lined the harbour front – all freshly painted and neat as Thomas Telford had planned them to be. In some ways, with these boats arriving there, it seemed history had travelled in a circle. Further up the coast in Sutherland, there was Rispond on Loch Eriboll, where reputedly the first boats taking herring from Scotland to both St Petersburg and Imperial Russia had arrived; holiday home, too, at one time to the Rootes family of motor-vehicle fame, whom Jon Winding-Sørensen had mentioned in his conversation.

There even used to be physical evidence of trade with this part of the world perched on kitchen dressers in many homes around the edge of Scotland. This took the form of little painted black bowls, made from birch decorated with red, gold and silver, called variously Baltic Bowls, Riga Cups or – most accurately of all, in terms of their geographical location – Skovy Kappes in Shetland. They were made in the Upper Volga region and brought back in the triangle of trade involving both timber and salt fish that existed between Scotland and that part of the world in the latter part of the nineteenth century. Since the Russian Revolution, however, the people from that part of the world had rarely been seen, and the long decades of absence made the new visitors more enigmatic and strange than ever. Sometimes I would try to peer through the sides of these vessels, attempting to puzzle out the secrets hidden on board. I was aware that there were times when there were around 9,000 inhabitants – Russians, East Germans, Bulgarians, Romanians, even sometimes Egyptians and those from West African states – concealed within their depths, far more than the 1,000 or so souls who lived in Ullapool. Occasionally I would catch a glimpse of them, an orange boiler suit, a steel helmet, and imagine a member of the Stasi, the KGB, the Romanian Securitate ... A bleak midwinter's day in Ullapool and even the wind seems to whip in from somewhere in the vicinity of Vladivostok.

It was to these vessels that the untaxed, unlicensed vehicles were being taken, heading for the broad thoroughfares of Murmansk, the backstreets of Bucharest. En route they were hoisted on to one of the Ullapool fishing boats and ferried out to vessels bearing names like *Olusha* or *Rybak Lanvir Artika*, their presence being announced not with the usual greeting of 'We bring you herring' or – more usually – 'We bring you mackerel', but instead, the even more odd announcement: 'We bring you cars.'

A man with long experience of the sea, having been a former sailor, an agent for a fishing company and employed by a company supplying fuel to boats, Donald John MacDonald also has a remarkable memory. Speaking to me by phone, he reeled out an account of the ships from the former Warsaw Pact countries and elsewhere that had creaked and groaned in the waters of Loch Broom during these years. In 1977 the first five boats arrived – three from Bulgaria, two from Russia. The following year saw the arrival of hundreds, largely old vessels unfit for stormy waters. It was, perhaps, for this reason that they arrived in Ullapool. Its sheltered waters offered more secure moorings than, say, Lerwick, where the seas were more stormy. Three Eastern European vessels sank in its waters during what are often referred to as the Klondike years, that word a reference to the heady days of the gold rush to the Yukon in north-west Canada.* As someone who had experience of both ports, as well as Falmouth in Cornwall, Bridlington near Hull and the Isle of Man, Donald John is well placed to make comparisons with them all.

'I was the agent for ten ships, getting mackerel and herring for these vessels. There were 2,000 tons of mackerel a day, 1,200 crans in the old measurement. Herring, too, when it could be obtained. These would be mainly caught on the North Atlantic

---

*An extraordinarily popular term in Scotland, where it has also come to refer to the early years of the oil boom in the north.

shelf during these years, fishing for herring in the Minch being banned in 1978.* And all of it would be gathered on board just the same way as it was in Harris when it arrived on Saturday night. Roused. That means it was left ungutted and sprinkled with salt.' He laughs. 'In Harris, we did that for religious reasons. Instead of breaking the Sabbath. I think that was the last thing on their minds.' He pauses for a moment, as if recalling his astonishment of what had happened at the time. 'They were huge crews. Around 230 of them on each boat. Both men and women.'

I nodded, recalling the sight of the women as we wandered around Ullapool, stranded there as a result of bad weather. They did not have the thick eyebrows and wide mouth, the boots, cigar, fur collar and greatcoat of their countrywoman, Madame Wolkova. Instead, both their faces and steep orange hairstyles were held in place by the heavy use of make-up and hairspray, the aroma of cheap perfume also keeping the stench of fish at bay. The men, too, had their own role. Going into the village shops, they would scout out bargains. Sometimes they would head to the rubbish dumps in places like Lerwick to see if any fridges, washing machines, VCRs or freezers had been left. Like the Ladas, they would be taken back to the ships.

'By the time they reached home, the engineers would get to work on them and make sure they were all hunky dory again,' said Andy Mitchell, smiling.

There is an American novel, *Polar Star* by Martin Cruz Smith, which attempts to portray life on an East European factory ship. For all that his vessel is on the Bering Straits between Alaska and Vladivostok, one imagines that life on

*There were occasional moments when it was allowed. On 9 August 1981, for instance, the *Herald* reported that about half a dozen deep-sea boats from the north-east sold 40 tonnes of herring to one of the Russian factory ships in Loch Broom.

some of these boats creaking, groaning and rusting outside Ullapool must have been similar. He describes it as 'the worst work for the worst pay. The crews are men on the run from their wives, from child support, maybe even manslaughter. No one cares because we need crews' on these kinds of vessels. Often covered with fish blood, the crews would move around the decks of the ships surrounded by posters urging them into working harder for the benefit of the state.

There were men on board who encouraged them not to look at these notices with the appropriate levels of irony but at least to show evidence of taking them seriously. These gentlemen were the emissaries of the Communist Party, members of the security service of the countries of the Eastern Bloc. They were the human, earthly equivalent of the signs I often used to see in the kitchens of my childhood village, which referred to 'the unseen guest at every meal, the silent listener to every conversation'. Donald John recalled to me the brooding presence of the commissar every time he talked to a member of the crew, taking in every word that passed between them. After Communism fell, he asked a crewman what had become of this figure who had loomed over their meetings for so long.

'Once he just used to sit and listen. Nowadays, he just sits and drinks,' the man answered.

Andy underlined some of the more unnerving aspects of the Communist system by noting how, out of the 130 members of the crew of a Romanian fishing boat, forty were members of the Securitate, Nicolae Ceauşescu's notorious state security service. This is unlikely to include the number of informants that were among the remainder. (Roughly 1 in 30 of the population were believed to be acting in that role.) Despite the poverty of the country, an array of 'bugging devices' was also among the more fashionable accessories of Ceauşescu's rule, no doubt tucked at irregular intervals along the deck or within fish tanks.

It may be the case that, as has been suggested to me, these vessels doubled up as prison ships for those who were either criminals or implacably opposed to the government. (The central figure of Martin Cruz Smith's novel fits into this category – Arkady Renko, a detective in disgrace and on a factory ship after questioning the corruption of the Soviet state.) It could be the case, too, that the vessels also acted as spy ships. There is, after all, a great deal of precedent for this. During the First World War, German maps of Shetland, for instance, were far more detailed and accurate than their Royal Navy equivalents, courtesy of the herring fishermen from German ports who had been going there for years.[*] It is difficult, though, to determine what kind of important information spying on places like Peel, Lerwick or Ullapool in the early 1980s would have gained anyone. Perhaps there was a stray letter from the Department of Agriculture and Fisheries urging those involved in the trade to: 'Increase Production in the Agro-Industrial Complex! Strive for a Decisive Upswing in the Supply of Fish Protein.'

For all the presence of some of the nastier aspects of the countries of the Warsaw Pact, the visitors also displayed an extraordinary fascination for both the good and bad sides of Western capitalism. Andy told me how the renowned Scots film-maker Bill Forsyth based the character of Victor in the film *Local Hero* on a ship's captain he had seen in the Ceilidh Place Hotel in Ullapool wheeling and dealing, contriving – in true capitalist style – to funnel a little additional cash into his pocket. This seaman became transformed into an unlikely

---

[*]There is a lovely story attached to this. When a German ship was captured near Lerwick in the First World War, a prisoner was greeted by a cry of 'Hello, Ralf!' from one of the Shetlanders gathered on the pier. Moments later, the Shetlander was arrested and interrogated about how he'd come to know the man. It turned out that Ralf had often visited Shetland before the conflict and the two men had become great friends.

country-and-western star, crooning 'Lonesome for a Lone Star Like Me' before an audience of locals in the film.

Some of the others showed this fascination in different ways. Stepping into the newsagent in Ullapool, one was often aware of a number of the men from the factory ship clustering around the pornographic magazines, often – or so I was told – bringing them back home for use as currency. For this reason, too, Western video players were popular and often taken home on the ships with the men. (Those sold in Eastern Europe used tapes of different size from those stocked on the shelves of the countries of the West. It was a way of ensuring that any wicked combination of Clint Eastwood, Scooby Doo and Linda Lovelace would not undermine the existence of governments there.) In Falmouth in Cornwall, there were apparently plans to close the local Marks and Spencer until those from Eastern European ships began to visit the town. The financial acumen of these visitors from behind the Iron Curtain was also seen in their fascination for catalogues. They would spend hours flicking through the pages of Freemans or Littlewoods, trying to add a little colour to their lives, perhaps taking the catalogues home as souvenirs for their wives.

Then there were those whose time of exile was marked by loneliness. Sometimes a few might go to the Thule Bar in, say, Lerwick and nurse a half-pint of beer, adding little 'top-ups' from small bottles in their inside pockets. Others – particularly a group of Nigerians stranded in Ullapool for around a year – might volunteer to help those who were more helpless in the community, adding a daub of paint there, mowing a lawn here. There was one Russian individual who used to spend much of his day in a flat occupied by some young men in Lerwick, watching hour upon hour of daytime TV. Perhaps *Neighbours* inspired him and his fellow East Europeans, for, as Andy Mitchell testified, there came a time when 'neighbours became good friends'. With the beginnings of perestroika, he was sometimes employed by Decca to provide new radar and electronic systems for some of the ships anchored outside Ullapool. There would be smiles and words exchanged, a few over-strength beers proffered and shared.

Working in Edinburgh, Iain MacSween, the Chief Executive of the Scottish Fishermen's Organisation, also noticed the change brought about by perestroika. For years, his meetings with his Russian counterparts had always taken place in Moscow, the fishermen making their way from the nation's vast coastline to its capital. In 1997, however, this altered. For the first time he travelled to Murmansk, a city that for much of the previous decades – since men like my Skye grandfather had sailed there in Arctic convoys during the Second World War – had been blocked to Westerners. After he spent some time gathering in the sights – the statue of Lenin, looking more forlorn than ever; the huge figure of the Alyosha, the Russian soldier, staring out over the port he and his kind defended – he sat down and spent some time discussing the same issues as had been mentioned when they were in the shadow of the Kremlin: the quota set for mackerel; the shortage of herring in parts of the North Atlantic.

In the last years of the Communist regime, matters became even worse for those on board these ships. The system was crumbling; old certainties fading away. It is likely, for instance, that wages were no longer being paid, supplies no longer delivered. A friend of mine in Lerwick recalled some of the consequences of this – how he caught one of the men from the factory ship trying to steal a car in the town, his eyes narrowing in a threat when he was noticed. I was aware, too, of signs appearing in the Ullapool shops when I travelled through to Stornoway. Written in Cyrillic, I thought for some time that it was a wonderful message of warm welcome to the visitors. I discovered some time later that, in fact, it was just like the notices shopkeepers sometimes place on their windows when they are invaded by hordes of children, forbidding entry to more than two at a time.

It was a period, too, when men like Allan Paterson, working in the Ullapool harbourmaster's office, began to notice more and more something of which he had always been dimly aware – that the Soviet Union was 'not just one big happy family', that there were cracks and divisions within it, some almost impossible to heal. It was mainly Latvians and Lithuanians who revealed this to him: an odd remark let slip from mouth or tongue; a grimace; an averting of the eyes. Now the commissar was no longer a 'silent guest at every conversation', those from the Baltic States were divulging what had hitherto been held secret. The fishermen from Latvia, Lithuania and Estonia did not always get on with those who came from within the Russian borders.

There were reasons for this. Some went back to the times when Soviet troops invaded the Baltic States, in June 1940 and also, more especially, later, in 1944 – a state of occupation that lasted till the early 1990s. Disliking even the prospect of rule from Moscow, many Estonians, for example, fled the conflict and the approach of the Red Army. They did this mainly by boat, using German transportation and hospital ships from different ports of Estonia. People from southern Estonia were evacuated to Latvia first and from there – from Liepāja and other ports – by ship to Germany. Those from the north-western part of Estonia and the islands of Saaremaa and Hiiumaa mostly left by small boats, such as fishing vessels, for Sweden.

In short, these escapes left very few boats on the Estonian coastline. The larger ones never returned to the country, staying mainly in the United Kingdom where they continued to work. (During wartime they became part of the British transport system. Later, crewed largely by Estonians, they sailed under the flag of Panama, unable to journey home.) Their numbers were decreased even further by the actions of the Communist government. The fishermen were forced to give their boats away, as they had now become common or state property, just like their farms. The ones that were not suitable for this purpose were destroyed.

This was a process repeated throughout the Baltic States. On the Livonian coast, part of Latvia, the boats were taken from the fishermen and burned or destroyed in other ways. Areas were restricted. Men were not allowed to fish near the coastline of Hiiumaa, where the Soviets had an airbase. Parts of the sea outside Saaremaa were watched zealously by silent commissars. Hours in which boats were permitted to catch the Baltic herring – the national fish of Estonia – were limited and restricted. Even the shoreline was affected. The Soviet soldiers ploughed the sand at various times of the day, allowing them to see if anyone had left footprints on its surface, plotting or even attempting to escape. They also patrolled the shoreline every day and night, seeking to prevent people escaping to the West, those driven to the continent's edge by their fear of Siberia and the gulag.

But there were some who slipped away and decided to go further. After they escaped from Estonia in a leaking boat that took them to Sweden, members of the family of Maaja Keays decided they would be better off outside Europe. This was the result of how insecure they felt in Malmö, where her parents were employed in a textile factory. For all that they were content with life in their new surroundings, there were a number of anxieties, some caused by the politics of the time and particularly the actions of the Swedish government, which was trying to fend off the Soviets at the border.

'When the Swedish government caved in to demands from the Soviets to send back to the Soviet Union Estonians who they considered "war criminals", there was general fear in the Estonian community. I don't think many individuals were deported but it was unsettling for the Estonian migrants in Sweden. Another reason my parents wanted to leave Sweden was that they didn't feel at home there. My parents felt that they would always be immigrants there and not fully accepted by the Swedish community.'

It was Argentina to which they first considered going. There were opportunities there, especially for those from northern Europe. Maaja's mother, Hiljaa, even began to learn Spanish in preparation for the move, especially attractive because of the way her father, Armand, was a trained butcher, a necessary trade in a country where beef was of prime importance. One morning, however, he went to examine the vessel that was supposed to take them to South America. He returned home shaking his head. By that afternoon, his plans had altered. He arrived back at their house with the idea that they should travel on the *Astrid*, a fishing smack that was going to be heading in the direction of Newfoundland, at that time not only a separate island but a separate country from the Canadian mainland to which it is nowadays linked. There would be twenty-nine people crammed on board that small vessel; seven of them, including Maaja, were young children. All of them paid a highly unusual fare.

'My mother told me that everyone, even the children, had shares in the *Astrid*. She had to borrow some money from her boss in Sweden to buy our share of the boat. It took her a long time to pay it back. She did after we settled in Toronto by sending cans of coffee from Canada to Malmö. This seems strange now, but I never asked her why that method of payment was agreed upon.'

She recalled too the moment they left Gothenburg. While her parents took in the quayside, the greyness of the day with the gulls squabbling over her head, the little girl's recollections were somewhat different.

'I remember putting my hand into a can of oil on the deck and trying to hide that from my mother. As the boat started to leave the dock, I remember feeling afraid even though I had been having fun with the other children on board.'

Maaja had good reason to feel anxious. The *Astrid* was in fact embarking on a momentous journey on that day in July 1948. Their voyage across the Atlantic would have been momentous at any time of year. However, the time of year when they were sailing is also a period when the seas of the North Atlantic are at their most fierce and unpredictable, the waters swirling around a vessel that was built for the – relatively – more sheltered waters of the Baltic Sea. Coupled with this, the captain they had hired for the voyage, Herman Vilnu, was more used to large-scale, ocean-going cargo vessels than skippering a tiny fishing boat across the open waters of the North Atlantic. All of that was hidden from Maaja, her recollections being those of a child.

'Most of my memories of the journey are of being below deck. I shared a bunk with my mother. My father had to sleep on the deck under a lifeboat. There was not enough room for him below deck. Later my parents spoke about the waves being as big as high-rise buildings. I don't remember being very seasick. I do recall people saying that Captain Vilnu's wife suffered terribly from seasickness. I don't remember the meals, only the rusty drinking water. I don't know what we did to occupy ourselves and I don't remember playing with the other children on deck or below during the actual voyage. I do remember singing some of my Estonian songs to one of the other passengers to pass the time. I don't think anyone knew what the journey would be like. My mother bought herself a two-piece bathing suit before our departure and envisioned she would be sunbathing on the deck – possibly the most useless article in our suitcase.'

There is one other aspect of the voyage that Maaja fails to remember – how the boat arrived, with its engine block cracked,* in Stornaway on July 12. Drawn by curiosity to this intrusion from the wartime politics of Europe, the locals congregated around the small vessel, making its people welcome in their town. Some offered baths and changes of clothing. They were fed with herring dipped in Oatmeal and fried in the Scottish style. A concert was arranged, complete with Gaelic song and bagpipes. The mother of Stornoway's former Lord Provost and Council Convener Sandy Matheson cashed in her entire chocolate ration that day, giving it to the children on board. ('Much to my disappointment,' Sandy confessed. 'I thought she was giving it all to me.') A cash collection from some of the town's businessmen was arranged. And when the time came for the *Astrid* to leave on the morning of July 16, as my Ullapool informant Donald John MacDonald, who witnessed it, informed me, the boat was surrounded by the town's fishing fleet, accompanying the boat towards the Butt of Lewis and the open sea, in the direction of Newfoundland.

It was a journey which, after the small vessel arrived in that harbour in Newfoundland, the mayor of St John's compared to one undertaken by those herring fishers of a much earlier time, the Vikings. For once, the comparison was both fitting and apt.

---

*In fact, its engine black had been cracked since the *Astrid* left Sweden. It was the task of Mr Paesüld, believed to be a marine engineer, to keep it going. This problem was also cited as one reason why they decided on the short, sharp and risky dash across the North Atlantic.

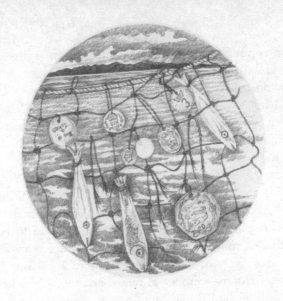

CHAPTER ELEVEN

'Spirit in the Sky'

'My Judaism is linked to the kitchen,' Ida Schuster Davis told me when I called her at home in early 2015.

The veteran Scottish actress went on to prove the truth of her statement, going on to talk of the number of ways she prepared herring. When her parents had arrived in Glasgow from Vilnius in Lithuania, they had taken with them their relish of that fish, part and portion of their lives in a city once described by Napoleon as 'the Jerusalem of the North'. At one time, in the census undertaken by the Russian Empire in 1897, they had made up the greatest percentage of inhabitants of that city – 61,847 or 40 per cent out of 154,500 – the others being Poles, Russians and a smattering of other groups, including the native Lithuanians. In the twentieth century, culminating in the Holocaust, they had seen their numbers being whittled away, their people destroyed by the combined threat of poverty, privation and pogrom that had stalked them on the continent of Europe.

Yet something survived of that way of life. It was a legacy I had been aware of even before I spoke to Ida on that day. Its spirit was present in the stories of a number of the Nobel Laureate winners I had encountered in my youth. There were the tales of Isaac Bashevis Singer, whose father was a Hassidic rabbi in – among other places – a poor, Yiddish-speaking area of Warsaw. His books, set in both Poland and New York, drew me into a world that was far away from my Hebridean home; the only connections seemed to be the way that so much was inspired by the Old Testament, the book that was the favoured reading of so many Lewis Presbyterians; the number of references, too, to the herring that so often boiled and bubbled on our stove. Then, later on, there was the work of Saul Bellow. Such was his obsession with the fish that the first food his son Greg had been fed with after he had been weaned was pickled herring. (Perhaps, free of bones, the initial meal some of my contemporaries at home had tasted was the boiled variety – but I somehow doubted even this.) I was reminded of this connection a few years ago when I stepped into the home of my fellow villager and fellow writer Alasdair Campbell.* On his kitchen wall there was a painting from the Russian-Jewish artist, Marc Chagall. Within it, there was a fish motif, one with a set of wings – placed there 'out of respect' for his father who was employed by a herring merchant in Vitebsk in present-day Belarus. His childhood, he said, 'smelled of smoked herring', something that can also be said of Alasdair's and my own.

*No relation of Tony Blair's former adviser, though that particular Alastair Campbell also probably had herring in his background. His ancestors, like some of mine, came from the inner Hebridean isle of Tiree.

Yet there seemed to be – in a number of ways – a greater variety and vitality in the culinary inheritance that Ida gained from her parents and from the fish that lay at its centre, the herring. Not for her just the kipper, the boiled or salted fish, the one dipped in oatmeal and fried. Instead, she performed a variety of operations on it that would have seemed outlandish to the average Hebridean – chopping it, adding vinegar and brown sugar to the mixture before flaking it and adding a sprinkling of crushed chocolate biscuits to its surface. When I expressed doubts about this recipe, there was a tinkle of laughter.

'But it's delicious,' she assured me.

Then there were the other methods she espoused: adding grated hard-boiled eggs, vinegar and sugar to the chopped herring. The sheer range of dressings she envisaged for herring reminded me a little of a statement I had read by Chaim Bermant, the late Scottish Jewish writer. His childhood must have been not unlike that of another famous Scottish Jew, Ivor Cutler. He declared: 'On Sunday, one had a pickled herring, on Monday soused herring, on Wednesday baked herring, on Thursday herring fried in oatmeal and on Friday herring with sour cream.'

There were even differences between the ways people prepared their chopped herring. There was the Litvak method of preparing the fish. This refers to people who came from the easternmost areas of the Pale of Settlement – the parts of tsarist Russia where Jews were allowed to live. There was also the fish preparation method used by the Galitzianer Jews. They lived in Galicia, then part of the Austrian Empire, now divided between Poland and the Ukraine. Galitzianers, for instance, often made their famous herring salad with tart green apple, preferring a sour taste like the Poles – a nation whose members often drain the pickled herring they obtain in the shops in Great Britain, finding it too sweet for their tastes. Litvaks, according to legend, add only chopped hard-boiled eggs to their herring salad. Other recipes use breadcrumbs, vegetable oil, onion, even gingersnaps.

The Jewish cookery writer Claudia Roden told me how this came to be. 'In Eastern Europe herring was the cheapest fish,' she stated. 'It arrived pre-salted in barrels from Norway, Holland, England and Scotland. Jews were prominent in the herring trade, importing and transporting the herring by rail to Germany, Poland and Russia and selling it in stores and from pushcarts. This poor man's food – turned these days into a rich man's delicacy – was an all-important part of the diet of the Jews. In the 1920s the Polish-French gastronome Edouard de Pomiane wrote that the Jews of Poland ate a herring a day.'

The fish came in a variety of forms, but two were most important. There was *matje* herring, consumed in areas near the quayside of Europe. There was also *schmaltz* herring, barrel-stored, fatty fish which is cured by being covered with coarse salt and left with a weight on top for up to four days. Before it can be used, this needs to be soaked for up to two days in a few changes of cold water to remove the salt. This was a valuable source of protein, especially because, as Ida explained to me, 'where meat has to be kosher, fish can be easily obtained'. This was especially the case in areas where there are few of the Jewish faith, as in Shetland where Ethel G. Hofman, author of *Mackerel At Midnight*, spent her childhood. She tells of her mother, faithful to her Jewish heritage, obtaining meat from a kosher butcher in Glasgow. By the time this came on the steamer from Aberdeen, it was 'crawling with maggots', so much so that she had a dramatic reaction to its arrival. '"My God, the meat's being eaten alive,"' she screamed, tossing chops, roast and flanken into the trash can.'

It was an encounter that forced her to make a decision. 'There's no question. My children must have meat whether it is kosher or not,' she concluded. For all this compromise, she continued to keep to the dietary laws that were explained to me in her home by Ida Schuster Davis. She did not serve pork, provide milk and meat together on the table, or boil meat in milk. She also avoided all kinds of shellfish – or, as Ida put it, fish without a backbone, such as lobster, prawns or shellfish.* Though she does not mention this, there is little doubt that she would not have eaten rabbits, pigeons or other 'lower order' animals, too.

Yet herring was permissible – and there was a great deal of it in Shetland at that time. For Ethel's family in the Protestant environs of Lerwick, Shetland, it would have been commercial suicide for them to treat Saturday as a day of rest. However, they still kept the Shabbat, preparing the food on a Friday night for the following day. It was, in her words, 'a much anticipated feast' in which the herring had pride of place. Along with gefilte fish, or deboned whitefish balls, garnished with carrot, there were bowls of pickled herring 'draped with bay leaves and dill'. Chopped herring, mixed with hard-boiled eggs, vinegar, onions and brown bread, was also on display. It was served in this way because it avoided *borer*, the picking of bones out of fish, which is not allowed under the Shulchan Aruch, one of the sources of Jewish law. (This has more than a passing resemblance to some of the rules that applied within my Presbyterian home where I grew up, though, of course, applied largely to the Sunday.) It also was the practice on Jewish holy days such as Yom Kippur, the day of repentance and fasting as atonement for the sins that had accumulated over the previous year. Again no work – like cooking – would be done. Bagels, cured and smoked fish, and pickled herring were ideal for serving on these occasions.

*Other societies share similar attitudes to certain shellfish, most notably limpets. It is a sign of the complete degradation of the Highlands after the Clearances there that some of the central characters in Neil Gunn's *The Silver Darlings* are shown to have no choice but to eat limpets.

Throughout the past century, some of the pickling of 'kosher herring' was done on the quaysides of these islands. James MacNab, originally from Fraserburgh but now living in Lerwick, recalled seeing it done around fifty years ago in Great Yarmouth. A rabbi of a kind known as a *mashgiach*, learned in Jewish dietary law, would come to the yard where they were working. In order for the herring to become kosher, he would say a few words in Hebrew over the barrel, laying a few scraps of black material on its surface to seal the fish, and tell Jewish clients that the fish was fit for eating. When this was done, he would walk away, unaware that one reason the marinated herring possessed the desirable light shade was that it had been treated with peroxide, a treatment now banned.

Nowadays, establishments involved in the creation of pickled herring – guaranteed peroxide-free – can be found far from the quayside. One, the makers of Silver Tide, can even be found on the edge of Grantown-on-Spey, a small Highland town where all sight of the sea is hidden by the Grampian mountains or the woodland that surrounds its streets. Within a small, anonymous building on its industrial estate, a wonderful alchemy takes place as skinless fillets of herring are transformed into a range of marinated herring – from rollmop to dill, mustard to tomato, garlic and herb to sherry – to be sold not only under its own label but also on the shelves of Marks and Spencer and Tesco. At regular intervals, its premises too are inspected by a visiting rabbi, who remains for three days, checking the pipework and containers, blessing every component that plays a part in the work, ensuring that the herring never comes into contact with shellfish and tying off the barrels with unbreakable seals.

It was Liverpool-raised Jackie Flusk who explained to me the way things were done. She pointed out the large vats where acetic acid first cooks the fish, softening the bones. It is a process that takes thirty days. The herring are sometimes stirred by rolling the barrel.

'The more you handle them, the softer they are,' Jackie declared.

It was after that she took me through their premises which used to be called Daniel's Sweet Herring before their fish were labelled and sold under the name Silver Tide. (The name 'Silver Darlings' was already used elsewhere. I must admit I liked this linking between two of Gunn's major novels, *The Silver Darlings* and *Morning Tide*.) As she did so, I heard about her life – how she had moved north from her native city, working at the fishing harbours in Scotland's north-east. Her daughter Anne – whom I also met when I was there – was a buoyant, cheerful individual who had followed her mother into the trade. She spoke too about the safety practices, the mesh of measures that were put in place to keep bad practice and bad hygiene away. I nodded, experiencing a slight sense of déjà vu as they were explained to me. This intensified the moment I stepped into Wellington boots, slipped on a hairnet, and put on an apron and a set of overalls. I felt then as if I had waltzed back in time. Way back in my student days, I had worked at Rolf Olsen, a Norwegian-owned factory that once existed in Stornoway harbour. My employment there was as a *Mackerel Transfer Technician*. This largely consisted of shifting the contents of large blue vats filled with mackerel, grading them quickly for size, and placing them on racks within a giant freezer. When I walked in there, I was subject to an ethereal metamorphosis. In the cold, my frozen apron would lift upwards like some form of celestial nightshift. A halo would be formed by my breath and settle above my hairnet. My boots would form invisible wings in my rush to escape the cold quarters in which the fish were stored.

It was worse when there was herring. It was there I learned to work out if a fish was fresh or on the verge of rotting. A touch was all that was required to determine whether it was firm or soft, greasy or dry. Along with men like Alex Crichton and Tom Maciver, under the eye of the manager, Alice Macleod, we came together to empty the vat as soon as possible, shifting all the herring as quickly as we could, the only way to undertake the task. There was one time, however, when we were shifting the catch from the large container on which it was held upon the fishing boat, and my hand became trapped between the machine hoisting it and the hard blue plastic in which it was stored. I yelled out in agony. My legs buckled and swam below me. I noticed Alex and Tom looking up in alarm in my direction. Seconds later, they had grappled with the machine, freeing my wrist and forearm from its grasp.

For all that my arm was swollen for some time afterwards, that moment was not my abiding memory of working there. There was Tom, with his wonderfully expressive face. A talented actor, he had the ability to tell a joke with a turn of his mouth, a lift of his eyebrow. Alex, too, was, in his own taciturn way, a gifted storyteller. He told me a tale about my uncle, who was at that time a missionary in the Church of Scotland, taking a bag of mothballs to the sermon with him one time, and presenting one to a fellow churchgoer who never brought his own sweets – an essential accompaniment at that time for any Highlander attending a church service. At this time, a few months after both my brother and I had lost our sole remaining parent, my father, their humour and storytelling did much to embolden me, strengthening me for the next session of university life.

It seemed to me that there were a number of aspects that distinguished this kind of working life now from the time around thirty years ago when I had been employed in that factory on the quay. The places in which people were employed are now much safer and hygienic than their equivalents some time ago. (No fly cigarettes within the walls. No draughts whistling around the building. No trudging in the same set of boots both outside and in.)

A change had clearly occurred on these islands over the last thirty years. It had become a rarer event to hear the country's native languages – whether Gaelic, English, Scots or even Manx – on the lips of those who worked in the fish industry. Instead, it was – with the exception of people like Jackie and Anne – largely people from Eastern Europe who were employed, whether this was young men like Oleg in Peel, Isle of Man, or those who speared herring with wooden spikes in places like Grantown-on-Spey. I asked one of the management in Grantown why this was the case. He shrugged his shoulders.

'I don't know. It's not as if we haven't tried.'

It is tempting to suggest that it is the English dislike of fish that has seeped – both north and west of its border – into Scotland and the Isle of Man. There are exceptions, of course, to this. The perennial British meal of fish and chips is one; rollmop herring another. It should be noted that neither is an innovation that originated in this soil. Fried fish are, in fact, the creation of Sephardic Jews from Portugal – as opposed to those of the Ashkenazi variety from northern Europe. In 1860, on the streets of the East End of London, a 13-year-old Jewish boy called Joseph Malin had the bright idea of combining fried fish with chips. The very term 'rollmop' comes from German, from *rollen*, to roll, and *Mops*, a pug dog. In Kate Colquhoun's book, *Taste*, she suggests a number of reasons why this is so. Among them is the condition of the fish sold in – especially inland – areas of England, often rotten and badly preserved. Another is the resentment that many English people felt at being forced to eat this food at both times of Lent and during other occasions in the Catholic religious calendar. This can even be seen in Shakespeare's *King Lear*. When Kent is asked by Lear, 'What dost thou profess?', he answers: 'I do profess to be no less than I seem; to serve him truly that will put me in trust: to love him that is honest; to converse with him that is wise, and says little; to fear judgment; to fight when I cannot choose; and to eat no fish.'

The mere eating of fish – and especially of herring, a fish that turned rotten sooner than most – was regarded as being a sign of a Catholic. Its dietary restrictions and the poor quality of the fish that were sold at that time in many inland areas of England were among the reasons people spurned the Catholic faith around the time of Shakespeare. This was, however, not a feature of religious life in Scotland, which, with its long jagged coastline, allowed the sea to make inroads into its land.

On the contrary, one could argue that fish – and most especially the herring – was central to Calvinism and other similar branches of Protestantism, especially the plain, unvarnished form that existed not only in the Netherlands but also on the coast of Scotland and sometimes further south on the eastern edge of England. At one time this was the faith of fishermen, one that distinguished them, say, from the Catholic merchant class that sold and traded in fish and that, in at least the early days of Dutch independence, owed its loyalty to the Spanish monarchy. One can see its legacy everywhere – from the meeting house in Lerwick which once served as a house of worship for Dutch fishermen working in that area, to the many churches, now sometimes converted to other purposes, found on the east coast of England. It appears, albeit in another form, in the Norwegian community portrayed in Isak Dinesen's short story 'Babette's Feast', and later, in the film based on the tale – a favourite of mine – where the Lutheran community has been shifted to northern Jutland. Its diet of fish and distrust of anything that even resembled comfort, never mind luxury, possessed great similarities to the community with which I grew up.

This bare, stark form of the Protestant faith has echoes even today, especially in the Netherlands. Its influence can be found in the Presbyterian Party that still goes campaigning in Urk, one of the fishing ports I visited in the Netherlands. The men employed on the modern-day Dutch fishing boats moored up in North Shields who refuse to take their vessels out of harbour on the Sabbath are the direct descendants of those fishermen from the Netherlands who went on strike in the eighteenth century in protest against how their government imposed a new, faster way of singing psalms in their domain. Their struggle has been portrayed by a modern Dutch novelist, Maarten 't Hart, in his novel *Het Psalmenproer.*

One can still hear or see signs of that Calvinist inheritance, even where one would least expect it. In the national fishing museum in Grimsby, one of its employees spoke wistfully of the difference between men from that port and those from the north-east coast of Scotland, traditionally one of Scotland's Bible Belts. 'In some ways, they were better prepared for a life at sea than we were,' he declared. 'They had their faith to support them. Put limits on their behaviour which our boys didn't have.' In his wonderfully eccentric museum in Great Yarmouth, the Potteries, Ernie Childs told me in 2014 of the Gaelic herring girls and their meetings near the harbour, their voices reeling, blending with gulls, as they rang out their accompanied psalms. 'It was both spooky and beautiful,' he declared. 'I've never heard anything like it again.' Further down the coast in Lowestoft, it was these same girls who inspired the English composer, Benjamin Britten, into composing a number of his pieces. Apparently he used to go down to the quayside with his nurse when he was young, the mixture of both sacred and secular songs that spilled from their lips when they were working coming to his mind when he created works like *A Charm of Lullabies*, and most especially 'Highland Balou'. The foreshore which this music haunted is largely lost now. What was not destroyed by the Great Storm of 1953, or the proximity of these towns to German bombers during the Second World War, has been laid waste by the oil and gas industry, which destroyed much of the gutting sheds and herring-girl quarters to be found near its storefront. One Klondike giving way to another.

Yet for all the rows of gambling machines, the talents of Jim Davidson and Roy Chubby Brown who were about to appear at Great Yarmouth's theatre when I was there recently, there was a time when faith was endemic to these places. A succession of evangelical reawakenings flourished among the fisherfolk of these towns. The last of these occurred in East Anglia in 1921, where it was the preaching of Rev. A. Douglas Brown that moved and caused people to fill the churches in ports like Lowestoft and Great Yarmouth. By and large, this occurred within Baptist, Congregationalist and Methodist denominations, though, according to Brown, it also happened within the Anglican faith. (He told a reporter of the *People's Journal*, a newspaper that used to be brought to my house up to and including my teenage years, that there 'was a revival' in Great Yarmouth, 'when Anglican and Free Church ministers were working hand in hand to secure God's blessing on the town'.) The movement touched not only the townspeople and local fishermen, but also the Scottish people who were in the locality. They – bolstered by preachers like Jock Troup, a former cooper from Wick who is still remembered as a legendary preacher in Scotland – travelled north and brought their new-found knowledge of the Gospel with them. Apart from the Hebridean Revival of 1949, which brought to faith many in the Western Isles, including some of my own relatives, it was the last large-scale spiritual awakening of its kind to have occurred within the Protestant tradition of these islands – the visits of Billy Graham in the mid-1950s notwithstanding.

It left its mark in some parts of Scotland, up and down its east coast. There are still remnants to be found in small towns like Portsoy, Banff and Buckie in the north-east. It is at its most dramatic around the isolated harbour of Gardenstown (Gamrie). Here houses cling, with that stubborn tenacity that still characterises the faith of many of its inhabitants, to a slope that inclines to the perpendicular in places. Its streets give little room or consideration to the modern car. Driving along, vehicles have to reverse into tight spaces, give way or hold firm when others come their way. Parking space, too, is at a premium. Sometimes it is marked out by an oil drum wheeled and rolled out in front of a house. No four-wheeled intruders will be welcome here, the householders seem to declare.

That stubborn quality is present in the faith. Churches and prayer groups divide continually. Congregations split at the slip or the drop of a doctrine – 'as fissiparous as they are fundamental' as a friend of mine once noted. This was even occurring in the Church of Scotland while I was there. The minster and his flock were beginning the new year as part of a new institution, no longer able to countenance the new ideas and doctrines that were emerging in their Mother Church, especially the ordination of gays. A walk around the village and one could find evidence of this happening again and again. A plethora of gospel halls, some now fallen into disuse, could be found within its boundaries. On its edge, out on the main road passing the community, a Free Presbyterian Church stood, which I was told was not connected with the Scottish church bearing that name but was part of the Northern Irish branch, the one that once had the Rev. Ian Paisley as a member of the clergy. In some ways, it all reminded me of the Presbyterian community back at home where splinter and secession appeared to be built into the religious psychology of the community. 'No man is an island,' John Donne may have said. He did appear, however, to have the capacity to form his own church.

There were other ways in which modern life appeared to be bypassing the community of Gardenstown. There were a number of houses brandishing 'For Sale' signs in their windows. Shops had closed in recent years; the baker and butcher had laid aside their mixing bowl and cleaver and shut their doors some time ago. The harbour, too, is largely empty. It is protected like so many on the east coast by a concrete breakwater. (The nearby village of Crovie provides evidence of what can happen when such insurance is not taken out. The Great Storm of 1953 washed its way into many of the houses there – and a number of its inhabitants moved out, refusing ever to return.) Nowadays some of the buildings in the town look like the old fishing communities that cluster around the coastline of Europe. Souvenirs – a galaxy of starfish, a constellation of lighthouses – collect in house windows, complete with price tags tangling around them like sea kelp or tarred rope.

Apart from regretting the loss of their community, it is difficult to be sure what the locals make of the change. Certainly there is little doubt that they have been long used to artists coming among them, either drawing pictures or taking photographs of them at their work. The black-and-white images of Frank Sutcliffe summon up the ghosts of Whitby, which I visited on my travels. Boats cluster around harbours now occupied by holidaymakers snacking on ice cream or even buying kippers from the foreshore shops. In their portrayals of the port of Newhaven, not far from Edinburgh, the images of the photographers David Octavius Hill and Robert Adamson even have their own didactic purpose. Closely allied to one of the founders of the Free Church of Scotland, Thomas Chalmers, himself a native of the fishing port of Anstruther, their images are remarkable in the way they ascribe so much dignity to those frequently snapped at with a camera by other 'gentlemen' coming to their community. All neat, pressed and tidy, some of the herring girls are portrayed gathering around a preacher, anxious to discover more about the Bible in his hands in *The Pastor's Visit*. One of another woman, Elizabeth Johnstone Hall, is captioned: 'It's no fish ye're buying, it's men's lives'; a reminder of tragedies like the one in which a hundred men drowned at Peterhead in 1848. There is also a further one of *Fishwives with Washing*, which is linked with the words of a song:

> The herring loves the merry moonlicht,
> The mackerel loves the wind.

But the oyster loves the dredging song,
For it comes of the gentle kind.

These communities have also spawned their own artists, riven by the tensions that can be found within these coastal towns and villages. Some of them have shown the human being at his or her most creative. There is the writer Christopher Rush. The title of one of his books, *Hellfire and Herring*, seems best to sum up – what was once – a description of the community of St Monans, where he was raised in the forties. One of the most remarkable artists is the Scottish painter John Bellany, who grew up around the same time among the fishing boats and gospel halls of Port Seton near the Firth of Forth, spending his holidays in Eyemouth, where his grandparents lived and worked. His paintings belong to both Scottish and northern European tradition, where much of the art reflects the world of work; his painting is part of that continuity, both involved in and commenting on the fishing industry it portrays. His art combines images of both the sacred and profane. In *Bethel*, for instance, we are reminded of the Crucifixion. Christ is at its centre dressed in red and white and holding a fish that is one of the motifs of the Christian faith; the two thieves stand on either side of him, holding blades in their hands. In *Kinlochbervie*, the gutting table with its fishermen standing behind becomes a form of *The Last Supper*. In *Scottish Fish Gutter*, he portrays the herring girl – one of the iconic figures of the Scottish fishing industry – complicit in the slaughter of fish. Based on a woman who was part of a small religious sect in Port Seton, he asks a question that could be directed at a number of the Christian fishermen involved in the trade. How could people who are a part of a tradition that is supposed to honour and uphold God's covenant with other forms of life be part of the excesses that have so often marked man's dealings with the creatures found within the oceans of the planet on which we live?

It is a question the art critic John McEwen deals with in his essay introducing John Bellany's work. He points out that 'one benign consequence of the Second World War' was that the restrictions on fishing which the conflict put into place allowed fish stocks to recover. There was the possibility of revitalising the oceans of the world, restoring life to them. However, the opposite occurred. The post-war generations have wiped the sea beds clean of the life – even sponges, sea kelp and other forms of existence – that once clung to them. McEwen links this to the loss of Christian faith that once characterised these fishing communities (and others) in the latter half of the twentieth century. Restraints and shackles were now completely shaken off. More efficient nets and boats were introduced. Traditional customs, such as the ban on fishing on Sunday, in itself an effective conservation measure, were forgotten. In short, greed – always an important aspect of man's relationship with the ocean – held further and greater sway.

It was an aspect of fishing I touched upon during a number of my conversations with fishermen during the last year. One was with Peter Johnson, a remarkable man who came from the Skerries on the outer edge of Shetland. He spoke of his early life within its tight confines, of the herring girls who used to visit there safe within its sheltered voes, even its brushes with history – like the moment a German warplane visited its shores. A remarkable place, its existence has become more frail and uncertain in recent years. The secondary school has recently closed. Its links with the mainland of Shetland by sea or flight are occasionally threatened by the vagaries of wind and tide. An existence that was marginal in terms of its geography now merits that description in other ways. He also told of his faith and how it helped men to cling on to life, believing that no matter how dangerous the seas became, there was a divine providence overseeing all.

On the other side of Scotland, Murdo Maclennan, from Marvig in South Lochs in the Isle of Lewis, shares a similar attitude. For all that he was in his eighties and had gone through two cancer operations in recent years, he was out working in his garden when I met him, looking after a small crop of cabbages he had grown in thin, unpromising soil. Even then he kept a weather eye looking out to sea. Most days, when wind and wave were not too savage or fierce, he would go out there, bringing back a clutch of fish – or a fry – for his neighbours. He'd look out, too, to the Minch for other reasons, still able to spot the gleam of herring in the distance, cherishing the sight as many more are doing these days, even in places as far away as Lough Swilly in the north of Ireland.

'They're coming back, Donald,' he told me. 'They're coming back.'

But he, too, mourned the lost days, before the time when he had to set aside his own boat, the *Providence*, because of the narrow vision and even narrower mesh of others. He had seen other boats – from the east coast and from other nations – coming into waters which both he and the community had sought to protect for years.

'You know Hebrideans would never have acted like that. They understand the responsibility that's on them.'

Perhaps. There is no doubt that the likes of Murdo would not have been so grasping anyway. Modest in his material needs, immense in his faith, he would have understood what others may have struggled with.

The limits set on man.

CHAPTER TWELVE

'Will You Still Love Me Tomorrow?'

There are a number of possible endings to this book.

It might have come to a close at an evening in Stornoway where a number of musicians and singers gathered to celebrate the fish. They included a trio of Gaelic songsters – flame-haired Ceitlin Smith, silver-voiced Norman Macleod and one of Scotland's best traditional singers, Mairi Smith – like Ceitlin a distant relative of mine. They sang of the battle with the sea that Hebrideans have always fought, sometimes with the elements, occasionally too with others, such as the Bucaich or Buckie men who are reputed to have looked on when a boat from my home village was upturned during bad weather and some fishermen from my village were drowned.

Then there was a singer, Alan Fish, not originally from Stornoway but now a vital part of the musical scene there. Guitar in hand, he sang 'The Shoals of Herring', words that were so familiar to me it seemed, as one fisherman was reputed to have told its composer, the folk singer Ewan MacColl, that 'he had always known it, that it had always been there'. What, of course, was even more remarkable was that it had only been written in 1960, when the herring fishing had already enjoyed its heyday. One of a number of songs called 'Singing the Fishing' he composed, charting the life of both fishermen and those ashore, as part of the BBC Radio ballads series, it was, in so many ways, the creation of a folk artist with a remarkable imagination – one that had been able to summon up the ghosts of his home place of Salford in 'Dirty Ol' Town' and stir into life the initial magical moments of a love affair in the song, 'The First Time Ever I Saw Your Face'. Those in the audience did what I have seen so many attending a musical session in either pub or concert hall do when that song was being played. Both males and females shut their eyes and opened their lips and imagined that they were the ones sailing out of port. Such is the power of melody and words to allow listeners to recall the romance involved in that trade, forgetting much of its back-breaking, skin-bruising, gut-reeling reality.

Then Alan sang an even older song, one that I think I first heard in a pub in the north-east of England where I spent a week or so on a training course during my teenage years in the mid-seventies. (It was in Billingham, near Middlesbrough, and a severe shock to a young lad just out of Stornoway, who had rarely if ever seen an industrial smokestack with a plume of dark cloud.) It was there among the white-fogged, dark brown glasses of Newcastle Brown ale that I saw someone first stand up and ask the question:

'What shall we do with a herring's head?'

Out of place in that landscape dominated by high flats, tenements and factories, it appeared to be a much more sensible question to be asking in the port of Stornoway, where that fish had been at one time ubiquitous. Based on my research, I felt like shouting out that it might serve as a hangover cure, or even as the small whistle to which it had apparently been transformed by some on the Baltic coast. Or better still add my own verse, which responded to the question:

'What shall we do with a herring's bones?'

My response might have been based on a 'Herring Cordial', which Ernie Childs from Great Yarmouth uncovered and included in *My Little Book of Herring*. Apparently it was the creation of an eminent medical practitioner called J. S. Dodd who – way back in 1752 – mixed what remained of 'ten pounds of herring bones' after being burnt in a hot furnace and transformed into an oil with 'rectified spirit of nitre', 'one pound of diaphoritic antimony', four ounces of 'volatile salt of tartar', 'an ounce of oil of nutmeg' and similar quantities of 'oil of cinnamon'. Apparently, this was digested for ten days and was 'good for food in the plagues'. Even I realised, however, that this response was more than a little tortuous and complex when put into the context of a song.

The rest of the audience was more restrained and respectable, however, and went on to answer a similar query when it was directed towards the remainders of the herring's anatomy, whether its eyes, fins or tails, in a song that – unlike MacColl's 'The Shoals of Herring' – has much greater claim to be timeless. Versions of this have existed throughout these islands, whether in the north-east of Scotland, the east coast of England or even the edge of Ireland. Perhaps it's just as well I did not blurt out my own original response. I did not know at this time that the herring's scales were sometimes transformed into tiny pearls to decorate a girl's comb. It took me till my visit to Iceland to find this out, seeing one there in a display case sparkling like a miniature tiara, suitable for a herring queen.

Another possible ending for this book might have referred to my visit to the marine biologist Johannes Hamre, who worked in the Marine Research Centre in Bergen. He came to find me in May 2014 when I was undergoing one of my regular experiences on the Continent – being lost and bewildered in a city's streets. (There are some, small disadvantages in being brought up on an island. Having only two routes to choose from, either 'to' or 'from' town, one never quite acquires a sense of direction.) On that remarkably warm day in Norway, he stepped towards me wearing light-coloured trousers and a brightly shaded Bermuda shirt. A lean, fit man who had survived a severe stroke a number of years before, he looked and acted nothing like the majority of those whom I have met in their mid-eighties. There were ripples still, however, following his health crisis. For two years he couldn't speak at all. Even today he was unable to write or pour a bottle. The main legacy of the earlier incident in terms of his speech was a slight hesitation sometimes as he searched and struggled for the right word to use. He assured me, however, that this sometimes afflicted him in Norwegian as well as the English he employed with me. It all added, however, to the impression I had of a man who was as exact and precise in his language as he was in his approach to his work.

It was an employment that had been brought about by the Second World War. Johannes told me that this was the reason his father, the captain of a fishing boat, had urged him towards an academic career. Having four sons, of whom Johannes was the second youngest, the old man was conscious that there was always the possibility that his vessel might be struck by a mine or, perhaps, be sunk by a bomb or a strafe of gunfire shot from either an Allied or German plane, or a ship operating in the area. Wanting to ensure that at least one son survived into adulthood, he persuaded young Johannes to apply to go to university.

Or at least that was the version Johannes told me. I suspect there was more to it than this – that Johannes probably showed remarkable intelligence at an early age, acquiring great fluency in whatever subject he tackled. (This included his mastery of the English language, about which he was so modest.) There is little doubt that his quick intellect made him at ease in the academic world. When he married, it was to the daughter of one of Norway's most gifted scholars, a man called Vilhelm Bakren, who was responsible for working out the solution of a pure mathematical theorem. Since then his own family circle had increased. He had fathered three children and was now the grandfather of six.

Yet way back in the early 1970s, the local media intruded into the quiet and private world of the scholar. After examining the dwindling stocks of herring to be found in Norwegian waters, Johannes came to the conclusion that what remained had to be conserved. There could be no more fishing for herring legally in Norwegian waters for a few years, otherwise there would be none left. It was a decision that according to one of the national newspapers made him for a while 'The Most Hated Man In Norway'.

He smiled wryly as he recalled this, noting that while there might have seemed to be plenty of herring left for the small boats fishing within fjords that still appeared to be full of fish, that was not less the case with those that went out into the open waters of the North Atlantic. They had noticed for some time that there were far fewer herring where they cast their nets – no rippling in the water as if a sudden, localised rain shower had fallen – and were aware that something had to be done. For all the loss in their income, they knew that measures like these were required. And so, as is the way of most small communities and countries, Johannes probably had their reassurance and support, often expressed in whispers. He also had the support of the scientific community to which he belonged, which knew that the approach of this fisherman's son to his work was both conscientious and precise. After a few years, in 1986, when the furore was over and herring could be netted once again, Johannes enjoyed the irony of being heralded by the same men and newspapers as 'The Man Who Saved the

Herring', and also receiving a gold medal from the King of Norway for his labours. It all seemed a much more fitting tribute for the quiet and modest man I met in Bergen, though one senses that neither headline troubled him overly much. It was the nature of his work that mattered most to him, the sense of a job being done with a great deal of exactness and attention to detail.

There were other moments, too, that would have served as the conclusion to this book. They include a wonderful dramatic performance of Gunn's novel *The Silver Darlings* I saw in Edinburgh a few years ago, where a wooden platform served as both fishing boat and the high cliffs and precipices which the central character Finn had to climb, gathering eggs on the Flannan Isles on the outer, western edge of Scotland. The tightness and economy of the storyline; the life and energy of the actors: all made me feel as giddy with excitement as the first time I read the book when I was a 17-year-old schoolboy in Stornoway. This told the story of my hometown as well as how the Highlands and Islands from which I come had emerged from the days of the Clearances, showing how the people who had once been driven from rough and mountainous land had learned to master rough and mountainous seas. Rather extraordinarily, as well as providing a sense of the romance of that period, it also provided much historical detail – showing how the government's payment of a bounty to the fishermen had encouraged the industry, how the landlords who had been responsible for 'clearing' the population from the glens now provided a new life for the people in the form of the hunt for the Silver Darlings – all for their own selfish economic reasons.

All things considered, though, it is none of these times that provided me with the true conclusion to the book. Instead, this took place in Siglufjörður at the north-western edge of Iceland. I arrived there in February 2015 on a morning when snowflakes whirled and whirred around the airport in

Akureyri, obtaining a lift into the town of the same name from a local pharmacist and her daughter who took pity on my lost and hangdog looks as I gaped into the blizzard. A quick swish of gloved hands across the windscreen and we were on our way, travelling down a frozen, snow-packed road to where the bus to Siglufjörður was probably waiting.

Or so we reckoned. Unfortunately, though, it had gone, revving down the twisting roads some twenty minutes before – right on schedule. A few minutes later and I was taking shelter in the local music hall where a Tom Jones tribute band – complete with singing 'Welshmen' at various stages in the man's long career – was appearing a short time later. Instead of sitting there longing for the 'Green, Green Grass of Home', I decided it might be best to take a walk around the small town, my footsteps crunching as I made my way along its streets. At one time I was aware of a rather loud and ominous bang behind me. I turned round to see that two cars had crashed. The wheels of one had skidded in my direction, ending a short distance away from where I stood. From the calmness of the two drivers who lifted up the debris from the surface a short time later, one had the sense that in winter at least, events like this were – to use Sir Tom's words – 'not unusual'.

And then, at last, there was the ride to Siglufjörður. The driver went there like a 'bat out of hell', to borrow a phrase from another tribute band that was playing in Akureyri a few weeks later. He skipped from one side of the road to the other, driving on the opposite of whichever side of its slippery surface seemed most dark and without the shifting weight and drift of snow. There were times, too, when we were submerged and swallowed by darkness, when the bus entered the tunnels that had been ground out in the mountains of northern Iceland. The last of these was built in 2010; one that stretched out till it appeared almost as long as its name, Héðinsfjarðargöng (the tunnels of Héðinsfjörður).

Between them, we looked out at the long inlet of the sea that lay between the mainland and the island of Grímsey. I discovered that in summer its waters were often visited by schools of whales. They stirred and thrashed the surface as they swam back and forth, enjoying, perhaps, both their prey and play.

After that we came to Siglufjörður. Stepping out of the bus as its last passenger, I looked around at a small town blurred and lost in a whirl of snow. For decades, since the beginning of the 1970s, it had been 'lost' in other ways too – its buildings crumbling under the weight of neglect and cold weather, its population drifting elsewhere after the years of what fishermen sometimes termed El Dorado or even – in shades of the Dutch fishermen I had met – 'Sodom' had come to an end. It seemed to be retreating in scale till it once more became the tiny village it had been in 1900. Back then, its main trade had been in shark hunting. There was no market even for that these days, all swallowed by the jaws of time.

Two or three major changes had altered its isolation. The first was Héðinsfjarðargöng. When that tunnel was gored from rock, it offered access to visitors arriving by plane, say, from Akureyri to ski down its slopes and walk around its harbours. The other innovation which – together with the folk-music centre and the renovation of old buildings for various purposes – had helped if not to save the town at least to staunch the flow of life from within its borders, was the work of a group of townspeople led by Örlygur Kristfinnsson. This was the herring museum, based in the Roaldsbrakki (Roald Station), a large red building that once possessed four large piers.

It was the renowned writer and neurologist Dr Oliver Sacks who had told me about its existence. I had written to him on impulse, having read of his fondness for *schmaltz* herring and his belief in the benefits of the fish's oil for human intelligence. He had responded with a short letter and a copy of an article in which he had extolled the attractions of the Herring Museum in Siglufjörður. He had claimed that it was the finest of its kind in the world. As a practised visitor to such places, there was no doubt in my mind that the good doctor had been right. Part of this was its location. As I walked in its direction with Örlygur the following morning, there was both the time and calmness to appreciate its setting. Eider ducks – the females with a deeper, richer, browner shade than their feathery equivalents in Scotland – dabbled in the quiet waters of the fjord. Long-tailed ducks called out their strange, three- or four-note cries. ('Wade out to me,' they were reputed to say in Icelandic folklore, tempting a traveller who was about to cross a deep river. Heaven help the poor souls who obeyed them here. They would be plunged in deep icy water in no time.) Occasionally, too, a raven would fly across the harbour, its wings a stark and glossy black against the white crests of Siglunesmúli and the other mountains surrounding the township. On the other side of the fjord, there were the ruins of a Norwegian salting station and the first fishmeal factory in Iceland. Both a stone wall and nine human lives had been crushed under the rolling weight of an avalanche of snow in 1911, creating a wave that caused huge damage to the town's piers and boats. The buildings stood there with doors and windows gaping as if uttering a warning to the men on the opposite side of the shoreline about the human folly of ever trying to achieve anything of note in this far northern edge of Iceland. Only an occasional arctic fox probed there now, searching for some life to give it sustenance. It seemed a far more promising hunting ground for the vulpine breed than it did for poor, frail humanity.

And then there were the buildings that made up the herring museum. Roaldsbrakki stood alongside various other structures in this part of the fjord. There was one that had not been completed yet. Shipped to Siglufjörður from the shores of the White Sea, it had been used for whaling at one time.

Nearby there was an old freezing plant. The true centre of
the collection, however, consisted of three structures – all of
which combined to provide the most detailed picture of the
herring industry that flourished in the town throughout
the first six or so decades of the twentieth century, providing
the degree of wealth and self-confidence that led the
Icelandic nation to secure its independence from Denmark
in 1944. The country was designated a republic, but there was
little question that for many years it was also a land where
the herring was king. In Siglufjörður, too, were found a
goodly number of its palaces, for all that there were few
remaining of the twenty-three salting stations and nine
factories that once stood there. One had been magicked into
a restaurant; another into an information centre. One could
imagine the latter-day equivalent of Óskar Halldórsson here,
the character on whom Iceland's Nobel Prize-winning
novelist Halldór Laxness had based the central figure of his
later work, *Guðsgjafaþula* (A Litany of God's Gifts) written in
1972. (*Guðsgjöf*, God's Gift, is one of the terms for herring in
Iceland, like Silver of the Sea, Iceland's Gold and Diamond
Herring.) With your eyes half shut in a snowstorm you could
see his thickset form, complete with coat and Homburg hat,
coming towards you, counting the barrels stacked on the
seven or so kilometres of piers to be found there, say, in 1927,
making deals, too, to expand his empire, standing in the
shade of the 50-metre-high chimney that was among the
tallest structures in Iceland at that time. It was an age, after all,
when according to the Nordic film created for the Great
Expo in New York in 1939, the 116,000 inhabitants of Iceland
exported two tons of herring per head, considerably more
than any other country in Europe, even the Norwegians
who had first begun the industry there, arriving in
Siglufjörður with their nets and vessels in the early years of
the twentieth century.

The three buildings at the centre of the museum reflected
the era of Óskar Halldórsson's lordship of the herring in

various ways. The one they called Grána told of the industrial history of the fishing, centring on a small factory from 1940 which showed – through a fine collection of machines – how the catch was transformed into fishmeal for animal feed and fish oil for many products including soap. The reek of tar and diesel oil swirled throughout. With remarkable exactness, even down to the smell of salt and spices when its door was squeezed open, the exhibition in the Boat House mirrored what life might have been like in the typical fishing port of the 1950s. Nine boats of various kinds were moored at the harbour, each one looking shipshape and precise. Wander around it and one could gain a sense of the unerring quality of Örlygur's vision. There was even a small fisherman's store, the objects on its shelves recalled from the days of his childhood. They were all there, the ropes, oil-lamps, winches, a collection of mopheads, their presence in the shop's stock a reminder that Örlygur had spent twenty years or so working as an art teacher. His trade may have changed but the keen eye had never altered. It was present, too, in his books. There were two he had written about the town's characters, including such figures as the tiny strong man known as Alli King Kong, and Ágúst Gíslason who waved his Bible and shook his fist against Communists, ignoring the fact that those of that political persuasion were among the kindest to him. There was one, too, he had illustrated for children to tell the story of the heyday of Siglufjörður – *Saga úr Síldarfirði*. The drawings are meticulous in their detail, resurrecting a time when according to the reaction of one Icelander visiting London, the crowds thronging the main street of that small town in the north of the country could be compared to those cramming the shops and stores of Oxford Street in the English capital.

He guided me through the buildings of the museum, a nimble man for all the greyness of his beard, the fact that he was in his mid-sixties, and the way he spoke of retiring from time to time. One could sense, however, that he was testing the sound of the word on his lips, checking it out for taste. He spoke of the two young ladies, Anita and Steinunn, who would one day take over from him and whom I met later that evening, consoling himself with the thought that – like him – they both had strong ties to the community to which they belonged, that there would still be a role for him.

'I'll still come in from time to time,' he said. 'Working as a volunteer. Finding out how they were doing.'

I was aware that he might be trying to convince himself, let the words take root there, as he attempted to wrench himself free from the work of a museum which was, to a large extent, his personal creation. He could then spend more time working both on his art and in the company of his wife, Guðný, the individual who – more than anyone else – had convinced him to undertake this project. I spent some time with them, and it was clear she was someone with whom he shared a number of interests, including a love of Iceland folk song, a form of music that on their lips was as intricate and delicate as the choral singing of the medieval Church, utterly different from the songs of the herring girls he played to me in the museum.

'It's about this young girl sending a message to her lover, by way of a seagull flying over the sea,' he said. 'He is working on a boat far away from home.'

The music reverberated around the walls of the building, reaching up to the top storey of the Roaldsbrakki where, in tight and cramped quarters, the Icelandic herring girls had slept until the end of the 1960s, when those still seeking the motherlode of the fisherman's El Dorado moved elsewhere – to the country's east fjords, where girls from as far away as the Faroe islands worked at one time. In these tiny rooms, the girls often slept side by side in a bed, their best clothes draped on hangers, their heavy armoury of bras, corsets and nylons drying in a small room at the side. On the walls beside their bunk beds, they often wrote the titles of the American songs they were increasingly hearing over the airwaves. 'One

Night With You', one scribbled, dreaming, perhaps, of the fisherman lover a previous generation had tried to deliver airmail to by employing the wings of a seagull. 'Will You Still Love Me Tomorrow?' another asks, somewhat plaintively on behalf of the decaying town where she is stationed, noting that its centre no longer bears a resemblance to London's Oxford Street. Norwegian and Icelandic fishermen and merchants did not bustle through its centre. The best Icelandic dance groups had stopped coming, too, to perform there in their white shirts and combed-back hair, tribute bands, perhaps, to Elvis Presley or Jerry Lee Lewis, bringing 'All Shook Up' and 'Great Balls of Fire' to a nation already known for its volcanic and seismic activity.

To return to the young lady's question, there is little doubt that the work of Örlygur Kristfinnsson and those who gave him help and assistance proves there are at least a few men and women who still love Siglufjörður yesterday, today and tomorrow. In creating the museum, they have done much to halt the port's decay. In creating what seems to me the finest museum of its kind in Europe, these individuals are also challenging the sense of fatalism that so often afflicts people in the north who all too frequently feel that the roll of history cannot be diverted or altered when it passes like the northern equivalent of tumbleweed through their empty streets. Their example recalls for us, too, the fact that without the herring, Iceland – like so many other places on the edge of Norway, Scotland and elsewhere – would not have possessed a modern society. In Siglufjörður, helped in some ways by the collapse of that town after its final passing, Örlygur has helped to fashion that industry's finest monument. Elsewhere in Europe, many of its buildings have been superseded and replaced by ferry terminals, gas and fuel installations, and the trammels of modern tourism. Only in that northern Icelandic port do they still stand aloft.

And there could yet be more than monuments. All around the coast of northern Europe, there are signs that the herring is coming back. Its presence glinted in the keen eyes of Murdo Maclennan as he stood outside his home in Marvig in Lewis. I heard tell of it filling the nets once more of the fishermen from Aran Island off the coast of Donegal in the north of Ireland; seen it, too, in the fish shops of Buckie. This is despite the fact that there is still much to concern ourselves about the state of our seas. I heard this spoken about on a number of occasions – from the mouths of marine biologists, old fishermen and sometimes the staff of museums intimately connected with the sea. Most powerful and strange of all, though, I heard about the sense of loss that many feel when they contemplate the ocean in the songs of Inge Thomson from Fair Isle in Shetland. In a concert which took place in Hillswick on the west side of the Shetland Mainland, not far from where Hanseatic merchants used to trade, she occupied the stage with the rest of her five-piece band. An unusual-looking figure with her blue dress, grey top and a loose band around her throat, her music was often strange and unworldly, trying continually to mimic the sights and sounds of the ocean around her island home.

'I want to create music that is in layers, imitating both all you can see and what we are often suspended above,' she said at one point. 'A little sparkling of tings and pings, like mareel [phosphorescence]. The bivalves and mussels. All that lies in rock pools too. The seaweed with their shades of green, purple, brown.'

Her rhythms mimicked, too, the sound of an old boat setting off from the harbour in Fair Isle, the low rumble of its engine, how it altered when it moved across different depths and shallows, moving away from the shelter of the land. She tried to mark out in her music the triangulations and landmarks old fishermen employed when they threw out their nets or sought out banks and channels in which a catch might be found, working out the progress of their voyage in a way that was as precise and exact as Inge's pattern of sound, moving beyond the land-bound steps of others in a precise and magical journey known only to those who followed their craft and trade. Again and again, it was the exactness of the observation that impressed, fitting for someone who came from generations of lighthouse keepers, their eyes scanning the oceans for all the minute changes that take place from season to season, year to year. Despite its remote location, it was not in some ways an isolated place. Norwegian and Dutch fishermen moored their boats there. Scots and mainland Shetlanders visited, seeking the whitefish that swam around the shoreline.

There was a sense of loss in much of her music. Some of Inge's words came from the pen of her friend and relative Lise Sinclair, whose life had come to an end in her early forties only a short time before. Her voice rang out sometimes with the emotional intensity of the grief that underpinned many of her lyrics. 'Something's gone. Something's lost. Something's broken,' she declared when singing of how there was no longer a snowstorm of kittiwakes greeting the plane when it touched down on the airfield at Fair Isle. The musical piece 'Dark Stacks' evoked a change in the cliffs that towered over the sea on that island. At one time they were white with guano from the seabirds that nested there. Now, with each year, they were becoming darker; the dark shade of the rock coming through as fewer and fewer birds rested and raised their fledglings there, abandoning the shoreline from where they had taken off for years, no longer able to find food in the seas nearby.

And this will continue – the absence of fish paradoxically making our skies and land more empty spaces, depriving us of both bird life and much of the human population in some of our coastal towns – until our governments stop seeing fishing in large-scale terms and start focusing on the smaller, human population. We saw this in May 2014 when the European Commission proposed a ban on all drift-net fishing. It threatened to impose this on all fishermen, regardless of the size of their vessels or their catch, whether they catch ten or a hundred tons a year, whether they sailed out of a small, isolated port like, say, Gairloch in the West Highlands of Scotland or some of the major harbours in the Netherlands or Norway. The measure also confused issues. There is little doubt that there are times when drift nets have been used as ten-mile 'walls of death' in some parts of, for instance, the Pacific or the Mediterranean, trapping whales, dolphins, turtles and sharks. In contrast, many of these smaller fishermen use around sixteen nets that are 35 metres in length. Their work – especially if done in conjunction and cooperation with conservationists – would be helpful to the environment and not in any way hazardous. Rather than the uniform policies that are currently in place, this approach would help men in smaller fishing boats maintain and restore their livelihood. It would help the communities they come from, too.

There is a requirement, too, to protect the environment. There is little doubt that for many years the bottom of the sea was scraped and scoured by fishing nets. They swept up both marine life and 'landscape' with them, destroying all that came into their clutches. In doing so, they damaged the bottom of the sea, where, as noted earlier, maerl exists, vital for allowing the herring and other fish to flourish and spawn. Allow this to revive and one can find again reasons for small towns and ports to exist all around the jagged coastlines of northern Europe. Because the maerl reviving is beyond our viewpoint and impossible for either our eyes or our reason to fathom does not mean that we should forget about it or deny its existence.

For many of these communities are failing. Go to the once great town of Great Yarmouth and you will see a people struggling to earn a livelihood. Instead of capturing shoals within their nets, they are now intent on catching the casual visitors by luring them on to their streets with gambling machines, the dubious attractions of Roy Chubby Brown and pole-dancing clubs. Go to my hometown of

Stornoway, or Wick, and you will see, year upon year, much of its younger population drifting away, unable to earn a living in towns that were once made rich by the Silver Darlings. Go to Mallaig and you will find a port that is – perhaps too precariously – dependent on the twin attractions of Harry Potter and farmed salmon. Go to Siglufjörður and only the most fanciful could compare its streets to those in the metropolis of London. The same can be said of many of the German towns I visited – whether Kappeln, for instance, or Glückstadt. It may be that these locations will never be the same as they once were when they were known as Herringopolis, but if they die – or even worse, to quote the words of Mick Jagger, be allowed to 'fade away' – the continent of Europe will be poorer for their loss. They were at one time as vital to our existence as the steel and coal industry, adding a richness and depth to our cultural life.

Their role in our past, present and future should be celebrated, and not forgotten.

Bibliography

Books

Abrams, Lynn. 2010. *Myth and Materiality in a Woman's World*. Manchester University Press, Manchester.

Brown, George Mackay. 2011. *A Calendar of Love*. Polygon, Birlinn, Edinburgh.

Byrne, Michael, ed. 2002. *The Collected Poems and Stories of George Campbell Hay*. Edinburgh University Press, Edinburgh.

Clover, Charles. 2005. *The End of the Line*. Ebury Press, London.

Colquhoun, Kate. 2007. *Taste*. Bloomsbury Publishing, London.

Coull, James R. 2007. *Fishing, Fishermen, Fish Merchants and Curers*. Shetland Amenity Trust, Lerwick, Shetland.

Cruz Smith, Martin. 1989. *Polar Star*. Random House, London.

Cutler, Ivor. 1998. *Life in a Scotch Sitting Room Vol. 2*. Methuen Publishing, London.

Davidson, Alan. 1983. *Food In Motion: The Migration of Foodstuffs and Cooking*. Penguin Books, London.

Day, Francis. 1884. *The Fishes of Great Britain*. Kessinger Publishing, Whitefish, MT.

Dinesen, Isak. 2002. *Seven Gothic Tales*. Penguin Books, London.

Dinesen, Isak. 2011. *Babette's Feast*, Penguin Books, London.

Dòmhnallach, Tormod Calum and Leslie Davenport. 1987. *Clann-nighean an Sgadain*. Acair Books, Stornoway, Isle of Lewis.

Dunlop, Jean. 1978. *The British Fisheries Society, 1786–1893*. John Donald Books, Birlinn, Edinburgh.

Fischer, Dr Ludwig et al. 2005. *Das Wattenmeer*. Theiss-Verlag, Darmstadt.

Grass, Günter. 2008. *Peeling the Onion*. Vintage, Random House, London.

Grass, Günter. 2010. *Tin Drum*. Vintage, Random House, London.

Griffin, Stanley C. 1992. *A Forgotten Revival*. Day One Publications, Leominster.

Gunn, Neil M. 1978. *The Silver Darlings*. Faber & Faber Ltd, London.

Gunn, Neil M. 2010. *Belief In Ourselves*. Whittles Publishing, Caithness.

Hartley, Keith, and Sandy Moffat. 2012. *John Bellany*. National Galleries Scotland Publishing, Edinburgh.

Hay, George Campbell. 2002. *Seeker, Reaper*. Edinburgh University Press, Edinburgh.

Hay, J. MacDougall. 2010. *Gillespie*. Canongate, Edinburgh.

Hofman, Ethel G. 2004. *Mackerel At Midnight*. Camino Books Inc., Philadelphia, PA.

Israel, Jonathan. 1998. *The Dutch Republic: Its Rise, Greatness and Fall*. Clarendon Press, Oxford.

Jardine, Lisa. 2009. *Going Dutch: How England Plundered Holland's Glory*. Harper Collins, London.

Johnson, Laureen. 2010. 'Rhythms', from *White Below*, edited by John Cumming. Hansel Cooperative Press.

Killip, Margaret. 1975. *The Folklore of the Isle of Man*. Batsford, Pavilion Books, London.

Kingshill, Sophia, and Jennifer Westwood. 2012. *The Fabled Coast*. Random House, London.

Kristfinnsson, Örlygur. 2010 and 2011. *Svipmyndir Ur Sildarbae* (1 & 2). Uppheimar, Iceland.

Kristfinnsson, Örlygur. 2011. *Saga úr Síldarfirði*. Iceland Herring Museum, Iceland.

Kurlansky, Mark. 1999. *Cod*. Vintage, London.

Kurlansky, Mark. 2003. *Salt: A World History*. Vintage, London.

Laurenson, Sarah et al. 2013. *Shetland Textiles: 800 BC to the Present*. Shetland Museums, Shetland.

Macdonald, Norman Malcolm. 2000. *Portrona*. Birlinn, Edinburgh.

Mackay, Catherine. 2004. *It Must Be Stornoway*. Argyll Publishing, Edinburgh.

Mackenzie, Roderick. 1988. *Tales and Legends of Lochbroom*. Ullapool Bicentenary Committee, Ullapool.

Mak, Geert. 2001. *Amsterdam: A Brief Life of the City*. Vintage, London.

Manx Sea Fishing 1600–1960. 1991. Manx Heritage Foundation, Isle of Man.

Martin, Angus. 1997. *The Ring-net Fishermen*. John Donald Books, Birlinn, Edinburgh.

Martin, Angus. 2001. *The North Herring Fishing*. House of Lochar, Isle of Colonsay, Argyll.

Martin, Angus. 2002. *Herring Fishermen of Kintyre and Ayrshire*. House of Lochar, Isle of Colonsay, Argyll.

Poulsen, Bo. 2008. *Dutch Herring: An Environmental History c. 1600–1860*. Aksant, Amsterdam University Press, Amsterdam.

Pye, Michael. 2014. *The Edge of the World*. Viking, London.

Roberts, Professor Callum. 2007. *The Unnatural History of the Sea*. Island Press, Washington, DC.

Roden, Claudia. 2007. *A Book Of Jewish Food: An Odyssey From Samarakand and Vilna to the Present Day*. Knopf Doubleday, New York, NY.

Ruhe, Stella. 2013. *Dutch Traditional Ganseys*. Forte Uitgevers, Baarn.

Rush, Christopher. 2007. *Hellfire and Herring*. Profile Books, London.

Russ Federman, Mark. 2013. *Russ and Daughters*. Schocken Books, New York, NY.

Schama, Simon. 2004. *The Embarrassment of Riches*. Harper Collins, London.

Sebald, W. G. 2013. *The Rings of Saturn*. Vintage, London.

Shorto, Russell. 2013. *Amsterdam*. Little Brown, London.

Sinclair, Douglas. 2010. *A Glimpse of Lerwick's Waterfront History*. Millgaet Media, Shetland.

Slavitt, David R. 2012. *Bottom of the Barrel*. Outpost19, San Francisco, CA and New York, NY.

Smylie, Mike. 2004. *Herring: A History of the Silver Darlings*. History Press, Stroud.

Stam, Huib. 2011. *Haring*. Meulenhoff, Amsterdam.

Stephenson, Frank. 2007. *Herring Fishermen*. The History Press, Mount Pleasant, SC.

Stevenson, Sara. 2002. *Facing the Light: The Photography of Hill and Adamson*. National Galleries of Scotland Publishing, Edinburgh.

Thompson, Gladys. 2000. *Patterns for Guernseys, Jerseys and Arans*. Dover Publications Inc., Mineola, NY.

Thompson, Paul, with Tony Wailey and Trevor Lummis. 1983. *Living the Fishing*. Routledge & Kegan Paul, London.

Thomson, Derick and Ruaraidh MacThomais. 1981. *Creachadh na Clarsaich*. Gairm Publications, Glasgow.

Ube, Kirmen. 2014. *Bilbao–New York–Bilbao*. Seren Books, Bridgend.

Unsworth, Christopher. 2013. *The British Herring Industry: The Steam Drifter Years 1900–1960*. Amberley, Stroud.

Wilson, James. 2012. *A Voyage Round the Coasts of Scotland and the Isles in 1941*. General Books.

Others

Allen, Woody. 1975. *Love and Death*, film.

Coull, James R. and Malcolm Poole. 2004. *Fishing In Mallaig*.

Coull, James R. 2005. *The Story of Fishing In Gairloch*.

'Follow the Herring' promotional material, 2014. Customs House, South Shields.

Haaland, Anders and Bjorn Djupevag. Date unknown. *Arbok 1999*. Norges Fiskerimuseum.

Haaland, Anders and Årstein Svihius. Date unknown. *Coastal and Maritime Norway*. Museumvest, Bergen.

Jay, H.H. Date unknown. *Fishy Tales: A Nostalgic Record of the Lowestoft Fishing Industry*. Heritage Workshop Centre, Lowestoft.

MuseumVest Guide. 2005. Bergen.

Nordhagen, Per Jonas. 1992. *Bergen: Guide and Handbook*.

Parrish, B.B. and Saville, A. *Biology of North East Atlantic Herring*, source and date unknown.

Poulsen, Bo. *Talking Fish: Co-operation and Communication in the Dutch North Sea Herring c. 1600–1850*, source and date unknown.

Scots Magazine. 1981. 'Eyemouth Remembers'.

Sutherland, Ian. Date unknown. *The War of the Orange or The True Story of Sabaid Mhor Inbhir-Uig*.

Thomson, Inge. *Da Fishing Hands*, Inge Thomson records 2015.

Time and Tide Museum brochure, 2014. Great Yarmouth.

Unger, Richard W. *The Netherlands Fishing Industry in the Late Middle Ages: The False Legend of William Beukels of Biervliet*, source and date unknown.

Note

At one time fishermen used not to call herring 'fish', differentiating it in this way from, say, cod, haddock, whiting and so on. As constant reiteration of this would be repetitive, I have avoided it in writing. (I am also not sure of its logical basis!) For a very different reason, I have avoided writing about the different kinds of boat involved in herring fishing. There were so many regional and national names for kinds and types of fishing boat even within these islands that it would have required another book.

'Reasons to be Cheerful'

Over the past year or so, I have had – to paraphrase yet another rock star, the late Ian Dury – many reasons to be grateful. The first of these was the support of two of the men who I met in the early stages of this journey, Arstein Svihus of the Norwegian Fisheries Museum in Bergen, Norway, and Huib Stam from Amsterdam in the Netherlands. Both encouraged me, recognising the value of what I was attempting to do. In fact, for all that it is very different from mine, it was Huib's own book about herring that, together with Simon Schama's *The Embarrassment of Riches*, provoked much of the thought behind these pages. I am grateful for their help and inspiration. I trust and hope that this book meets with their approval. It owes much to them.

Yet they were by no means alone. In Norway, I met a number of people who gave their time freely. They included Margerethe Kallestad, Anders Haaland, Bjorg Christopherson,

Ross Murray (from my own native Isle of Lewis who – through his own experiences of Bergen – was extremely valuable in helping me to meet people in this part of the world), Johannes Hamre, Einar Sandal, editor of *The Fish Book*, Natascha in the fish restaurant who guided me in his direction, Jon-Winding Sorensen, Marianne (who acted as an unpaid tourist guide during my time in Bergen) and the entire population – or so it seemed – of Floro. (A special mention goes to Mike, Elaine and Celia of Legend. I bet that when they sang at the festival that day, they would never have imagined ending up in a book about herring.) In Germany, there were many I met along the way, but especially Norbert Fischer and the Ross family of Holm. The assistance of Barbara Ziehm and Peter and Marleen Haviland was also of great benefit to me while in that country. In the Netherlands I encountered so many people to whom I am grateful. Most of these meetings were the result of the kindness of Roel Bosch and his wife Marleen Berg. I owe them a great debt of gratitude for their hospitality and help. They are truly wonderful people whom I hope to meet again and again. I would also like to thank Arie and Riet Westerduin from Scheveningen, who very kindly provided some of their family photographs for inclusion in the plates. On the Estonian story, there were a number of individuals who were helpful, including Andrea Dey, Toomas Ojassu, Les Kreinin and Simpson Buglass.

In Iceland, too, I was met with kindness. My friends Adalstein Asberg Sigurdsson and Gyrdir Eliasson gave me their customary help and hospitality, the former providing me with a roof over my head when I stayed in Reykjavik. Both are talented men and gifted individuals, their writing as impressive as their kind nature. Orlygur, Gudny and the staff at the Herring Era Museum, Anita and Steinnin were outstanding. They even made me forget the chill of the February snow that kept billowing and blowing outside. After they took me to a talk about vampires in the evening, it was as if young, fresh blood was flowing in my veins.

Closer to home I was given further support and help. The Isle of Man seemed to me to have a remarkable community. I was given assistance there by John Quirk and all those involved in the annual Manx Litfest, Julie Matthews and the staff at Bunnscoill Ghaelgagh, those working for the National Library and Archives, Moore's Kipper Factory and the Isle of Man Fisheries Association. I would like to thank John especially for his kind invitation to speak there. Both he and Julie are wonderful people whom I feel privileged to have met.

The same was true on my journey around the east coast of England. In Lowestoft there were the men of the Maritime Heritage Museum. In Great Yarmouth there was both the remarkable Time and Tide Museum and Ernie Childs at the Potteries. (The latter especially was great company as well as a wonderful source of information.) Further up the coast, I came across extraordinary people and places. They ranged from the Olde Ship Inn in Seahouses to the Old Low Light on the Fish Quay in North Shields. I really appreciated both the energy and enthusiasm of the staff at the Customs House in South Shields, especially Esen Kaya who granted me a great deal of time in explaining the 'Follow the Herring' project to me.

North of the Border, the kindness continued. Among others I am grateful to the Fenty family who provided me with food and shelter when I visited Eyemouth on my travels; John Goodlad and Matthew Maciver who commented on the early chapters of this book; Mairi Smith and Margaret Stewart (and her mother) who taught me a little of all they know of Gaelic song; Deborah Moffat; the staff of the Scottish Fisheries Museum, Anstruther; Silke Reepelong; Joni Buchanan; Douglas Sinclair who spent time with me explaining Lerwick's history; so many more too – in the Hebrides, Shetland and the mainland of Scotland. Some of the bearers of that kindness are mentioned in the preceding pages; others are not. I hope I may be forgiven my neglect on this occasion. Otherwise, I would be required to write another book filled with their names! I will, however, have to express my great and unending gratitude to the people everywhere whom I found both kind and considerate. My thanks to the staff of both Stornoway and Lerwick libraries and museums for tolerating my eccentricities while putting together this book. I also wish to put on record my gratitude to Donald Anderson and his predecessor Alex Cluness, both Literature Development Officers at Shetland Arts. I owe a great debt, too, to the late Norman Malcolm Macdonald and Iain Crichton Smith, and the very much alive Ian Stephen and Tom Clark for their help and encouragement over the years. *Tapadh leibh uile*.

I would like to acknowledge the kindness of Michael Hance and the W. L. Lorimer Trust Ltd, care of the Scots Language Centre, A. K. Bell Library, Perth in granting me permission to reproduce the extract from George Campbell Hay's poem, *Seeker, Reaper,* and Laureen Johnson for allowing me to use an extract from her work.

There is also the financial and material help I was given in the course of this book. This included assistance from both Pròiseact nan Ealan and Fèisean nan Gàidheal, who helped provide me with singers; Bryan and Carla who run Creative Retreat in Gardenstown; the staff and management of the various workplaces I visited (all mentioned in the book); Northlink who gave me support in taking me and my car from Lerwick to Aberdeen and back again; the Isle of Man Steam Packet Company, which provided me with free travel to and from Douglas; Caledonian Maritime, Caledonian MacBrayne and the shipping yard in Flensburg for enabling me to visit the new *Loch Seaforth*: my old friend Donald Farmer who – suddenly and unexpectedly – granted me the wonderful gift of air miles he had earned through Icelandair; Sandra Laurenson and the staff at Lerwick Port Authority who provided financial help; their equivalents at Stornoway Port Authority who commissioned me to write my last book, *SY StorY* and as a result, also assisted in this one, and especially Creative Scotland which, by granting me a travel bursary, made all of this possible. Words cannot express my gratitude.

I would also like to thank the fishermen I knew in my youth who fished for herring without greed or causing destruction to the ocean bed, and the legions of forgotten women who stood behind them, waiting on the pier for the catch to arrive. I would especially like to express my gratitude to my late aunt, Bella Morrison of 41 South Dell. A herring girl in her youth, she was like a mother to me, showing strength, love and tolerance while at the same time enduring great physical pain. Sometimes life places angels alongside us, for all that we – especially as children – are unaware of their presence. I will never forget her smile or the silver coins she used to – secretly – press in my fingers. I still miss her very much.

Finally, there are those who help and support me professionally. These include Judy Moir, my agent, for her enduring support, Stephen Moss who invited me to Stamford to talk about guga, Julie Bailey for all her hard work at Bloomsbury and Mari Roberts, who performed the impossible when editing this book. My gratitude is due to Andrew Noble for this invaluable assistance with the captions for the photographs. I would also like to thank Doug Robertson, who has worked with me for many years now. In the course of that time, he has also become that rare and special person – a warm and reliable friend. Thank you very much for being there.

Lastly there is Maggie, my wife. Each evening, as I spend time in her company, I marvel at her love and patience. She is – in her own way – as integral to this book as she is to my life.

Donald S. Murray
July 2015

Index

Photograph Credits

Bloomsbury Publishing would like to thank the following for providing photographs and for permission to reproduce copyright material within the plate section of this book. While every effort has been made to trace and acknowledge all copyright holders, we would like to apologise for any errors or omissions, and invite readers to inform us so that corrections can be made in any future editions.

1 Print Collector/Gettyimages; 2 Shetland Museum & Archives; 3 t UniversalImagesGroup/Gettyimages, b Stornoway Historical Society; 4 t Topical Press Agency/Gettyimages, b Pictorial Parade/Gettyimages; 5 t Topical Press Agency/Gettyimages, b Fox Photos/Gettyimages; 6 t ...es; 7 t Fox ...rs Margaret ...Shader and ...r; 10 all Arie ...l Advertiser; ...& m Donald ...Firdaposten;